Adobe® Photoshop® Lightroom® 5

CLASSROOM IN A BOOK®

The official training workbook from Adobe Systems

Adobe Photoshop Lightroom 5 Classroom in a Book

Adobe Press books are published by Peachpit, a division of Pearson Education located in San Francisco, California. For the latest on Adobe Press books, go to www.adobepress.com. To report errors, please send a note to errata@peachpit.com. For information on getting permission for reprints and excerpts, contact permissions@peachpit.com.

Printed and bound in the United States of America

ISBN-13:   978-0-321-92848-1
ISBN-10:   0-321-92848-2

9 8 7 6 5 4 3 2 1

WHERE ARE THE LESSON FILES?

Purchasing this Classroom in a Book gives you access to the lesson files that you'll need to complete the exercises in the book, as well as other content to help you learn more about Adobe software and use it with greater efficiency and ease. The diagram below represents the contents of the lesson files directory, which should help you locate the files you need. Please see the Getting Started section for full download instructions.

CONTENTS

PHOTOGRAPHY SHOWCASE: JOHN BATDORFF 236

7 CREATING A PHOTO BOOK 240

GETTING STARTED

Adobe® Photoshop® Lightroom® delivers a complete workflow solution for the digital photographer—from importing, reviewing, organizing, and enhancing images to publishing photos, producing client presentations, creating photo books and web galleries, and outputting high-quality prints.

The user interface is highly intuitive and easy to learn, yet Lightroom has all the power and versatility you'd expect from an Adobe application, using state-of-the-art technologies to manage large volumes of digital photographs and to perform sophisticated image processing tasks.

Whether you're a home user, a professional photographer, a hobbyist, or a business user, Lightroom enables you to stay in control of your growing photo library and to easily produce good-looking pictures and polished presentations for both web and print.

About Classroom in a Book

Adobe Photoshop Lightroom 5 Classroom in a Book is part of the official training series for Adobe graphics and publishing software developed with the support of Adobe product experts.

Each lesson in this book is made up of a series of self-paced projects that give you hands-on experience using Adobe Photoshop Lightroom 5.

If you're new to Lightroom, you'll learn the fundamental concepts and skills that will help you master the application; if you've used earlier versions of Lightroom, you'll find that this Classroom in a Book® teaches advanced tips and techniques, and covers the many innovative features that Adobe Systems has introduced in the latest version.

What's new in this edition

This edition covers many new features in Adobe Photoshop Lightroom 5, such as configurable grid and guide overlays, drag and drop geocoding, advanced content-aware retouching, and smart previews that enable you to go on editing the photos in your Lightroom library while you're on the road, though the original files are on the hard disk of your desktop computer at home.

New exercises will show you how to make feathered local adjustments and create custom off-center vignettes with the Radial Filter tool, how to remove unwanted objects with the enhanced Spot Removal tool, and how to correct perspective effects with a single click using the new Upright feature.

This edition also covers enhancements to both the Book and Slideshow modules, introduces the latest addition to the Publish Services panel—a link to the Behance service, and showcases the inspirational visions of seven guest photographers.

Prerequisites

Before starting on the lessons in this book, make sure that you and your computer are ready by following the tips and instructions on the next few pages.

Requirements on your computer

You'll need about 500 MB of free space on your hard disk for the downloaded lesson files (*see Accessing the Classroom in a Book files on the facing page*) and the work files that you'll create as you work through the exercises.

Required skills

The lessons in this book assume that you have a working knowledge of your computer and its operating system.

Make sure that you know how to use the mouse and the standard menus and commands, and also how to open, save, and close files. Can you scroll (vertically and horizontally) within a window to see content that may not be visible in the displayed area? Do you know how to use context menus, which open when you right-click (Windows) / Control-click (Mac OS) items?

If you need to review these basic and generic computer skills, see the documentation included with your Microsoft® Windows® or Apple® Mac® OS X software.

Installing Adobe Photoshop Lightroom

Before you begin the lessons in *Adobe Photoshop Lightroom 5 Classroom in a Book*, make sure that your system is set up correctly and that you've installed the required software and hardware.

You must purchase the Adobe Photoshop Lightroom 5 software separately. For system requirements and complete instructions for downloading, installing, and setting up the software, see the topics listed under the header "Up and running" at http://helpx.adobe.com/lightroom.html.

Accessing the Classroom in a Book files

In order to work through the exercises in this book, you'll need to download the sample image files and other resources from your Account page at peachpit.com. You can either download the entire Lessons folder before you begin, or download the files for individual lessons as you need them.

Your Account page is also where you'll find any updates to the lessons or to the work files. Look on the Lesson & Update Files tab to access the most current content.

Downloading the Lesson files

1   Go to www.peachpit.com/redeem, and enter the code found at the back of this book. If you don't yet have a Peachpit.com account, follow the prompts to create one.

2   Click the Lesson & Update Files tab on your Account page to see a list of downloadable files. Click the links to download either the entire Lessons folder or the work folders for individual lessons to your computer.

3   Create a new folder named **LR5CIB** inside the *username*/My Documents (Windows) or *username*/Documents (Mac OS) folder on your computer.

4   If you downloaded the entire Lessons folder, drag the downloaded folder into the LR5CIB folder on your hard disk. If you downloaded the work folder for an individual lesson, first create a Lessons folder inside the LR5CIB folder; then, drag the downloaded folder to your LR5CIB/Lessons folder.

You'll import these sample images into your Lightroom library and learn to organize them using the catalog file that is central to many of the projects in this book. Keep the lesson files on your computer until you've completed all the exercises.

● **Note:** The downloadable sample images are practice files, provided for your personal use in these lessons. You are not authorized to use these files commercially, or to publish or distribute them in any form without written permission from Adobe Systems, Inc. and the individual photographers who took the pictures, or other copyright holders.

Understanding Lightroom catalog files

The catalog file stores information about all the photos in your library. It includes the location of the master files, any metadata you've added in the process of organizing your images, and a record of every adjustment or edit you've made. Most users will keep all their photos in a single catalog, which can easily manage thousands of files. Some might want to create separate catalogs for different purposes, such as home photos and business photos. Although you can create multiple catalogs, you can only have one catalog open in Lightroom at a time.

For the purposes of working with this book, you'll create a new catalog to manage the image files that you'll use in the lessons. This will allow you to leave the default catalog untouched while working through the lessons, and to keep your lesson files together in one easy-to-remember location.

Creating a catalog file for working with this book

When you first launch Lightroom, a catalog file named Lightroom 5 Catalog.lrcat is automatically created on your hard disk. This default catalog file is created inside the folder *username*/My Documents/My Pictures/Lightroom (on Windows) or *username*/Pictures/Lightroom (on Mac OS).

You'll create your new work catalog file inside your LR5CIB folder, right beside the Lessons folder containing your downloaded work files.

1 Start Adobe Photoshop Lightroom 5.

2 From the Lightroom menu bar, choose File > New Catalog.

3 In the Create Folder With New Catalog dialog box, navigate to the LR5CIB folder you created on your hard disk.

4 On Windows, type **LR5CIB Catalog** in the File Name text box; then, click Save. On Mac OS, type **LR5CIB Catalog** in the Save As text box; then, click Create.

● **Note:** In this book, the forward arrow character (>) is used to denote submenus and commands found in the menu bar at the top of the workspace or in context menus; for example, Menu > Submenu > Command.

5   If you see a notification about backing up the current catalog before loading your new catalog, choose your preferred option to dismiss the message.

In order to be sure that you're always aware of which catalog you're working with as you progress through the exercises in this book, you will now set the preferences so that you'll be prompted to specify the LR5CIB catalog each time you launch Lightroom. It is recommended that you keep this preference set as long as you're working through the lessons in this book.

6   Choose Edit > Preferences (Windows) / Lightroom > Preferences (Mac OS).

7   In the Preferences dialog box, click the General tab. From the Default Catalog menu, choose Prompt Me When Starting Lightroom.

● **Note:** In the remainder of this book, instructions that differ for Macintosh users and those working on Windows systems are given in a compact format as follows; the forward slash character (/) is used to separate equivalent terms and commands for Windows / Mac OS, in the order shown here.

8   Click OK (Windows) / the Close button (⬤) (Mac OS) to close the Preferences dialog box.

Next time you start Lightroom the Select Catalog dialog box will appear, giving you the opportunity to make sure that your LR5CIB Catalog is selected before Lightroom launches.

▶ **Tip:** Even if you've set Lightroom to load the most recent catalog by default, you can open the Select Catalog dialog box by holding down the Clrl+Alt / Control+Option keys immediately after you launch Lightroom.

Getting help

Help is available from several sources, each one useful to you in different circumstances:

Note: You don't need to be connected to the Internet to view Help in Lightroom. However, with an active Internet connection, you can access the most up-to-date information.

Help in the application: The complete user documentation for Adobe Photoshop Lightroom is available from the Help menu, in the form of HTML content that displays in the Adobe Community Help application. Even without the Community Help application, this content will display in your default browser. This documentation provides quick access to summarized information on common tasks and concepts, and can be especially useful if you are new to Lightroom or if you are not connected to the Internet.

The first time you enter any of the Lightroom modules, you'll see module-specific tips that will help you get started by identifying the components of the Lightroom workspace and stepping you through the workflow.

You can dismiss the tips if you wish, by clicking the Close button (x) in the upper right corner of the floating tips window. Click the Turn Off Tips checkbox at the lower left to disable the tips for all of the Lightroom modules. You can call up the module tips at any time by choosing Help > [*Module name*] Tips.

In the Help menu you can also access a list of keyboard shortcuts applicable to the current module.

Help on the Web: You can also access the most comprehensive and up-to-date documentation on Lightroom via your default browser. Point your browser to http://helpx.adobe.com/lightroom.html.

Help PDF: Help is also available as a PDF document, optimized for printing; download the document at: http://livedocs.adobe.com/en_US/Lightroom/1.0/help.pdf.

Additional resources

Adobe Photoshop Lightroom 5 Classroom in a Book is not meant to replace documentation that comes with the program or to be a comprehensive reference for every feature. Only the commands and options used in the lessons are explained in this book. For comprehensive information about program features and tutorials, please refer to these resources:

Adobe Photoshop Lightroom 5 Help and Support You can search and browse Help and Support content from Adobe at http://helpx.adobe.com/lightroom.html.

Adobe Forums http://forums.adobe.com lets you tap into peer-to-peer discussions, questions and answers on Adobe products.

Adobe Creative Cloud Learn https://helpx.adobe.com/creative-cloud/tutorials.html provides inspiration, key techniques, cross-product workflows, and updates on new features. The Creative Cloud Learn page is available only to Creative Cloud members.

Adobe TV http://tv.adobe.com is an online video resource for expert instruction and inspiration about Adobe products, including a How To channel to get you started with your product.

Resources for educators www.adobe.com/education includes three free curriculums that use an integrated approach to teaching Adobe software and can be used to prepare for the Adobe Certified Associate exams.

Also check out these useful links:

Adobe Photoshop Lightroom 5 product home page
http://www.adobe.com/products/photoshop-lightroom.html

Adobe Labs http://labs.adobe.com gives you access to early builds of cutting-edge technology, as well as forums where you can interact with both the Adobe development teams building that technology and other like-minded members of the community.

Adobe Design Center www.adobe.com/designcenter offers thoughtful articles on design and design issues, a gallery showcasing the work of top-notch designers, tutorials, and more.

Adobe certification

The Adobe training and certification programs are designed to help Adobe customers improve and promote their product-proficiency skills. There are four levels of certification:

- Adobe Certified Associate (ACA)
- Adobe Certified Expert (ACE)
- Adobe Certified Instructor (ACI)
- Adobe Authorized Training Center (AATC)

The Adobe Certified Associate (ACA) credential certifies that individuals have the entry-level skills to plan, design, build, and maintain effective communications using different forms of digital media.

The Adobe Certified Expert program is a way for expert users to upgrade their credentials. You can use Adobe certification as a catalyst for getting a raise, finding a job, or promoting your expertise.

If you are an ACE-level instructor, the Adobe Certified Instructor program takes your skills to the next level and gives you access to a wide range of Adobe resources.

Adobe Authorized Training Centers offer instructor-led courses and training on Adobe products, employing only Adobe Certified Instructors. A directory of AATCs is available at http://partners.adobe.com.

Visit http://training.adobe.com/certification.html for information on the Adobe Certified programs.

1 A QUICK TOUR OF PHOTOSHOP LIGHTROOM

Lesson overview

The first part of this lesson will help you understand how Lightroom works and introduce you to the seven Lightroom workspace modules:

- The Library Module, where you'll import, review, and organize your images so that you can access them quickly and easily
- The Map Module, where you can make use of GPS information recorded by your camera to help manage your photos
- The Develop Module, a digital darkroom where you can correct, adjust, retouch, and enhance your photos
- The Book Module, where it's easy to produce stylish photo books
- The Slideshow Module, where you can quickly create dynamic, expressive presentations to showcase your work
- The Print Module, where you can quickly set up professional-looking print layouts and manage output settings with ease
- The Web Module, where you'll find everything you need to share your photos in your own interactive web gallery

The exercises in the second part of the lesson will guide you through a typical workflow: you'll import, review, organize, and edit images, and then share them as e-mail attachments.

 You'll probably need between one and two hours to complete this lesson. If you haven't already done so, download the Lesson 1 work files from the Lesson & Update Files tab on your Account page at www.peachpit.com.

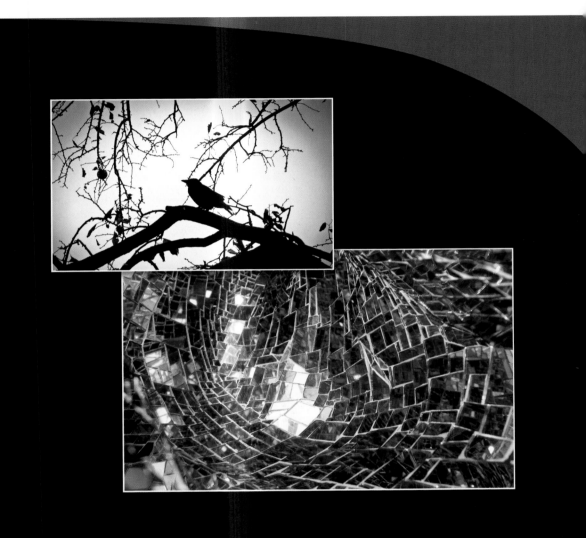

In this lesson, you'll get an overview of how Lightroom works. You'll familiarize yourself with the workspace, panels, tools, and controls, as you explore the Library, Develop, Map, Book, Slideshow, Print and Web Modules.

Understanding how Lightroom works

Working with Lightroom will be easier and more productive if you have an overview of how Lightroom works—and how it differs from other image processing applications in the way it handles digital images.

About catalog files

Note: A single catalog can easily manage thousands of files but you can create as many catalogs as you wish, depending on the way you prefer to work. For example, you may wish to use different catalogs to separate your personal library from your professional work.

Lightroom stores information about your images in a catalog file. The catalog file is central to the way Lightroom works: when you bring a photo into your library, Lightroom does not actually import the image file itself but merely creates a new entry in the library catalog to record the file's location. Once an image has been registered in this way as part of your Lightroom library, any operation you perform on the photo in Lightroom will be recorded in its catalog entry. Whenever you edit the image, assign it a rating, tag, or flag, group it in a collection with other photos, or publish it online, your actions are recorded in the catalog file.

The images in your Lightroom library can be located anywhere on your computer hard disk, or even on external storage media; the catalog file stores references to their locations. If you wish to rename or move an image file that you've already imported into your library, you should only do so from within Lightroom so that the changes can be tracked by the catalog file; otherwise, Lightroom will report the renamed or moved file as missing and you'll be asked to reestablish the link so that the information in the catalog file can be updated.

Managing photos in a library

To work with a photo in Lightroom you must first add it to your library catalog by importing it from your computer hard disk or from external storage media, or by downloading it directly from a digital camera or card reader.

Even during the import process, Lightroom offers you a range of options to help you manage your photos. The intuitive import interface (see the illustration below) makes it quick and easy to set up your own import presets that will save you time and effort by batch-processing your image files as they are imported.

You can choose to leave your image files at their current locations, copy them to a new location leaving the originals intact (the option illustrated below), or move them and delete the originals to avoid duplicating files. If you choose to copy or move your files during the import process, you can either have Lightroom replicate the original folder structure in which they are stored, reorganize them into subfolders based on capture date, or consolidate them into a single folder.

You can also have Lightroom rename your image files during import, create duplicates for backup purposes, attach keyword tags and other metadata, and even choose from a wide range of developing presets—all before you've opened a single image! You'll learn more about the import options in Lesson 3, "Importing."

Non-destructive editing

The catalog file records each step you take when you modify or edit a photo. When you crop the image, correct the color, adjust exposure, or apply effects, Lightroom writes the changes to the photo's library catalog entry—effectively saving a set of instructions for the edits you make—rather than applying the changes directly to the original image file. This is called non-destructive editing.

As you work on your photo, Lightroom will show you a preview of the effects of your work, but the original image actually remains unaltered. The modifications you make are applied only when you export or output the image. In this respect, Lightroom works very differently from image processing applications such as Photoshop or Photoshop Elements, which save changes directly to the source file.

There are many advantages in storing modifications separately from the image data. Non-destructive editing frees you to experiment with your images. Crop an image and later change your mind—no problem! You can undo, redo, or tweak any modification that you've made without ever losing any information from the original file.

The changes you make to an image will be applied only during output—while it is being exported as a preview to be displayed on-screen in Lightroom, as part of a print or book layout, or as a low-resolution JPEG image to be used in a web page. The original image data remains intact; the editing instructions captured in the catalog file are applied only to copies of the image created in the rendering process.

▶ **Tip:** You can specify your favorite external editor in the External Editing preferences. If you have Photoshop installed on your computer, it will be pre-selected by default.

Should you wish to edit an image using an external image processing application, you should always launch the process from within Lightroom. In this way, you can be sure that Lightroom will keep track of changes made to the file, and the edited copy will automatically be added to your Lightroom library. For a JPEG, TIFF, or PSD image, Lightroom gives you the option to edit the original file, or a copy— either with or without the adjustments that you've already applied in Lightroom. For files in any other file format, you can edit a copy to which your Lightroom adjustments have already been applied.

The Lightroom workspace

The Lightroom workspace is divided into six main panels. At the center of the workspace is the work area, flanked by the left and right panel groups. Above the work area and the left and right panel, the top panel displays an identity plate at the left and presents the Module Picker to the right. Immediately below the work area is the Toolbar, and below that, across the bottom of the workspace, the Filmstrip.

Note: The illustration at the right shows the Windows version of Lightroom. On Mac OS, the arrangement of the workspace is the same except for minor differences in style between the two operating systems. On Windows, for example, the menu bar is located under the title bar of the application window, whereas on Mac OS the menu bar is anchored at the top of the screen, above the title bar of the application window.

The basic arrangement of the panels is identical in all of the seven Lightroom workspace *modules*. Only the contents of the panels vary from module to module, to address the specific requirements of each working mode.

The top panel

The top panel displays an identity plate on the left and the Module Picker on the right. The identity plate can be customized to feature your own company name or logo and will be temporarily replaced by a progress bar whenever Lightroom is performing a background process. You'll use the Module Picker to move between the different workspace modules by clicking their names. The name of the currently active module is always highlighted in the Module Picker.

The work area

At center-stage is the main preview and working area. This is where you select, review, sort, compare, and apply adjustments to your images, and where you preview the work in progress. From module to module, the work area offers different viewing options, allowing you to see either one photo or multiple images at a range of magnification levels, and to preview your book designs, slideshow presentations, web galleries, and print layouts.

You can increase the size of the work area by hiding any or all of the surrounding panels. The work area is the only element of the Lightroom workspace that can never be hidden from view.

The left and right panel groups

The content of the side panel groups changes as you switch between the workspace modules. As a general rule, you'll use the panels in the left group to find and select items, and panels in the right group to edit or customize settings for your selection.

In the Library Module for example, you'll use the panels below the Navigator panel in the left group (Catalog, Folders, Collections, and Publish Services) to locate, select, and group the images you want to work with, and the panels below the Histogram panel in the right panel group (Quick Develop, Keywording, Keyword List, Metadata, and Comments) to apply changes to them. In the Develop Module, you can choose from develop presets on the left, and fine-tune their settings on the right. In the Slideshow, Print and Web Modules, you'll select layout templates on the left, and customize their appearance on the right.

The Toolbar

The tools available in the Toolbar also vary as you move from module to module. You can customize the Toolbar for each module independently to suit your working habits, choosing from a variety of tools and controls for switching viewing modes, setting ratings, flags, or labels, adding text, and navigating through preview pages. You can show or hide individual controls, or hide the Toolbar altogether until you need it. Most of the options presented in the Toolbar are also available as menu commands or keyboard shortcuts.

The Filmstrip

The Filmstrip always displays the same set of images as the Grid view in the Library module; it can show every image in the library, the contents of a selected folder or collection, or a selection filtered by subject, date, keyword, or a range of other criteria. You can work directly with the thumbnails in the Filmstrip—or the Grid view in the Library module—to assign ratings, flags and color labels, apply metadata and developing presets, and rotate, move, or delete photos.

The Filmstrip keeps the images you're working with accessible when you're using a view other than the Grid view in the Library Module, and while you're working in one of the other modules. Whichever module you're working in, you can use the Filmstrip to quickly navigate through a selection of images, or to move between different sets of images.

Customizing the workspace

All of the workspace panels are highly customizable. You can expand, collapse, resize, hide, and show panels and groups of panels, either manually or automatically. You can add or remove control elements, change the font size, background color, and more. All of these options will be covered in more detail in Lesson 2, "Introducing the Workspace."

The Lightroom modules

Lightroom has seven workspace modules: Library, Develop, Map, Book, Slideshow, Print, and Web. Each module offers a specialized set of tools and features tailored to the different phases of your workflow: importing, organizing and publishing, adjusting and enhancing, and generating output for screen, print, or web.

You can move effortlessly between modules to suit the task at hand. Some operations, such as creating backup copies or exporting images in various file formats, are not tied to any specific module and are always accessible via menu commands.

The Library module

In the Library module you can review and organize the images in your photo library. The work area offers several different viewing modes so you can browse, inspect, compare, or select images with ease.

You can move between the different viewing modes either using menu commands or the View Mode buttons at the left of the Toolbar. From left to right, the buttons invoke the Grid, Loupe, Compare, and Survey views.

You can customize the Toolbar for each of the viewing modes independently, choosing features, tools, and controls from the menu at the far right of the Toolbar.

Tools and controls that are currently visible in the Toolbar have a check mark beside their names in the menu. The order of the tools and controls from left to right in the Toolbar corresponds to their order from top to bottom in the menu.

In the Library module, the left panel group consists of the Navigator panel and any combination of the Catalog, Folders, Collections, and Publish Services panels, which help you to find, organize, and share the images in your library. At the top of the group, the Navigator panel is always available but you can show or hide any of the other four panels as you create additional folders and collections and move your photos between them.

The right panel group contains the Histogram panel, which can be collapsed but not hidden, and any combination of the Quick Develop, Keywording, Keyword List, Metadata, and Comments panels. Use these five panels to quickly apply developing presets, to make color corrections and tonal adjustments, and to review or edit any keyword tags, metadata, or published comments that are attached to an image.

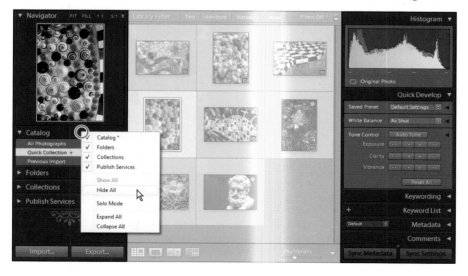

▶ **Tip:** To specify which panels are expanded, collapsed, displayed, or hidden in a panel group, right-click (Windows) or Control-click (Mac OS) any panel header in the group, and choose from the context menu.
To choose from options that affect the behaviour of the panel group as a whole, Right-click / Control-click the outer edge of the panel group (beyond the scrollbar).

The buttons below the panel groups give quick access to the Import, Export, Synchronize Metadata, and Synchronize Settings dialog boxes.

The Develop module

Although the Quick Develop panel in the Library module offers some basic image editing options, you'll work in the Develop module when you wish to make more detailed adjustments and modifications to your photos. You can correct the color balance or tonal range, crop or straighten an image, remove red eye, and apply a range of selective local adjustments—all non-destructively.

In the Develop module, the work area offers two viewing modes: the Loupe view, which enables you to view a single image at different levels of magnification, and the Before/After view (with a variety of layout options), which makes it easy to compare the original and edited versions of a photo. You can move between these viewing modes using the controls at the left of the Toolbar.

▶ **Tip:** You can make more space available for your working view by hiding any panels that you're not currently using, as has been done with the Filmstrip in the illustration below.

The Toolbar can be customized for each viewing mode independently by choosing from an array of controls—Flagging, Rating, Color Label, Navigate, Slideshow, and Zoom—available in the menu at the right of the Toolbar. Some tools are available only in one module, such as the Painter tool, which can be used to apply attributes and settings directly to your images in the Library module. Others appear only in a particular viewing mode, such as the Before & After controls, which let you swap or copy develop settings between the original and edited versions of a photo in the Before/After view of the Develop module.

The left panel group contains the Navigator panel, which can be collapsed but not hidden, and any combination of the Presets, Snapshots, History, and Collections panels, which can be shown or hidden to suit the way you prefer to work.

Develop presets are used to apply a series of develop settings with a single click. Lightroom ships with a set of default presets, and also allows you to add your own. Snapshots are development stages that you have chosen to save during the editing process. The History panel enables you to selectively undo or redo changes.

At the top of the right panel group you'll always find the Histogram panel and an array of editing tools—the Crop Overlay, Spot Removal, Red Eye Correction, Graduated Filter, Radial Filter, and Adjustment Brush tools. Below the editing tools, you can show or hide the Basic, Tone Curve, Adjustments (HSL / Color / B&W), Split Toning, Detail, Lens Corrections, Effects, and Camera Calibration panels. You'll use these panels to fine-tune your photos: adjust the tonal balance, create dual tone effects, correct distortion, or add film grain. The buttons below the panel groups simplify the process of copying and pasting settings between photos, applying previously used settings, and resetting an edited photo to its original state.

The Map module

Lightroom incorporates geotagging in the Map module, where you can see or mark where your photos were taken. Photos already tagged with GPS coordinates will automatically appear on the map. You can drag images captured without GPS information directly onto the map from the Filmstrip, and edit location details and other metadata in the panel at the right. The Filter bar above the map view lets you highlight just those photos at locations currently visible on the map or filter for tagged or untagged shots. In the Saved Locations panel at the left, you can save a list of your favorite places for easy access.

▶ **Tip:** You can also load a GPS tracklog from a mobile device and have Lightroom tag your photos automatically by matching their capture times to the locations recorded in the tracklog.

The Book module

The Book module delivers a suite of layout and type tools to help you create your own sophisticated photo book designs that can either be uploaded directly from Lightroom for printing through the online book vendor Blurb, or saved to PDF and output on your own printer.

You can work with a multi-page preview of your book layout, focus on your design spread-by-spread, or view single pages in the Book module's central work area, switching between these viewing modes and moving through the pages of your book using the controls in the Toolbar.

In the left panel group, the Preview panel displays a thumbnail preview of the page or spread you're editing and helps you to navigate the layout when you're working at high magnification. The Collections panel provides easy access to your photo collections and saved book designs. The right panel group presents the tools and controls you'll use to customize your photo book. Once you've chosen from size, cover style, and paper type options, you can either have Lightroom generate a layout and place your photos automatically or choose from a wide range of preset page templates, and then tweak your design with the controls in the Page, Guides, Cell, and Background panels. The Text and Type panels let you customize page and photo captions and edit type characteristics for titles and body text. The Book module Filmstrip has markers to show which images are included in your layout.

The Slideshow module

In the Slideshow module you can easily create stylish presentations from any image collection in your library. The images in your collection are displayed in the Filmstrip, where you can choose which photos you wish to include in your slideshow, and drag their thumbnails to change the order in which they will appear. The work area shows one image at a time in the Slide Editor view, where you can work on the slides individually, or preview your slideshow as a whole.

The left panel group contains the Preview, Template Browser, and Collections panels. The Template Browser offers a list of customizable slide layouts and the Collections panel allows you to navigate between your collections or create new ones. The right panel group can contain any combination of the Options, Layout, Overlays, Backdrop, Titles, and Playback panels. Use the Options, Layout, Overlays, and Backdrop controls to customize your slides. You can specify the way text or ratings appear, choose a background, or change the layout, and then save your customized settings as a new template. The Titles panel lets you add intro and ending screens, and the Playback panel offers options for adding a soundtrack, and controls for fades and timing. In the Toolbar below the Slide Editor view you'll find playback controls for the slideshow preview and tools for rotating images and adding text to your slides. Buttons below the left panel group make it simple to export a single slide or the entire presentation in either PDF or video formats.

The Print module

The Print module offers a range of preset templates and all the layout tools you'll need to quickly prepare any selection of images from your library for printing.

The photos in your collection are displayed in the Filmstrip, where you can select the images you want to print. You can drag the thumbnails in the Filmstrip to change the placement of your photos in the layout. The work area—the Print Editor view—shows your print layout, which may include only one image, a single image repeated at a variety of sizes, or multiple images.

The left panel group contains the Preview panel, the Template Browser, and the Collections panel. You can use the Collections panel to navigate between your collections or to create new ones, and the Template Browser to choose from a list of customizable print layout templates. The right panel group contains the Layout Style panel and a suite of other panels that varies slightly with your choice of layout style. Use the Image Settings, Layout, Rulers, Grid & Guides, Cells, and Page panels to customize your print layout. If you wish, you can save your settings as a custom template. The Print Job panel has settings for print resolution, color management and other output options.

The Toolbar below the Print Editor view contains controls for navigating through multiple-page print previews and buttons below the panel groups provide easy access to page setup and print settings.

The Web module

In the Web module you can build, preview, and then export or upload your own website to showcase your photos interactively.

As in the Slideshow and Print modules, the Template Browser in the left panel group offers a wide range of preset gallery templates which can be previewed in the Preview panel at the top of the group. The Collections panel provides easy access to your images and saved gallery designs. The panels in the right panel group contain settings and controls that enable you to choose between HTML and Flash® gallery styles, customize the appearance and functionality of the preset templates, add titles, captions, information, links, and graphics, and manage output.

The main work area—the Gallery Editor view—displays a working interactive preview of your web gallery that is updated as you work. The style and placement of the image thumbnails and playback controls for your gallery depends on your choice of layout style and gallery template. Buttons below the panel groups make it easy to test your gallery on the fly in your choice of web browser, before you export or upload your finished presentation.

The Toolbar below the Gallery Editor view presents controls for navigating the photos in a collection and a menu offering the option to include all of the images in the Filmstrip, a selected subset, or just those photos you have flagged. You can use the Filmstrip to change the order in which your photos will appear.

The Lightroom workflow

The modular Lightroom interface makes it easy to manage every stage of your workflow, from image acquisition to finished output:

- **Import** The Lightroom workflow begins in the Library module, where you can acquire images from your hard disk, from storage media or another application, download them from a camera, extract frames from video, and even bypass your camera's memory card and shoot photos directly into Lightroom.

- **Organize** You can set the options in the Import dialog box to apply a basic level of organization to your catalog at import by adding keyword tags and other metadata to your photos in batches. Once the photos have been added to your catalog, you'll use the Library and Map modules to manage them—to tag, sort, and search your image library and create collections to group your photos.

- **Process** You'll crop, adjust, correct, retouch, and apply effects to your images in the Develop module.

- **Create** In the Book, Slideshow, Print and Web modules, you can put together polished presentations and layouts to showcase your photos.

- **Output** Some output operations—such as exporting your edited images in a variety of digital file formats or sharing them as e-mail attachments—are not tied to any specific module and are always accessible via menu commands. The Book, Slideshow, Print and Web modules each have their own output options and export controls. The Library module hosts the Publish Services panel for sharing your images online.

▶ **Tip:** If you wish to process your images further in your favorite pixel-based editor, you can launch an external application from inside the Library or the Develop module.

In the exercises to follow, you'll step through a typical workflow as you familiarize yourself with the Lightroom workspace.

Importing photos

You can import photos into your Lightroom library from your hard disk, your camera, a memory card reader, or from external storage media. During the import process you can choose from many options to help you manage and organize your files. For the purposes of this Quick Tour we will ignore most of these advanced options; Lesson 3, "Importing," will go into more detail.

Before you start on the exercises, make sure you've set up the LR5CIB folder for your lesson files and created the LR5CIB Catalog file to manage them, as described in "Setting up a work folder" and "Creating a catalog file for working with this book" in the Getting Started chapter at the beginning of this book.

If you haven't already done so, download the Lesson 1 folder from your Account page at www.peachpit.com to the LR5CIB/Lessons folder, as detailed in the section "Accessing the Classroom in a Book files" in the chapter "Getting Started."

1   Start Lightroom. In the Adobe Photoshop Lightroom - Select Catalog dialog box, make sure that the file LR5CIB Catalog.lrcat is selected in the list of recently opened catalogs, and then click Open.

2   Lightroom will open in the screen mode and workspace module that were active when you last quit. If necessary, switch to the Library module by clicking Library in the Module Picker at the top of the workspace.

3   Choose File > Import Photos And Video. If the Import dialog box appears in compact mode, as shown in the illustration below, click the Show More Options button at the lower left of the dialog box to access all of the options available in the expanded Import dialog box.

Tip: If you can't see the Module Picker, choose Window > Panels > Show Module Picker, or press the F5 key. Note that on Mac OS the function keys are assigned to specific operating system functions by default and may not work as expected in Lightroom. If you find this to be the case, either press the fn key (not available on all keyboard layouts) together with the F5 key, or change the keyboard behavior in the system preferences.

The layout of the header bar of the Import screen reflects the steps in the import process: working from left to right, first specify the source location of the files you wish to import, select the appropriate type of import, and then choose from destination (for Copy and Move imports) and batch processing options.

4   In the Source panel at the left of the expanded Import dialog box, navigate to the Lessons folder that you copied into the LR5CIB folder on your hard disk.

5   Select the Lesson 1 folder. Ensure that all of the images in the Lesson 1 folder are checked for import.

6 In the import options just above the thumbnail previews, select Add so that the imported photos will be added to your catalog without being moved or copied.

7 In the File Handling panel at the right of the expanded Import dialog box, choose Minimal from the Render Previews menu and ensure that the Don't Import Suspected Duplicates option is activated.

8 In the Apply During Import panel, choose None from both the Develop Settings menu and the Metadata menu, and then type **Lesson 1** in the Keywords text box. Make sure that your import is set up as shown in the illustration below, and then click Import.

Thumbnails of the Lesson 1 images appear in the Grid view of the Library module and also in the Filmstrip at the bottom of the Lightroom workspace. If you don't see the Filmstrip, press the F6 key or choose Window > Panels > Show Filmstrip.

Reviewing and organizing

When you're working with a library that contains many images, you need to be able to find exactly what you're looking for quickly. Lightroom delivers numerous tools that will make organizing and finding your files easy and enjoyable.

You should make it a working habit to go through a few cycles of reviewing and organizing your files each time you import a new batch. Investing a little time in this way can save you a lot of effort later, making it much quicker and easier to retrieve the photos you want when you need to work with them.

You've already taken the first step towards structuring your catalog by applying the keyword tag "Lesson 1" to the lesson images as they were imported.

Tagging photos with keywords is perhaps the most intuitive and versatile way to organize your catalog, because it lets you sort and search your library based on whatever words you choose to associate with your images, making it easy to find the files you need, regardless of how they are named or where they are located.

About keyword tags

Keyword tags are labels (such as "Sculpture" or "New York") that you can attach to your images to make them easy to find and organize. Shared keywords create virtual groupings within your library, linking photos by association, although the image files may actually be stored in many separate locations.

There's no need to painstakingly sort your photos into subject-specific folders or rename files according to their content; simply assign one or more keyword tags to your images and you can easily retrieve them by searching your library using the Metadata and Text filters located in the Filter bar across the top of the work area.

You can create keyword tags to sort your photos into photographic categories, organize them according to content by tagging them with the names of people, places, activities or events, or associate them by season, color, or even mood; your imagination is the only limit.

Attach multiple keyword tags to your images to make retrieving the pictures you want even easier; you could quickly find all the photos that you've tagged with the keyword Sculpture, and then narrow the search to return only those that are also tagged New York. The more tags you attach to your photos, the more chances you have of finding exactly the right image when you need it.

For more detail on using keyword tags, see Lesson 5, "Organizing and Selecting."

Working in slideshow mode

As a convenient way to review the images you've just imported, you can now sit back and enjoy an impromptu slideshow:

1 Check the Catalog panel (below the Navigator preview in the left panel group) to make sure that the Grid view is displaying the images from the previous import. Choose Window > Impromptu Slideshow or press Ctrl+Enter / Command+Return to launch a full-screen slideshow. Press the spacebar to pause and resume playback. Press the left arrow key to return to the previous image or the right arrow key to advance to the next.

● **Note:** The slideshow plays according to the settings current in the Slideshow module and will repeat until you press the Esc key to return to the Library.

Even while the slideshow is playing, you can start organizing your catalog by using keyboard shortcuts to rank your photos with star ratings, flag images as picks or rejects, or attach color labels. This makes the impromptu slideshow a great first-pass review: you can quickly mark your images, and then use a search filter to isolate the shots you want to work with once you return to the Library.

2 To quickly assign a rating to the image currently displayed in your slideshow, press a number between 1 (for 1 star) and 5 (for 5 stars) on your keyboard. To remove the rating, press 0. You can attach only one rating to each photo; assigning a new rating will replace the old one. For the purposes of this exercise, mark three or four images with either 3, 4, or 5 stars.

Rating stars are displayed under the thumbnail images in all of the Library module views and in the Filmstrip, as shown in the illustration at the left.

▶ **Tip:** Whenever you use your keyboard to mark a photo in the impromptu slideshow, the rating, flag, or label you assign appears briefly in the lower left corner of the screen to confirm your action.

3 Press the P key on your keyboard to flag the image currently displayed in your slideshow as a pick (⚐), press the X key to flag it as a reject (⚑), or press the U key to remove any flags. Flag several of the Lesson 1 images as picks, and mark at least one as a reject.

You can choose to display flags, along with other information, in the image cells in the Library views and in the Filmstrip. Images flagged as rejects appear grayed out, while those marked as picks are indicated by a white border.

Use color labels to mark photos for specific purposes or projects. You might use a red label for images you intend to crop, green for those that need correction, or blue to identify photos you wish to use in a particular presentation. To help you remember the meaning of your labels, you can assign your own names to the colors by choosing Metadata > Color Label Set > Edit. You can create several label sets, and switch between them as needed. You could customize one set for working in the Library module and another to suit your workflow in the Develop module.

4   To assign a color label to the image currently displayed in your slideshow, use the number keys. Press 6 on your keyboard to assign a red color label, press 7 for yellow, 8 for green, or 9 for blue. There's no keyboard shortcut to assign a purple color label. To remove a color label simply press the same number again. Assign different colored labels to several of the images, and then remove one.

In the Library module's Grid View, and in the Filmstrip, a photo with a color label will be framed in that color when it's selected, and surrounded by a tinted image cell background when it's not, as shown in the illustration at the right.

If you prefer, you can change the view options so that color labels will appear only under the thumbnail images in the Grid view. You'll learn about customizing view options and more about assigning ratings, flags, and color labels, using both menu commands and the controls in the Toolbar, in Lesson 5, "Organizing and Selecting."

5   Press the Esc key to stop the slideshow and return to the Library module.

In the Library, you can use the Filter bar above the thumbnail grid to search your images by text or metadata content, and then refine your search by filtering for one or more of the searchable attributes—rating, flag status, label color, or file type—so that only those photos you want are displayed in the Grid view and the Filmstrip.

6   If the Filter bar is not already visible above the work area, open it by choosing View > Show Filter Bar. Click the Attribute filter. Click the fourth star, and choose Rating Is Greater Than Or Equal To from the Rating menu. Lightroom will now display only those photos with at least a 4 star rating.

7   Experiment a little with the attribute filters. Try searching different star ratings; then varied combinations of ratings, flags, and labels.

When you're working with only a few images, as you are in this lesson, rating, flagging, and filtering seems unnecessary, but as your photo library grows to contain more and more photos you'll find these tools invaluable. The objective of this step in your workflow is to organize your images so that you can retrieve them easily for processing in the Develop, Slideshow, Print, and Web modules.

Creating a collection

Once you've searched your library by keywords or text, and then filtered out the unwanted images using the attributes filters, you can group the resultant group of photos as a *collection*, so that you can easily retrieve the same selection at any time without repeating the search. You can choose between several types of collection:

- The Quick Collection: a temporary holding collection in the Catalog panel, where you can assemble a selection of images.

- A "standard" Collection: a permanent grouping listed in the Collections panel.

- A Smart Collection: a selection of images automatically filtered from your library according to whatever criteria you specify.

- A Publish Collection: a selection of images intended for publishing that will be listed in the Publish Services panel. A Publish Collection will keep track of images you've published, enabling you to check at a glance whether the versions you're sharing are up-to-date.

For this exercise, you'll create a standard Collection.

1   If the star rating filter is still active in the Grid view, clear this setting by choosing Library > Filter by Rating > Reset This Filter, or simply click None in the Filter bar above the Grid view to disable all active filters.

2   Ensure that Previous Import is selected in the Catalog panel; the Grid view and the Filmstrip should display all nine images.

● **Note:** A selected image is highlighted in the Grid view and the Filmstrip by a narrow white border (or a colored border if the image has a color label) and a lighter cell background color. If more than one photo is selected, the active photo is shown with an even lighter background. Some commands will affect only the active photo while others affect all selected photos.

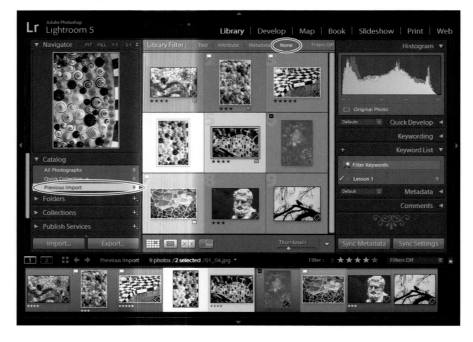

When you next import images, the Previous Import folder will be updated and you'll no longer be able to isolate this particular group of images by choosing from the entries in the Catalog panel. In this case, you could still retrieve your selection by working with the Folders panel or searching the Lesson 1 tag, but it would not be so easy to retrieve a group of photos (such as the results of a complex search) that didn't share a keyword or were spread across separate folders.

The solution is to create a collection, a virtual grouping that will be permanently listed in the Collections panel, so you'll be able to call up the same set of images at any time with a single click.

3 Choose Edit > Select All; then choose Library > New Collection. In the Create Collection dialog box, type **Niki de St Phalle** (the artist responsible for the featured mosaics) as the collection name. Under Location, leave the option Inside A Collection Set disabled. Under Collection Options, ensure that Include Selected Photos is activated, and the other options disabled; then, click Create.

Your new collection is now listed in the Collections panel. The listing includes an image count showing that the Niki de St Phalle collection contains nine photos.

▶ **Tip:** Folders in the Collections panel can be nested. For example, you could create a Portfolio folder, and then create subfolders named Portraits, Landscape, Product shots, Black & White, etc. Each time you import an outstanding image, add it to one of these collections to slowly build up your portfolio.

Rearranging and deleting images in a collection

While you're working with the images in the Previous Import folder or the All Photographs folder, source locations listed in the Catalog panel, the order of the photos in the Grid view and in the Filmstrip is fixed; the thumbnails are either ordered by capture time (the default) or by your choice of various other criteria from the sort menu in the Toolbar, such as file name, rating, or the order in which the photos were imported into your catalog.

If the image source is a single folder without subfolders, or a collection, however, you're free to rearrange their order in the Grid view and the Filmstrip, and even remove them from the working view without deleting them from the catalog.

1 If your new collection is not already selected in the Collections panel, click to select it now. Choose Edit > Select None.

2 In the Filmstrip, Ctrl-click / Command-click to select the fourth and sixth images (two portrait-format photos of mosaic surfaces) and drag the selection over the border between the second and third thumbnails in the Filmstrip. Release the mouse button when the black insertion line appears.

▶ **Tip:** You need to drag the thumbnail of one of your selected images, rather than the image cell frame.

The selected photos snap to their new positions in the Grid view and the Filmstrip.

3   Deselect the photos by clicking an empty area in the main work area. Click to select the first thumbnail in the Grid view and drag it over the border between the fourth and fifth images. Release the mouse button when the black insertion line appears. In the Toolbar, the Sort criteria has changed to User Order.

4   Choose Edit > Select None. Shift-click to select the last two thumbnails in the Grid view; then, right-click / Control-click either of the selected images and choose Remove From Collection from the context menu.

In the Collections panel (and in the header bar of the Filmstrip) the image count shows that the new collection now contains only 7 images.

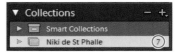

Although you've removed photos from the collection, they have not been deleted from your catalog. The Previous Import and All Photographs folders in the Catalog panel still contain all nine images. A collection contains only links to the files in your catalog; deleting a link does not affect the file in the catalog.

▶ **Tip:** Should you wish to edit the same image differently in two collections, you'll first need to make a virtual copy—an additional catalog entry for the image—for inclusion in the second collection. You'll learn about this in Lesson 6, "Developing and Editing."

You can include a single image in any number of collections—each collection will then contain its own link to the same file. If you apply a modification to a photo in a collection, the modification will be visible in each folder and collection that references the same photo. This is because Lightroom stores only one entry for each image file in its library catalog, and a record of all modifications is associated with that entry; any collection including that image links to the same catalog entry, and therefore displays the modified photo. Although the original image file itself remains untouched, its catalog entry has changed to include your modifications. For more information on collections, please refer to "Using collections to organize images" in Lesson 5.

Comparing photos side by side

Often you'll have two or more similar photos that you'd like to compare side by side. The Library module features a Compare view for exactly this purpose.

1   If you have any images selected in the Grid view, choose Edit > Select None. Select the first two images in the Filmstrip, and then click the Compare View button (XY) in the Toolbar to switch to the Compare view. Alternately, choose View > Compare, or press C on your keyboard.

2   The Select pane is active by default. In the Filmstrip, click on the third photo to replace the current Select image. Press the right arrow key on your keyboard repeatedly to cycle the Candidate pane through the Filmstrip to the last photo.

3 Press the Tab key on your keyboard, and then press F5 to hide the side and top panels so that your photos can be displayed at a larger size in the Compare view.

4 Click the Swap button ([XY]) in the Toolbar below the Candidate image to swap the Candidate and Select images; then, use the right arrow key to compare the new Select photo with the next candidate from the collection.

5 When you've made your choice, click the Done button at the right end of the Toolbar. The Select image will appear in the single-image Loupe view.

Comparing several photos

The Survey view lets you compare several photos at the same time and narrow your selection until only the best photo remains. Even while you're working in the Compare and Survey views, you can continue to organize your photos using menu commands and the Toolbar to assign ratings, flags, and color labels. If necessary, use the Content menu at the right of the Toolbar to show the controls you need.

1 Choose Edit > Select None. In the Filmstrip, Ctrl-click / Command-click any three of the landscape-format photos, and then click Survey view ([▦]) in the Toolbar. Alternatively, choose View > Survey, or press N on your keyboard.

The Survey view will display all the selected images; the more images you select the smaller the individual preview images in the Survey view. You can make more room for the images you're reviewing by hiding the Filmstrip and side panel groups as necessary. However, it may be helpful to show the right panel group where you can examine a histogram and metadata for the active photo, apply Quick Develop adjustments, and add keyword tags, titles, and captions. The active image is indicated by a thin white border; to activate a different photo, you can either click its thumbnail in the Filmstrip or click the image directly in the work area.

2   Drag any of the images to reposition it in the Survey view. The other images will be shuffled automatically to accommodate your action.

3   As you move the pointer over each of the images, a Deselect Photo icon ([X]) appears in the lower right corner. Click this icon to remove a photo from the selection in the Survey view.

As you eliminate candidates the photos remaining in the Survey view are progressively resized and shuffled to fill the space available in the work area. When you eliminate a photo from the Survey view, the image is simply dropped from the selection, not removed from the collection.

▶ **Tip:** If you eliminate a photo accidentally, choose Edit > Undo to return it to the survey selection, or Ctrl-click / Command-click the image in the Filmstrip. You can easily add a photo to the selection in the same way.

4   Eliminate another photo from the Survey so that your selection is narrowed down to a single image, and then press E on your keyboard to switch to the single-image Loupe view.

5   Press Shift+Tab (twice if necessary) to show all the workspace panels. Double-click the enlarged image to return to the Grid view. Choose Edit > Select None.

Developing and editing

The next step in the Lightroom workflow is to process your images, whether you wish to improve them technically by correcting color, tonal balance, and distortion, or enhance them creatively using customizable develop presets and effects.

You can start without even leaving the Library module, where the Quick Develop panel offers simple controls for basic color correction and tonal adjustment, and a choice of preset crop and develop settings. For a finer degree of control, the Develop module offers an extended suite of sophisticated image processing tools, in a more comprehensive and convenient editing environment.

Using Quick Develop in the Library module

In the following example you'll quickly improve the color tonal balance of an image, and then tweak the results with the controls in the Quick Develop panel.

1   In the Catalog panel, click the Previous Import folder so that you can see all nine of the lesson images.

▶ **Tip:** If the Filmstrip is not visible, choose Window > Panels > Show Filmstrip or press F6 on your keyboard.

2   In the Filmstrip or the Grid view, hold the pointer over the photo of a marble sculpture to see the file name and basic image details in a tooltip. Click the thumbnail to select it; the file name is also displayed in the status bar above the Filmstrip.

3   Double-click the selected image in the Filmstrip to open it in the Loupe view. If necessary, expand the Histogram and Quick Develop panels in the right panel group by clicking the arrows beside the panel names.

▶ **Tip:** To make more space for the image in Loupe view, use the commands in the Window > Panels menu to hide the left panels, the Module Picker, and the Filmstrip. Commands for showing and hiding the Toolbar and Filter bar are listed in the View menu.

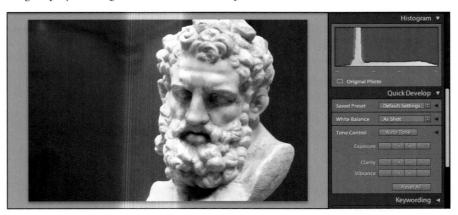

As you can see from both the image preview and the curve in the Histogram panel, this photo does not have a balanced tonal distribution; it is slightly overexposed and lacking in contrast, giving it a somewhat dull, flat look.

4 In the Quick Develop panel, watch the tone distribution curve shift in the Histogram panel as you click the Auto Tone button.

Although the automatic adjustment hasn't done a perfect job with this particular photo, there is substantial improvement; a lot of image detail has been recovered from the overexposed hair and face and there is more depth in the mid-tones. The contrast, however, remains unimpressive, and the darker areas still look flat.

▶ **Tip:** Click back and forth between the Reset All button at the bottom of the Quick Develop panel and the Auto Tone button to assess the results in the Loupe view.

5 Click the triangle to the right of the Auto Tone button to expand the Tone Control pane. Click twice each on the right-most buttons for both the Highlights and Shadows controls. Click twice each on the left-most buttons for Whites and Blacks, and twice on the right-most Clarity button.

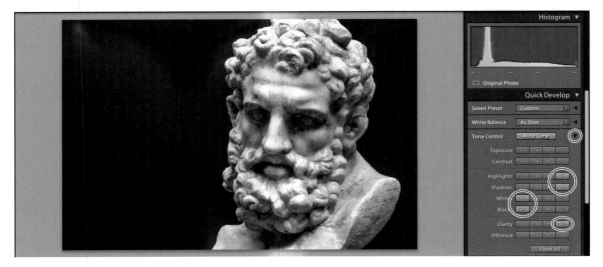

The histogram shows a more even tonal spread; there is more depth in the darker areas of the image, better definition in the midtones, and the upper highlights are more subdued. The adjusted image has more detail in both the lit and shadowed areas, and the overall contrast is greatly improved.

Working in the Develop module

The controls in the Quick Develop panel let you change settings but don't indicate absolute values for the adjustments you make to your images.

In our example there is no way to tell which parameters were modified by the Auto Tone adjustment, or by how much they were shifted. For finer control, and a more comprehensive editing environment, you need to move to the Develop module.

1   Keeping the image from the previous exercise selected, switch to the Develop module now by doing one of the following:

  •   Click Develop in the Module Picker.

  •   Choose Window > Develop.

  •   Press Ctrl+Alt+2 / Command+Option+2.

2   If necessary, expand the History panel in left panel group and the Basic panel in the right panel group by clicking the white triangle beside each panel's name. Collapse any other panels that are currently open, except the Navigator on the left and the Histogram at the right. Press F6 to hide the Filmstrip.

The History panel not only lists every modification you've made to a photo—even Quick Develop adjustments made in the Library module—but also enables you to return the image to any of its previous states. The most recent entry—the last Clarity adjustment you applied—is at the top of the History list. The earliest entry, at the bottom of the list, records the date and time that the image was imported. Clicking this entry will revert the photo to its original state. As you move the pointer over each entry in the list, the Navigator displays a preview of the image at that stage of development.

The Basic panel displays information about the adjustment settings that was unavailable in the Quick Edit panel. For our image in its most recent state, the Exposure is set to -0.80, Contrast is set to -14, Highlights, Shadows, Whites, Blacks, and Clarity are set to +33, +47, -27, -39, and +40, respectively.

3   In the History panel, click the entry for the first modification you made to this photo: the Auto Tone adjustment: Inspect the settings in the Basic panel.

For this image, clicking Auto Tone modified all of the settings in the Tone pane, but applying Auto Tone to another photo may effect fewer settings and produce very different adjustment values.

4   Click the top entry in the History list to return the photo to its most recent state.

5 In the Toolbar (View > Show Toolbar), click the small triangle to the right of the Before/After button and choose Before/After Top/Bottom from the menu.

▶ **Tip:** If you don't see the Before/After button in the Toolbar, click the triangle at the right of the Toolbar and activate Before And After in the Toolbar content menu.

By comparing the Before and After images, you can see how much you've improved the photo with just a few clicks.

Now let's look at how much difference your manual Quick Develop adjustments made after applying Auto Tone.

6 Leaving the most recent Clarity adjustment activated in the History panel, right-click / Control-click the entry for the Auto Tone adjustment and choose Copy History Step Settings To Before from the context menu.

There's much more to learn about the correction and adjustment tools in the Develop module, but we'll leave that for later. For now you'll straighten this slightly tilted photo, and then crop it.

Straightening and cropping an image

1 Press D on your keyboard to activate the Loupe view in the Develop module.

2 Click the Crop Overlay Tool (▦), located just below the Histogram in the right panel group. The Crop Overlay Tool enables you to both crop and straighten your image.

3 When the Crop Overlay Tool is active, a pane with additional controls opens below the tool buttons. Click the Straighten tool (⬤). The pointer changes to a crosshairs cursor, and the spirit level icon of the Straighten tool follows your movement across the image preview.

4 Look for a line in the image that should be either true horizontal or vertical. For this photo, the only reference is the out-of-focus line where the walls meet in the background. Drag a plumb line with the Straighten tool, from the corner of the ceiling down the junction of the walls. Release the mouse button; the image is rotated so that your plumb line becomes vertical and the Straighten tool returns to the Crop Overlay Tool controls.

▶ Tip: To maintain the original aspect ratio of an image when you crop it manually, make sure that Original is selected from the cropping Aspect menu and that the aspect ratio is locked.

Lightroom has overlaid a cropping rectangle on the straightened photo, automatically positioned to achieve as large a crop as possible with the original aspect ratio while trimming away the angled edges. If you wished to adjust the crop, you could drag any of the six handles on the cropping rectangle. To assist with manual cropping, you can choose from a variety of grid overlays in the Tools > Crop Guide Overlay menu, or hide the grid by choosing Tools > Tool Overlay > Never Show.

5 When you're done, apply the crop by clicking the Crop Overlay tool, the Close button at the lower right of the tool controls, or the Done button in the Toolbar.

You can reactivate and adjust the crop at any time by simply clicking the crop tool.

Adjusting lighting and tonal balance

In the previous project, you used the simplified Quick Develop tone controls to tweak the tonal range of an image that needed just a little attention. This time you'll work in the Basic panel to rescue a photo that may at first seem beyond redemption.

1 Press F6 and F7 (or use the Window > panels menu) to show the Filmstrip and hide the left panels. In the Filmstrip, click to select the photo 01_09.jpg.

This image is a very difficult case; captured in low light on an gloomy day, and back-lit by a flat overcast sky, the photo is badly underexposed. There is so little detail in the bird and branches that, at first glance, they appear to be mere silhouettes.

2 Inspect the histogram at the top of the right panel group. It's easy to see that the tonal distribution is uneven: data is clumped at both ends of the curve, with an obvious deficiency of information through the midtone range, and none at all in the upper highlights and whites.

3 In the Basic panel, click the Auto adjustment button at the top of the Tone pane, noting the effect on the histogram curve as well as the image in the work area.

The tone distribution curve has shifted to the right; the image is brighter, but it still looks dull and lifeless. The automatic adjustment has spread the peak formerly in the shadows range of the histogram into the lower midtones, bringing out more detail in the bird and branches; however, the central trough is unimproved, so the photo still lacks midtone contrast. Although it has shifted from the lower highlights into the whites, the peak at the right of the curve is still the dominant feature, reflecting the fact that the sky now appears almost completely burned-out to white.

4 Inspect the controls in the Basic panel. The Auto Tone adjustment has affected all six of the settings in the Tone pane.

As the automatic adjustment was relatively successful for this photo, you can use these settings as a starting point, and then make manual adjustments to tweak the tonal balance as you did earlier, using the simplified controls in the Quick Develop panel.

5 Auto Tone has already increased the Exposure as much as possible without losing information, so you can leave it as set. Watch the change in the histogram as well as the photo as you move the Contrast slider to the left, or type in the text box, to reduce the value to -**100**.

Reducing the Contrast may seem counter-intuitive but, as you can see, it has drawn image data inwards from the ends of the histogram toward the center, reducing the range most affected by the trough. In the illustration at the right, the red overlay shows the curve before reducing contrast.

At this point, the photo may actually look worse for the reduction in contrast, but the extreme tonal deficiencies in this image will require some adjustments that are equally extreme, and reducing the Contrast will help limit the damage.

6 Increase the Highlights value to **0** and decrease the Shadows setting to +**25**. Set the Clarity to +**100**, and set a value of +**50** for both Vibrance and Saturation.

The Clarity and Vibrance settings in the Basic panel's Presence pane affect the image as a whole, rather than a specific tonal range. Increasing the Clarity adds depth and definition to an image by heightening the local contrast between adjacent areas of the image. The Vibrance slider alters the saturation of color in a non-linear manner, boosting less saturated colors more than bolder areas.

And now, it's time for a dirty trick. Increasing the Whites value significantly will push the right end of the curve off the end of the graph, causing most of the sky to be "clipped" to pure white. In purist, technical terms this is not an acceptable result, but for our hard-case image the sky is already so devoid of color and detail that we can trade the barely noticeable loss against improvement elsewhere.

7 Use the slider to increase the Whites value slowly to +**100**. Watch the change in both the photo and the histogram curve when the value exceeds +**82**.

8 Press F7, or use the Window > panels menu, to show the left panels. In the History panel, click back and forth between the current state at the top of the list, the Import state at the bottom, and the Auto Tone entry just above it, comparing the changes in the histogram as well as the results in the Loupe view. When you're done, leave the image open in Loupe view for the next exercise.

Original photo   Auto Tone   Manual adjustments

Creating effects with the Radial Filter tool

You can use the Radial Filter tool—new in Lightroom 5—to create off-center custom vignettes, amongst other effects, by applying local adjustments to a selected area in an image through a feathered elliptical mask.

Unlike the centered post-crop vignette in the Effects panel, you can place the center of your Radial Filter adjustment anywhere in the photo, focusing attention on whichever part of the image you choose.

By default, your local adjustments are applied to the area outside the adjustable ellipse, leaving the inside unaffected, but the Radial Filter's Invert Mask option enables you to reverse the focus of the filter.

By applying multiple Radial Filter adjustments, you can treat the inside and outside areas differently, highlight more than one area in the same image, or create an asymmetrical vignette, as illustrated here.

You can experiment with adding custom vignettes to your own photos later. In this exercise, you'll learn how to work with the Radial Filter tool as you set up a more complex effect that will hopefully add a little color and atmosphere to our problem photo, which is still less than exciting.

You'll start by setting up a combination of adjustments that will be applied through your first Radial Filter.

1 Click to activate the Radial Filter tool—the fifth of the editing tools located right below the Histogram in the right panel group.

> **Tip:** Make sure the color swatch at the bottom of the local adjustments pane shows a black X on a white background (no color selected). If this is not the case, click the swatch and reduce the Saturation setting to 0.

2 Set up the local adjustment controls as shown in the illustration at the right. Set the Temperature to **-20** and the Tint to **-5**. Reduce the Exposure setting to **-2.20**, increase the Contrast to **45**, and decrease the Highlights to **-100**. Set the Shadows and Clarity values to **60** and **-50** respectively. Make sure that the Feather control is set to the default value of **50** and the Invert Mask option is disabled.

> ● **Note:** Holding down the Shift key as you drag with the Radial Filter tool constrains the adjustment to a circle. When dragging the control handles to scale an existing elliptical adjustment, holding the Shift key constrains the mask's proportions.

3 Hold down the Shift key and drag in the Loupe view with the Radial Filter tool's cross-hairs cursor, starting from a point at the back of the bird's neck. When you've created a circle as shown in the illustration at the right, release the mouse button, and then the Shift key.

Once established, the active Radial Filter adjustment is displayed with a circular "pin" at its center and four square control handles around its circumference. Whenever the Radial Filter tool is activated, you can select an existing filter by clicking its central pin, reposition it by dragging the pin, and resize the adjustment area or change its shape by dragging any of the square control handles.

> **Tip:** If the colors you see on-screen differ significantly from those illustrated, consider calibrating your display. See Windows / Mac OS help for instructions. Slighter differences may be a result of the CMYK printing process.

4 Hold Ctrl+Alt / Command+Option and click the pin to duplicate the filter. As you can see, duplicating the radial filter has doubled the effect on the image; you should keep it in mind that the effects of overlapping filters are cumulative.

5 Activate the Invert Mask option below the local adjustment controls. The same adjustments are now being applied both inside and outside the feathered mask, so that the entire image is affected evenly.

6   With your second Radial Filter adjustment still selected and active, change the Temperature and Tint values to **25** and **15** respectively. Set the Exposure to **1.30**, and the Contrast, Highlights, and Shadows to a common value of **-100**. Increase the Clarity setting to **100**, Saturation to **45**, and Sharpness to **100**. The new settings are applied inside the inverted mask.

7   Hold down the Shift key to constrain the shape of the filter as you drag the bottom control handle downwards. Enlarge the circle as shown in the illustration at the left, below. Be sure to release the mouse button before you release the Shift key. Drag the control handle on the left side of the circle (without the Shift key) until it lies just outside the left edge of the image, as shown on the right, below. The mask is enlarged horizontally, from its center.

8   Hold Ctrl+Alt / Command+Option and drag the pin to duplicate the active filter and reposition it as shown at the left, below; then, without holding the Shift key, drag the control handles at the top and left of the ellipse to enlarge the Radial Filter adjustment as illustrated at the right, below.

> **Tip:** Radial Filter adjustments scale from the center by default. Hold down Alt / Option to scale from one side.

9   Drag the central pin for the active Radial Filter to the left to center the ellipse horizontally, while maintaining its distance from the lower edge of the image. Set both the Temperature and Tint values to **33**, increase the Exposure to **1.60**, and reduce the Clarity and Sharpness to **0** and **50** respectively. You can leave the rest of the settings as they are.

10 Press the Esc key or click the Radial Filter tool below the Histogram to disable the tool and hide the local adjustment pins from view.

Editing in another application

You can open a photo from your Lightroom catalog in an external image editing application from within the both the Library and Develop modules. Lightroom gives you the option to edit either the original image or a copy—either with or without the edits and adjustments you've already applied in Lightroom. Lightroom will automatically update the catalog entry for an original file edited externally; a copy edited externally will be imported to the catalog automatically and grouped in a stack with the original image.

If you have Photoshop installed on your computer, it will be preselected as the default external editor, but in the External Editing preferences you can specify an additional application that will be also listed in the Photo > Edit In menu. If you like to work with several image editing applications, you can create multiple external editor presets, or set up several presets for the same application, each with differing file type, naming, and photo handling settings suited to specific editing tasks.

If your external editor is Photoshop CS4 or later, Lightroom lists additional commands in the Photo > Edit In menu. You can open an image in Photoshop as a Smart Object, open multiple shots as layers in a single file (ideal for photo-composites), merge a series of photos into a panorama, or produce a HDR (High Dynamic Range) image by merging several differently exposed pictures of the same subject.

Sharing your work by e-mail

Now that you've edited and enhanced your photos, the final step in your workflow is to present them to your client, share them with friends and family, or publish them for the world to see on a photo-sharing website or in your own interactive web gallery. In Lightroom, it takes only minutes to create a sophisticated photo book or slideshow, customize a print layout, publish your photos online, or generate a stylish interactive gallery ready to be uploaded directly to your web server from within Lightroom.

Lesson 7, "Creating a Photo Book," Lesson 8, "Creating a Slideshow," Lesson 9, "Printing Images," and Lesson 10, "Publishing your Photos," will provide much more detail on the many Lightroom tools and features that make it simple to create professional-looking presentations, layouts, and galleries to showcase your photos. In this exercise, you'll learn how you can attach your finished images to an e-mail without leaving Lightroom.

1   Press Ctrl+D / Command+D or choose Edit > Select None. In the Filmstrip, Ctrl-click / Command-click to select the images 01_08.jpg and 01_09.jpg—the two photos that you've edited in the course of this lesson.

2   Choose File > Email Photos.

Lightroom automatically detects the default e-mail application on your computer and opens a dialog box where you can set up the address, subject, and e-mail account for your message, and specify the size and quality of the attached images.

3   Click Address to open your Lightroom address book. Click New Address; then, enter a contact name and e-mail address and click OK.

● **Note:** For Windows users: if you have not specified a default e-mail application in Windows, the sequence of dialog boxes you see may differ slightly from that described and illustrated here (from Mac OS). The process is basically the same, but you may need to refer to steps 8, 9, and 10 to set up an e-mail account before returning to this step.

4   In the Lightroom Address Book dialog box, you can specify as many recipients for your message as you wish. For now, select the entry for your new contact by clicking the associated check box, and then click OK.

5 Now type a subject line for your e-mail.

6 Choose from the image size and quality options in the Preset menu.

7 If you intend to use your default e-mail application, you're ready to click Send and add a text message in a standard e-mail window.

8 If you'd prefer to connect directly to a web-based mail service, you need to set up an account. In the From menu, choose Go To Email Account Manager.

9 In the Lightroom Email Account Manager dialog box, click the Add button at the lower left. In the New Account dialog box, enter your e-mail account name and choose your service provider; then, click OK.

10 Enter your e-mail address and password under Credential Settings in the Lightroom Email Account Manager dialog box, and then click Validate.

Lightroom uses your credential settings to verify your account online. In the Lightroom Email Account Manager dialog box, a green light indicates that your web-based e-mail account is now accessible by Lightroom.

11 Click Done to close the Email Account Manager. Type a message in the text box above the thumbnails of your attached images, change the font, text size, and text color if you wish, and then click Send.

Getting help

Help is available from several sources, each one useful to you in different circumstances:

Help in the application: The complete user documentation for Adobe Photoshop Lightroom is available from the Help menu, in the form of HTML content that displays in the Adobe Community Help application. Even without the Community Help application, this content will display in your default browser. This documentation provides quick access to summarized information on common tasks and concepts, and can be especially useful if you are new to Lightroom or if you are not connected to the Internet.

● **Note:** You don't need to be connected to the Internet to view Help in Lightroom. However, with an active Internet connection, you can access the most up-to-date information.

In the Help menu you can also access a list of keyboard shortcuts for the current module, and module-specific tips that will help you get started by introducing you to the Lightroom workspace and stepping you through the workflow.

Help on the web: You can also access the most comprehensive and up-to-date documentation on Lightroom via your default browser, whether Lightroom is currently running or not.

Help PDF: Help is also available as a PDF document, optimized for printing; download the document at: http://livedocs.adobe.com/en_US/Lightroom/1.0/help.pdf.

Navigating Help in the application

1   Choose Help > Lightroom Help, or press the F1 key on your keyboard. Even if you are not currently connected to the Internet, the Adobe Community Help application (or, if the Community Help application is not installed, your default web browser) will open to the front page of the Adobe Photoshop Lightroom Help documentation that was installed on your computer together with the Lightroom application.

2   For quick access to Help documentation specific to the module in which you are working, press Ctrl+Alt+/ on Windows, or Command+Option+/ on Mac OS.

3   Press Ctrl+/ on Windows, or Command+/ on Mac OS to see a list of keyboard shortcuts for the current module.

4   Choose a topic from the table of contents. Click the plus sign (+) to the left of any topic heading to see a list of sub-topics. Click a sub-topic to see its content displayed on the right.

If you do have an active Internet connection, the Community Help application gives you access to the most up-to-date information about Lightroom and other Adobe products. You can search and browse Adobe and community content, and comment on or rate any article just as you would in your default browser. Search results will show not only content from Adobe, but also from the community.

You can also download reference content for use offline, and subscribe to new content updates (which can be downloaded automatically) so that you'll always have the most up-to-date information. Adobe content is updated based on community feedback and contributions. You can contribute in several ways: add comments to content or forums—including links to web content, publish your own content using Community Publishing, or contribute Cookbook Recipes. Find out how to contribute at http://helpx.adobe.com/community.html.

Accessing Help and Support on the web

You can access Lightroom Help, Support and other useful resources on the web, even if Lightroom is not currently running.

1   Do one of the following::

    • If Lightroom is currently running, choose Help > Lightroom Online.

    • If Lightroom is not currently running, point your default web browser to http://helpx.adobe.com/lightroom.html where you can find and browse Lightroom Help and Support content on adobe.com.

2   To search for a particular topic in the Help documentation, enter a search term in the Search text box at the top of the page, and then click Search.

3   Choose from the options just below the search field on the results page to show All Community Content or narrow the search to return Only Adobe Content.

You can find a list of additional resources that will help you to get the most out of Lightroom in the preceding chapter, Getting Started.

Congratulations—you've completed the first lesson. You have been introduced to the seven Lightroom workspace modules and learned how they fit into your workflow. You've imported photos, taken the first steps towards organizing your catalog in the Library module, explored some of the powerful editing tools in the Develop module, and seen just how easy it can be to share your images.

Before you move on to the next lesson, take minute or two to refresh your new skills by reading through the lesson review on the facing page.

Review questions

1 What is non-destructive editing?

2 What are the seven Lightroom workspace modules and how do they relate to your workflow?

3 How can you increase the viewing area without resizing the application window?

4 What advantage is there to grouping images in a collection, rather than by keyword?

5 Why is it recommended to create a special collection for each book, slideshow, print, or web project?

Review answers

1 Whatever modifications you make to an image in your library—cropping, rotation, corrections, retouching, or effects—Lightroom records the editing information only in the catalog file. The original image data remains unchanged.

2 The Lightroom workflow begins in the Library module: a hub where you'll import, organize, sort, and search your photos, manage your growing catalog, and keep track of the images you publish. You can leverage GPS metadata to organize your photos by location in the Map module. Move to the Develop module for a comprehensive editing environment with all the tools you need to correct, retouch, and enhance digital images and ready them for output. The Book, Slideshow, Print and Web modules each provide a range of stylish preset templates together with a suite of powerful, intuitive controls to help you customize them so that you can quickly create sophisticated layouts and presentations to share and showcase your work in its best light.

3 You can hide any of the panels and panel groups surrounding the work area. The working view automatically expands into the space available. The work area is the only part of the Lightroom workspace that you cannot hide from view.

4 The difference between grouping images in a collection and applying keyword tags is that, in a collection, you can change the order of the photos displayed in the Grid view and the Filmstrip, and you can remove an image from the group.

5 In a collection, you can change the order in which your images are displayed, which affects their placement in your project or layout. Images that are not included in a collection are displayed in a fixed order reflecting your choice of sorting criteria, such as capture date, file name, or star rating.

2 INTRODUCING THE WORKSPACE

Lesson overview

Whether you prefer to use menu commands and keyboard shortcuts or buttons and sliders, whether you use a single monitor or two—you can set up the flexible Lightroom workspace to suit the way *you* work. Customize each module individually so you always have your favorite tools and controls at hand, arranged just the way you like them.

To help familiarize you with the Lightroom workspace, this lesson will focus on the interface elements and skills that are common to all the workspace modules:

- Toggling between screen modes
- Adjusting the workspace layout
- Showing and hiding panels and panel groups
- Collapsing or expanding panels
- Changing and customizing view modes
- Working with a second display
- Personalizing the workspace
- Choosing interface options
- Using keyboard shortcuts

 You'll probably need between one and two hours to complete this lesson. If you haven't already done so, download the Lesson 2 work files from the Lesson & Update Files tab on your Account page at www.peachpit.com.

Make working with Lightroom even more pleasurable, and ultimately more productive, by personalizing the workspace so that you always have your favorite tools at hand. Lightroom streamlines your workflow, allowing you to move effortlessly between the different modules and viewing modes and freeing you up to spend less time in front of the computer and more time behind the lens.

Getting started

Before you start on this lesson, make sure you've set up the LR5CIB folder for your lesson files and created the LR5CIB Catalog file to manage them, as described in "Setting up a work folder" and "Creating a catalog file for working with this book" in the Getting Started chapter at the start of this book. Download the Lesson 2 folder from your Account page at www.peachpit.com to the LR5CIB/Lessons folder, if you haven't already done so, as detailed in the "Accessing the Classroom in a Book files" section in the chapter "Getting Started."

1 Start Lightroom. In the Adobe Photoshop Lightroom - Select Catalog dialog box, make sure that the file LR5CIB Catalog.lrcat is selected under Select A Recent Catalog To Open, and then click Open.

▶ **Tip:** If you can't see the Module Picker, choose Window > Panels > Show Module Picker, or press the F5 key. Note that on Mac OS the function keys are assigned to specific operating system functions by default and may not work as expected in Lightroom. If you find this to be the case, either press the fn key (not available on all keyboard layouts) together with the F5 key, or change the keyboard behavior in your system preferences.

2 Lightroom opens in the module that was last active. Switch to the Library, if necessary, by clicking Library in the Module Picker at the top of the workspace.

Importing images into the library

The first step is to import the images for this lesson into the Lightroom library.

1 Choose File > Import Photos And Video. If the Import dialog box appears in compact mode, click the Show More Options button at the lower left.

2   Under Source at the left of the expanded Import dialog box, disable Include Subfolders; then, navigate to the Lessons folder that you copied into the LR5CIB folder on your hard disk and select the Lesson 2 folder. In the thumbnail grid, ensure that all seven images in the Lesson 2 folder are checked for import.

3   In the import options just above the thumbnail previews, select Add so that the imported photos will be added to your catalog without being moved or copied.

4   Under File Handling at the right of the expanded Import dialog box, choose Minimal from the Render Previews menu and ensure that the Don't Import Suspected Duplicates option is activated.

5   Under Apply During Import, choose None from both the Develop Settings menu and the Metadata menu and type **Lesson 2** in the Keywords text box. Make sure that your import is set up as shown in the illustration below, and then click Import.

▶ **Tip:** The first time you enter any of the Lightroom modules, you'll see module tips that will help you get started by identifying the components of the Lightroom workspace and stepping you through the workflow. Dismiss the tips by clicking the Close button. To reactivate the tips for any module, choose [*Module name*] Tips from the Help menu.

6   If necessary, press the F6 key to show the Filmstrip across the bottom of the Lightroom workspace (on Mac OS, refer to the margin Tip on the facing page).

Thumbnails of the seven Lesson 2 images appear in the Grid view of the Library module and in the Filmstrip. You're now ready to start the exercises in this lesson.

Toggling screen modes

● **Note:** Whether you are running Lightroom on Windows or Mac OS, the workspace looks almost identical—any variations are simply due to the different user interface conventions on each platform.

In Lightroom 5, you can switch between four *screen modes* as you work. In the default mode the workspace appears inside an application window that you can resize and position on your screen. If you prefer, you can expand the workspace to fill the screen, either with or without a menu bar, or switch to a full-screen preview to see the photo you're working on without any distracting workspace elements.

1 Choose Window > Screen Mode > Normal to ensure that you are in the default screen mode.

In Normal screen mode on Windows, the Lightroom workspace appears inside an application window with the menu bar just below the window's title bar.

Normal screen mode on Windows.

In Normal screen mode on Mac OS, the Lightroom workspace appears inside a document window with the menu bar across the top of the screen.

Normal screen mode on Mac OS.

2 Choose Window > Screen Mode > Full Screen With Menubar.

In Full Screen With Menubar screen mode on Windows, the Lightroom workspace expands to fill the screen with the menu bar across the top of the screen and the Windows task bar across the bottom.

Full Screen With Menubar screen mode on Windows.

In Full Screen With Menubar screen mode on Mac OS, Lightroom expands to fill the screen with the menu bar across the top of the screen and the Dock, if it's not currently hidden, at the bottom.

Full Screen With Menubar screen mode on Mac OS.

3 Choose Window > Screen Mode > Full Screen. In Full Screen mode, the workspace fills the entire screen; the menu bar is hidden, as is the Windows task bar or the Dock on Mac OS.

4 Move the pointer to the top edge of the screen to see the menu bar; then, choose Window > Screen Mode > Full Screen And Hide Panels. Alternatively, you can use the keyboard shortcut Shift+Ctrl+F / Shift+Command+F.

5   In the Grid view, double-click any of the thumbnails to enter Loupe view.

A variant of Full Screen mode, Full Screen And Hide Panels maximizes the space available for the main work area, whether you're working with the thumbnail grid or with a single image in the Loupe view. Although the surrounding panels are all hidden, you can still access any of them when needed—using either keyboard shortcuts or your mouse—without changing the view. You'll learn more about showing and hiding panels later in this lesson.

6   Press T to hide the Toolbar at the bottom of the work area.

7   Press Shift+F repeatedly, or choose Window > Screen Mode > Next Screen Mode, to cycle through the three working modes. As you switch between the screen modes, you'll notice that the panels around the work area remain hidden.

8   To reveal all panels, press Shift+Tab once or twice. Press T to show the Toolbar.

9   Press the F key to see a full-screen preview of the selected image at the highest magnification possible, without the distraction of workspace elements; then, press Alt+Ctrl+F / Option+Command+F to return to Normal screen mode.

Adjusting the workspace layout

Working with the application window on Windows

In Normal screen mode on Windows, you can resize and reposition the application window just as you are used to doing with other applications.

1   Move the pointer to any edge of the window. When the pointer changes to a horizontal or vertical double-arrow icon, you can drag the window's edge.

2   Move the pointer to any corner of the application window. When the pointer changes to a diagonal double-arrow (↗), you can drag the corner.

3   Click the Maximize button (▣), located beside the Close button (✖) at the right of the title bar; the application window expands to fill the entire screen, though you are still in Normal screen mode with both the title bar and the menu visible. While the window is maximized, it's no longer possible to resize it as you did in steps 1 and 2, or reposition it by dragging the title bar.

4   Click the Restore Down button (▣) to return to the previous window size.

Working with the application window on Mac OS

1   In Normal screen mode on Mac OS, resize the application window by dragging its lower right corner.

2   Click the green Zoom button (●), located beside the Close and Minimize buttons at the left of the title bar. The application window expands to fill the screen. Click the Zoom button again to return to the previous window size.

3   Reposition the application window on your screen by dragging the title bar.

Using a secondary display

If you have a second monitor connected to your computer, you can use it to display an additional view that is independent of the module and view mode currently active on your main monitor. You can choose to have the secondary view displayed in its own window that can be resized and repositioned, or have it fill your second screen. Use the view picker at the top of secondary display to switch between Grid, Loupe, Compare, and Survey views.

If you have only one monitor connected to your computer, you can open the additional display in a floating window that you can resize and reposition as you work.

1   To open a separate window—whether you're using one or two monitors—click the Second Window button (![2]), located at the upper left of the Filmstrip.

▶ **Tip:** You can use keyboard shortcuts to change the view in the secondary display— Shift+G for Grid, Shift+E for Loupe, Shift+C for Compare, and Shift+N for Survey. If the second window is not already open, you can use these keyboard shortcuts to quickly open it in the desired viewing mode.

2   In the top panel of the secondary display, click Grid or press Shift+G.

3   Use the Thumbnails slider in the lower right corner of the secondary display to change the size of the thumbnail images. Use the scrollbar on the right side, if necessary, to scroll to the end of the Grid view.

The Grid view in the secondary display shows the same images as the Grid view and the Filmstrip in the main window. The source indicator and menu at the left of the secondary display's lower panel work the same way they do in the Filmstrip, and the top and bottom panels can be hidden and shown, just as they can in the main window. You'll learn more about working with panels later in this lesson.

4 In the secondary display, check the mode picker at the right of the top panel to make sure that Normal mode is selected. Click to select any thumbnail in the grid, and then click Loupe in the view picker at the left of the top panel.

When the secondary display is in Normal mode, the Loupe view displays the active image from the Grid view and Filmstrip in the main display.

5 Use the left and right arrow keys on your keyboard to select either the previous or next photo in the series. The new selection becomes the active image and the secondary display is updated accordingly.

6 Click Live in the mode picker at the right of the secondary display's top panel.

In Live mode, the secondary display shows the image that is currently under your pointer in the main window—whether that image is a thumbnail in the Filmstrip or the Grid view, or enlarged in the Loupe, Compare, or Survey view.

● **Note:** If your secondary display is open in a window rather than on a second screen, you may need to change the focus for any keyboard input by clicking inside the main window or on its title bar.

You can set a different zoom level for the secondary display by choosing from the picker at the lower right of the secondary window.

7   Select an image in the Filmstrip; then, switch the secondary window to Locked mode by clicking Locked in the mode picker at the right of the top panel. The current image will now remain fixed in the secondary display until you return to Normal or Live mode—regardless of the image displayed in the main window.

8   Change the zoom level for the secondary display by choosing from the picker at the right of the lower panel: click Fit, Fill, or 1:1, or choose a zoom ratio from the menu at the far right.

9   Drag the zoomed image to reposition it in the secondary window, and then click the image to return to the previous zoom level.

10 (Optional) Right-click / Control-click the image to choose a different background color or texture from the context menu. These settings will apply to the secondary display independently of the options chosen for the main window.

11 Choose Compare from the view picker at the left of the secondary window's top panel. In the main window, select two or more images—either in the Grid view or in the Filmstrip.

The image in the left pane of the Compare view is the *Select* image; the image in the right pane is the *Candidate*. Click the Select Previous Photo button (◀) or the Select Next Photo button (▷) to change the candidate image. If you have more than two images selected, only images from the selection are considered as candidates. To replace the Select image with the current Candidate, click the Make Select button (⧉).

12 In the main window, select three or more images—either in the Grid view or in the Filmstrip, and then click Survey in the top panel of the second window. Use the Survey view to compare more than two images at the same time (*see illustration on next page*). To remove an image from the Survey view, move the pointer over the unwanted image and click the Close button (x) that appears in

the lower right corner of the image. You'll learn more about using the Compare and Survey views later in this book.

13 Click to un-check Show in the Window > Secondary Display menu, or click the Close button (☒ Windows) / (⊖ Mac OS) to close the secondary display.

Resizing panels

You can customize the layout of the Lightroom workspace to suit the way you work or to make more space for the task at hand by adjusting the width of the side panel groups and the height of the Filmstrip panel, or by hiding any of these elements.

1 Move the pointer over the right edge of the left panel group; the cursor changes to a horizontal double arrow (↔). Drag to the right and release the mouse button when the panel group has reached its maximum width.

The central work area contracts to accommodate the expanded panel group. You might use this arrangement to maximize the Navigator preview.

2 Click Develop in the Module Picker to switch to the Develop module. You'll notice that the left panel group returns to the width it was when you last used the Develop module.

Lightroom remembers your customized workspace layout for each module independently, so that the workspace is automatically rearranged to suit the way you like to work for each stage in your workflow as you move between modules.

3 Press Alt+Ctrl+Up Arrow / Option+Command+Up Arrow to return quickly to the previous module.

4 In the Library module, drag the right edge of the left panel group to return the group to its minimum width.

5 Move the pointer over the top edge of the Filmstrip panel; the cursor changes to a vertical double-arrow (↕). Drag the top edge down until the Filmstrip reaches its minimum height.

The work area expands to fill the available space. This arrangement keeps the Filmstrip visible while increasing the space available for the Grid view when you're selecting photos, or for reviewing images in the Loupe, Compare and Survey views.

● Note: For the side panel groups, double-clicking the border will produce a different result. This is discussed in the next section, "Showing and hiding panels or panel groups."

6 Switch to the Develop module. The Filmstrip remains unchanged as you move between modules. Whichever module you switch to, the Filmstrip will remain at its current height until you resize it.

7 Move the pointer over the top edge of the Filmstrip panel; the pointer changes to a vertical double-arrow cursor. Double-click the top edge of the Filmstrip to reset the panel to its previous height; then switch back to the Library module.

8 Drag the top border of the Filmstrip to its maximum height. The thumbnails in the Filmstrip are enlarged and, if necessary, a scroll bar appears along the bottom of the Filmstrip. Scroll to view all the thumbnails; then, double-click the top edge of the Filmstrip with the vertical double-arrow cursor to reset the panel to its previous height.

● **Note:** You can't change the height of the top panel, but you can hide or reveal it as you wish.

Showing and hiding panels or panel groups

By adjusting the size of the side panel groups and the Filmstrip, you can allocate more space for the controls you access most frequently and reduce the prominence of features you use less often. Once you've set up the workspace as you like it, you can maximize your working view as needed by temporarily hiding any, or all of the surrounding panels. In some screen modes, Lightroom even hides the title and menu bars and the Windows task bar or Mac OS Dock.

1 To hide the left panel group, click the Show / Hide Panel Group arrow (◀) in the left margin of the workspace window. The panel group disappears and the arrow icon is reversed to face right.

2 Click the reversed Show / Hide Panel Group arrow (▶) to reinstate the left panel group.

▶ **Tip:** You don't need to be accurate when you click the Show / Hide Panel Group arrows. In fact, you can click anywhere in the workspace margins to hide and show panels.

You can use the arrows in the top, right, and bottom margins of the workspace to show and hide the top panel, the right panel group, and the Filmstrip.

3 Disable the menu option Window > Panels > Show Left Module Panels or press the F7 key to hide the left panel group. To show the group again, press F7 or choose Window > Panels > Show Left Module Panels. Disable the menu option Window > Panels > Show Right Module Panels or press the F8 key to hide the right panel group. To show the group again, press F8 or choose Window > Panels > Show Right Module Panels.

4 Disable the menu option Window > Panels > Show Module Picker or press the F5 key to hide the top panel. To show it again, press F5 or choose Window > Panels > Show Module Picker. To hide the Filmstrip, press the F6 key or disable the menu option Window > Panels > Show Filmstrip. To show it again, press F6 or choose Window > Panels > Show Filmstrip.

5 To hide or show both side panel groups at once, press the Tab key or choose Window > Panels > Toggle Side Panels. To hide or show the top panel and the Filmstrip as well as the side panel groups, press Shift+Tab, or choose Window > Panels > Toggle All Panels.

▶ **Tip:** On Mac OS, some function keys are assigned to specific operating system functions by default. If pressing a function key in Lightroom does not work as expected, either press the fn key (not available on all keyboard layouts) together with the respective function key, or change the keyboard behavior in the system preferences.

Lightroom also offers options that make the workspace even more flexible and convenient by showing and hiding panels or panel groups automatically in response to your movements with the pointer, so that information, tools and controls will appear only when you need them.

6   Right-click / Control-click the Show / Hide Panel Group arrow (◀) in the left margin of the workspace window. Choose Auto Hide & Show from the context menu.

7   Hide the left panel group by clicking the Show / Hide Panel Group arrow (◀); then, move the pointer over the arrow in the left margin of the workspace. The left panels automatically slide into view, partly covering the work area. You can click to select catalogs, folders, and collections; the left panel group will remain visible as long as the pointer remains over it. Move the pointer outside the left panel group and it will disappear again. To show or hide the left panels independently of the current settings, press the F7 key.

8   Right-click / Control-click the Show / Hide Panel Group arrow (◀) in the left margin of the workspace window and choose Auto Hide from the context menu. Now the panel group disappears when you are done with it and does not reappear when you move the pointer into the workspace margin. To show the left panel group again, click in the workspace margin, or press the F7 key.

9   To turn off automatic show and hide for this panel, right-click / Control-click the Show / Hide Panel Group arrow (◀) in the left margin of the workspace and choose Manual from the context menu.

10   To reset the left panel group to its default behavior, activate Auto Hide & Show in the context menu. If either of the left or right panel groups is still hidden, press the F7 key or the F8 key respectively, to show it again.

Keep it in mind that Lightroom remembers your customized panel layout for each module independently—including your choice of show and hide options—so you can set these options differently in each module to suit the way you like to handle each stage of your workflow. The options you choose for the Filmstrip and the top panel, however, remain unchanged as you move between modules.

Working with the left and right panel groups

Up to this point in our lesson, we've dealt with the left and right panels only as groups. Now you'll learn to work with the individual panels within the groups.

Expanding and collapsing panels

1   If you are not already in the Library module, switch to it now. Create more space to work with the side panel groups by hiding both the top panel and the Filmstrip. *(See step 4 in the previous exercise.)*

In the Library module, the left panel group contains the Navigator, Catalog, Folders, Collections, and Publish Services panels. Each panel within a group can be *expanded* to show its content or *collapsed* so that only the panel header is visible. A triangle next to the panel name indicates whether a panel is expanded or collapsed.

2   To expand a collapsed panel, click the triangle next to its name; the triangle turns downward and the panel expands to show its content. Click the triangle again to collapse the panel.

▶ **Tip:** You don't need to be accurate when you click the triangle. Clicking anywhere in the panel header will do, as long as you don't click any other control that might be located there, such as the Plus icon (+) in the header of the Collections panel.

Folders within a panel—such as the Smart Collections folder in the Collections panel—can be expanded and collapsed by clicking the triangle next to the folder name, or by double-clicking the folder header.

3   Open the Window > Panels menu; panels that are currently expanded and fully visible in the panel group show a check mark in front of their names. Choose any of the panels from that menu and toggle its display status.

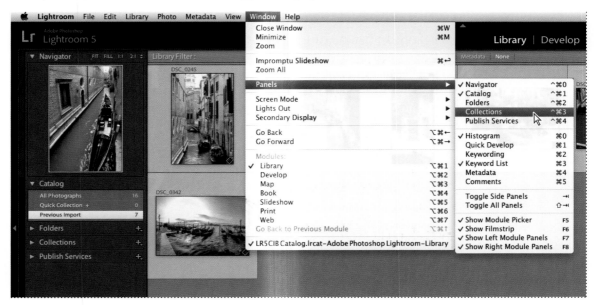

4 In the Window > Panels menu, look at the keyboard shortcuts for expanding and collapsing the individual panels. For the panels in the left group, the keyboard shortcuts begin with Ctrl+Shift / Control+Command followed by a number. The panels are numbered from the top down, so you press Ctrl+Shift+0 / Control+Command+0 for the Navigator panel, Ctrl+Shift+1 / Control+Command+1 for the Catalog panel, and so on. For the panels in the right group, the keyboard shortcuts begin with Ctrl / Command followed by a number. Press Ctrl+0 / Command+0 to collapse the Histogram panel. Press the same keyboard shortcut again to expand it. These keyboard shortcuts may be assigned to different panels in another workspace module, but this should not be too confusing if you remember that the panels are always numbered from the top of the group, starting at 0.

With one click, you can expand and collapse all panels other than the topmost in each group, or have all the panels other than the top panel in the group and the one you're working with close automatically. The top panel in each group has a special role and is not affected by these commands.

▶ **Tip:** You can also right-click / Control-click the empty area below the bottom panel to access the panel group context menu.

5 To collapse all panels in either of the side groups, right-click / Control-click the header of any panel other than the top panel in the group, and then choose Collapse All from the context menu. The top panel remains expanded.

6 To expand all the panels in either group, right-click / Control-click the header of any panel—other than the top panel in each group—and choose Expand All from the context menu. Once again, the top panel remains unaffected.

▶ **Tip:** Alt-click or Option-click the header of any panel to quickly activate or disable the Solo mode.

7 To collapse all the panels in a group other than the one you're working with, right-click / Control-click the header of any panel—other than the top panel in the group—and choose Solo mode from the context menu. Only one panel will remain expanded. The triangles beside the panel names change from solid to dotted when Solo mode is activated. Click the header of a collapsed panel to expand it. The previously expanded panel collapses automatically.

Hiding and showing panels

If you use some panels in a group less often than others, you can hide them from view to create more space to expand the panels you use most frequently.

1 To hide all the panels in a group other than the topmost, right-click / Control-click the header of any panel and choose Hide All from the context menu. All the panels in the group are now hidden, except the Navigator panel at the top.

2 To show all panels, right-click / Control-click inside the empty space below the visible panels and choose Show All from the context menu.

3 To show or hide an individual panel, choose it from the same context menu. Panels that are currently visible have check-marks in front of their names.

Working with the main display area

The main display area—the work area—in the center of the application window is where you select, sort, and compare images, and then preview your work as you make adjustments and create presentations. The work area serves different purposes in each of the workspace modules. In the Library and Develop modules the work area offers a choice of view modes to suit a range of tasks, from organizing your photos to editing them. In the Book, Slideshow, Print, and Web modules, the work area presents a working preview of your projects and presentations.

Depending on your workspace setup in the Library module, you may see the Filter bar across the top of the work area. You can use filters to limit the images that are displayed in the Grid view and the Filmstrip so that you'll see only those photos with a specified rating, flag status, or containing particular metadata content.

![Library Filter grid view with thumbnails DSC_0245, DSC_0268, DSC_0272, DSC_0289, DSC_0311, DSC_0327, DSC_0342]

▶ **Tip:** You'll learn more about using the Filter bar controls in Lesson 5, "Organizing and Selecting."

The Toolbar, located at the bottom of the work area, is common to all the workspace modules but contains different tools and controls for each.

1 If you're not already in the Library module, switch to it now.

2 If the Filter bar is not already visible at the top of the work area, show it by pressing the backslash character (\) on your keyboard or by activating the menu option View > Show Filter Bar. Press backslash again or disable the menu option View > Show Filter Bar to hide it.

3 If the Toolbar is not already visible, press T to show it. Press T again to hide it. Switch to the Develop module. If the Toolbar is not already visible, press T to show it. Switch back to the Library Module. In the Library module the Toolbar is still hidden from step 3; Lightroom remembers your Toolbar setting for each module independently. Press T to show the Toolbar in the Library module.

4 Double-click an image in Grid view to switch to Loupe view. The Loupe view is available in both the Library and Develop modules, but the controls available in the Loupe view Toolbar differ for each of these modules.

▶ **Tip:** If you activate more tools than can be displayed in the width of the Toolbar, you can increase the Toolbar's width by hiding the side panel groups, or disable tools that you don't need at the moment.

5 To hide or show individual tools, click the white arrow at the right end of the Toolbar and choose their names from the pop-up menu. Tools that are currently visible in the Toolbar have a checkmark in front of their names.

Navigating the Loupe view

In Loupe view, you can view your images at different levels of magnification. The zoom controls in the top right corner of the Navigator panel in the left panel group enable you to switch quickly between preset magnification levels. You can choose from Fit, Fill, 1:1, or choose another option from a menu of ten zoom ratios.

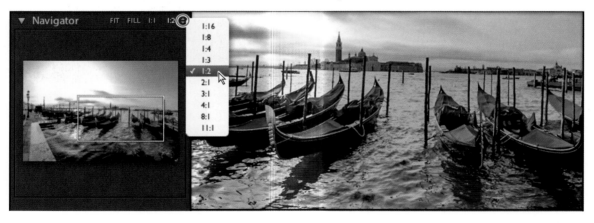

You can toggle between zoom levels by choosing View > Toggle Zoom View, or pressing Z on your keyboard. To better understand the Toggle Zoom View command, you should be aware that the magnification controls in the Navigator panel are organized into two groups: Fit and Fill are in one group, and the zoom ratio settings are in the other. The Toggle Zoom View command toggles between the magnification levels last used in each group.

1 Click Fit in the zoom controls in the top right corner of the Navigator panel. Now click the 1:1 control. Choose View > Toggle Zoom View, or press Z. The zoom setting reverts to Fit. Press the Z key; the zoom setting reverts to 1:1.

2 Click Fill in the zoom controls in the top right corner of the Navigator panel. Now choose a zoom ratio from the menu at the far right of the Navigator panel header; we chose 2:1. Click the image in the Loupe view. The zoom setting reverts to Fill. In the Loupe view, clicking the image is equivalent to pressing the Z key, or choosing View > Toggle Zoom View, except that the zoomed view of the image will be centered on the area you clicked. Press Z to zoom to 2:1.

3 While the view is magnified, drag the zoom rectangle in the Navigator preview, or drag in the Loupe view to change the area currently visible in the work area. At higher zoom levels you may find using the Navigator panel more convenient; dragging in the Loupe view is better suited to working at lower zoom levels.

4 Using keystrokes to navigate an image can be helpful when you wish to inspect the entire image in close detail. Press the Home key (fn+Left Arrow) to position the zoom rectangle at the upper left of the image; then press the Page Down key (fn+Down Arrow) repeatedly to scroll through the magnified image one section at a time. When you reach the bottom of the photo the zoom rectangle jumps to the top of the next column. To start in the lower right corner of the image, press the End key (fn+Right Arrow); then use the Page Up key (fn+Up Arrow).

5 Show the Filmstrip; then, select another photo with the same orientation and click in the Navigator preview to move the zoom rectangle to a different part of the image. Return to the previous image; the zoom rectangle returns to its previous position for that photo. Choose View > Lock Zoom Position, and then repeat the first part of this step; the position of the zoom rectangle is now synchronized. This can be useful when comparing detail across similar photos.

6   In the View menu, un-check the Lock Zoom Position option to disable it.

The zoom controls and the Navigator panel work the same way for the Loupe view in both the Library and Develop modules. You'll learn more about using the Grid, Loupe, Compare, and Survey views in Lesson 4 and Lesson 6.

Grid and Loupe view options

You can choose from the many options in the Library View Options dialog box to customize the information Lightroom displays for each image in the Grid and Loupe views. For the Loupe view and thumbnail tooltips you can activate two sets of options, and then use a keyboard shortcut to switch between them.

1   Press G to switch to Grid view in the Library module.

2   Choose View > View Options. The Library View Options dialog box appears with the Grid View tab already selected. Position the Library View Options dialog box so you can see some of the images in the Grid view.

3   At the top of the Grid View tab, un-check Show Grid Extras. This disables most of the other options.

4   The only options still available are Tint Grid Cells With Label Colors and Show Image Info Tooltips. If they are not already activated, click the checkboxes for both of these options. As the images have not yet been assigned color labels, activating the first option has no visible effect in the Grid view. Right-click / Control-click any thumbnail—you can do this while the Library View Options dialog box is open—and choose a color from the Set Color Label menu.

In the Grid view and the Filmstrip, a color-labeled image that is currently selected will show a thin colored frame around the thumbnail; a color-labeled image that is not selected has a tinted cell background.

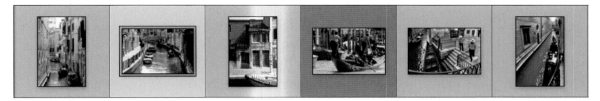

5   Position the pointer over a thumbnail in the Grid view or the Filmstrip; a tooltip appears. In Mac OS you'll need to click anywhere in the Lightroom workspace window to bring it to the front before you can see the tooltips.

By default, the tooltip will display the file name, capture date and time, and the cropped dimensions. You can specify the information to be displayed in the tooltip by choosing from the Loupe View options.

6   On Mac OS, if the Library View Options dialog box is now hidden behind the main application window, press Command+J to bring it back to the front.

7   Activate the Show Grid Extras option and choose Compact Cells from the menu beside it. Experiment with each setting to see its effect in the Grid view display. Activate and disable the settings for Options, Cell Icons, and Compact Cell Extras. Position the pointer over the various icons in the image cells to see tooltips with additional information.

8 Under Compact Cell Extras, click the Top Label menu to see the long list of choices available. For some choices, such as Title or Caption, nothing will be displayed until you add the relevant information to the image's metadata.

9 Now choose Expanded Cells from the Show Grid Extras menu. Experiment with the Expanded Cell Extras options to see the effects in the Grid view. Click any of the Show Header With Labels menus to see the many choices available to customize the information that is displayed in the cell headers.

10 Click the Loupe View tab. The work area switches from Grid to Loupe view so you can preview the effects of the changes you'll make in the Library View Options dialog box.

For the Loupe view, you can activate the Show Info Overlay option to display image information in the top left corner of the view. Choose items from the menus in Loupe Info 1 and Loupe Info 2 to create two different sets of information, and then choose either set from the Show Info Overlay menu. When you choose an information item such as Capture Date And Time, Lightroom extracts those details from the image metadata. If the image's metadata does not contain the specified information, nothing will be displayed for that item. For both the Grid and Loupe view options you can choose the information item Common Attributes, which will display the flagged status, star rating and color label for each image.

You can reset either group to its default state by clicking the Use Defaults button. Activate the Show Briefly When Photo Changes option to show the info overlay for only a few seconds when a new image is displayed in the Loupe view. Activate the Show Message When Loading Or Rendering Photos option to display a notification in the lower part of the view while the image preview is updated. It is recommended that you keep this option activated so that you don't inadvertently make judgments about the quality of an image before the update is complete.

11 Click the Close button (x) / (⊖) to close the Library View Options dialog box.

12 You can choose which of the two information sets will be displayed by choosing an option from the View > Loupe Info menu, or by pressing the I key to cycle the info overlay through Loupe Info 1, Loupe Info 2, and its disabled state.

13 Switch to the Grid view. From the View > Grid View Style menu you can choose whether or not to display additional information, using either the Compact Cells layout or the Expanded Cells layout. Press the J key to cycle through the Compact Cells layout, with and without additional information, and the Expanded Cells layout.

Dimming lights

Lightroom gives you the option to darken the workspace so that you can focus on the image or images with which you're working. In the Library and Develop modules, everything is dimmed or darkened except your selected photos. In the other three modules, everything except the presentation preview in the work area is dimmed or darkened. All tools and controls will still work in the Lights Dim or Lights Off modes—if you can find them! You could pick up the crop tool for example, and then switch to either the Lights Dim or Lights Off mode to help you concentrate on achieving the best result.

1 To dim the lights, press the L key or choose Window > Lights Out > Lights Dim.

2 If you're in the Grid view, double-click an image to switch to Loupe view. Click the image to switch between zoom levels. If you can see the Filmstrip, click to select a different image. Switch to a different module. If you remember the keyboard shortcuts they can really come in handy now.

3 To darken the workspace around the image completely, press the L key again or choose Window > Lights Out > Lights Off—if you can still see the menu bar. To return to the normal display mode, press the L key a third time, or choose Window > Lights Out > Lights On.

Lightroom achieves the dimming and darkening effects by means of a black overlay applied to the interface—at a default opacity of 80% for Lights Dim and 100% for Lights Off. You can choose instead to have the workspace fade to white or a shade of grey. This might be useful, for example, if your images contain a lot of black or dark colors. You can also adjust the level of opacity for the Lights Dim mode so that you can still see the controls if necessary.

4 To change the Lights Out screen color or to adjust the opacity for the Lights Dim mode, choose Edit > Preferences / Lightroom > Preferences. In the Preferences dialog box, click the Interface tab and choose a new opacity value from the Dim Level menu in the Lights Out options. From the Screen Color menu, choose white or a shade of grey.

5 Click OK / the Close button (⊝) to close the Preferences dialog box, and press the L key repeatedly to see your new settings in effect. Return to step 4 to modify your settings or reinstate the defaults.

Personalizing the identity plate

If you're using Lightroom to make presentations to clients on your computer, or if you'd simply like to personalize the workspace with your name or company logo, you can change the graphic that is displayed as an identity plate in the top panel.

1 If the top panel is not currently visible, press the F5 key on your keyboard, or choose Window > Panels > Show Module Picker.

2 Choose Edit > Identity Plate Setup / Lightroom > Identity Plate Setup. Position the Identity Plate Editor dialog box so you can see both the dialog box and the identity plate in the top panel.

3 If not already selected, activate the Use A Styled Text Identity Plate option. Then activate the Enable Identity Plate option. You'll notice an immediate change in the appearance of the identity plate.

● **Note:** If your Identity Plate Editor dialog box differs from the one shown in the illustration—other than the text in the text box on the left and the font selection—click the Show Details button in the lower left corner.

To personalize the identity plate, you can either use styled text or place a graphic of your choice. If you wish, you can also change the typeface and text color used for the Module Picker at the other end of the top panel to better suit your design.

4 Select the text in the text box and replace it with your own.

5 Press Ctrl+A / Command+A to select your new text, and choose a typeface, font style, and font size from the menus beneath the text box. Use your company's corporate typeface or your own favorite—not necessarily mutually exclusive choices. Click the color box beside the font size menu and choose a new color from the Colors palette. Keep an eye on how your choices look in the top panel of the main window. Click OK to apply your changes or Cancel to reject them.

▶ **Tip:** You can use more than one typeface, font style, size, or color in your identity plate text. Simply select a portion of your text and make the desired changes.

▶ **Tip:** If your text is too long to be fully visible in the text box, either resize the dialog box or reduce the font size until you've finished editing.

6 (Optional) You can also change the typeface, font style, and font size used for the text in the Module Picker to better suit your new identity plate design. There is a second set of controls in the Identity Plate Editor dialog box for this purpose. Click the first color box to change the color used to highlight the name of the active module and the second to change the color used for the others.

7 To use an image as your identity plate, choose Edit > Identity Plate Setup / Lightroom > Identity Plate Setup. In the Identity Plate Editor dialog box, activate the Use A Graphical Identity Plate option, and then click Locate File. In the Locate File dialog box, navigate to and open the Extras folder inside your Lesson 2 folder, select the file Identityplate.png, and then click Choose.

● **Note:** On Windows, you can choose a JPEG, PNG, GIF, BMP, or TIFF image for your graphical identity plate. The image can contain transparent pixels and should not be more than 48 pixels in height. On Mac OS, images in PSD or PDF format are also supported and the image height can be up to 57 pixels.

8 (Optional) You can save several identity plate setups as presets that can be easily accessed for different situations. Choose Save As from the Enable Identity Plate menu, enter a name for your identity plate preset and click Save. Your identity plate presets will appear in the Enable Identity Plate menu.

9 Disable the Enable Identity Plate option, and then click OK to close the Identity Plate Editor dialog box.

Personalizing the side panels

Another great way to make the Lightroom workspace your own is to display your choice of ornament as a *panel end mark* below the bottom panel in each of the side groups. You can use a pre-installed design, load your own graphic, or choose not to display a panel end mark at all.

1 Right-click / Control-click in the space below the panels in either of the side groups and choose the Small Flourish ornament from the Panel End Mark submenu.

2 Right-click / Control-click the Small Flourish end mark and choose Panel End Mark > Go To Panel End Marks Folder.

3 Open another Windows Explorer / Finder window and navigate to the Extras subfolder inside your Lesson 2 folder. Drag the file Endmark.png from the Extras folder to the Panel End Marks folder; then, return to Lightroom.

4 Right-click / Control-click the Small Flourish end mark and choose Panel End Mark > Endmark.png from the context menu.

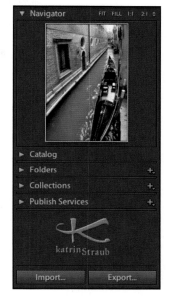

The same panel end mark is used for both side panel groups through all the Lightroom modules.

You can use your own design, which may include transparency, in PDF, JPEG, GIF, PNG, TIFF, or PSD format.

The names of any images you place in the Panel End Marks folder will appear in the panel group context menu. Alternatively, you can change the panel end mark, and also the size of the font used in the panels, in the Preferences dialog box.

5 Choose Edit > Preferences / Lightroom > Preferences. In the Preferences dialog box, click the Interface tab.

You'll find the End Marks and Font Size menus in the Panels options. The End Marks menu offers the same options you saw in step 4. From the Panel Font Size menu you can choose either Small (the default) or Large, although the difference is subtle. Changes to the font size will take effect next time you launch Lightroom.

6 Click Cancel / the Close button (⊜) to close the Preferences dialog box without making any changes.

Keyboard shortcuts

Press Ctrl+/ (Windows) / Command+/ (Mac OS) to see a list of keyboard shortcuts for the currently active module. When you're done reviewing the keyboard shortcuts, click to dismiss the list.

This concludes your introduction to the Lightroom workspace. You've learned how to switch between the different screen and view modes and how to arrange the workspace layout to suit the way you work in each module. You know how to hide, show, collapse, or expand panels and panel groups, how to customize the Toolbar, and how to use a secondary display. Finally, you've looked at ways to personalize the Lightroom workspace. Before you move on to the next lesson, take a minute or two to read through the review questions and answers on the following pages.

Review questions

1 How would you view an image at the largest size possible on your screen?

2 How do you adjust the size of the thumbnail images in the Grid view, the Navigator panel, and the Filmstrip?

3 What are the keyboard shorcuts to show or hide the four panels that surround the Lightroom workspace?

4 What do you do if you can't see the tool you're looking for in the Toolbar?

5 How can you personalize the Lightroom interface?

Review answers

1 In the Grid view, double-click the image thumbnail to enter the Loupe view. Choose Window > Screen Mode > Full Screen And Hide Panels, or use the keyboard shortcut Shift+Ctrl+F / Shift+Command+F. A variant of Full Screen mode, Full Screen And Hide Panels is ideal for viewing an image at the largest size possible on your display. Press the T key to hide the Toolbar, leaving nothing on screen but your photo. Press the F key to see a full-screen preview of the selected image at the highest magnification possible, without the distraction of workspace elements.

2 To change the size of the Grid view thumbnails on your main screen, use the Thumbnails slider in the Toolbar. In Grid view on a secondary display use the slider in the lower right corner of the window. The thumbnail images in the Navigator panel and the Filmstrip are resized automatically as you resize the left panel group or the Filmstrip.

3 The keyboard shortcuts to show or hide the top panel, the Filmstrip, the left panel group, and the right panel group are F5, F6, F7, and F8, respectively.

4 Check what module and view mode you are in. The Toolbar contains different tools for different views and modules. Click the triangle at the right of the Toolbar and activate the missing tool in the tools menu. If the tool is activated and you still can't see it, there may be too many active tools to fit across the Toolbar. Disable tools you are not using in the tools menu and they will be removed from the Toolbar.

5   Lightroom offers several options to personalize the interface:

- You can change the identity plate, the graphic that is displayed at the left corner of the top panel. You can either use styled text or place your own graphic.

- It's also possible to change the typeface and text color used for the Module Picker at the other end of the top panel to better suit your new identity plate.

- You can customize the panel end mark displayed in the left and right panel groups. Choose a pre-installed design or use one of your own.

- You can set the color and texture of the background that shows behind the images in many of the working views.

- Set the level of opacity for the Lights Dim modes in the Preferences dialog box.

- Show or hide different workspace panels to suit different tasks. Set panels to show and hide automatically. You can arrange the workspace differently in each of the Lightroom modules so that when you switch between modules, your tools are always set out the way you like them.

3   IMPORTING

Lesson overview

Lightroom allows a great deal of flexibility in importing your photos; you can download images directly from a camera, import them from your hard disk or external storage media, or transfer them between catalogs on different computers. During the import process you can organize your folders, add keywords and metadata to make your photos easy to find, make backup copies, and even apply editing presets.

This lesson will familiarize you with the many options available to you as you add more photos to your Lightroom library:

- Importing images from a camera or card reader
- Importing images from a hard disk or removable media
- Choosing file handling options
- Evaluating images before importing
- Organizing, renaming, and processing images automatically
- Applying keywords and metadata as part of the import process
- Initiating backup strategies
- Setting up automatic importing and creating import presets
- Acquiring images from other catalogs and applications

 You'll probably need between one and two hours to complete this lesson. If you haven't already done so, download the Lesson 3 work files from the Lesson & Update Files tab on your Account page at www.peachpit.com.

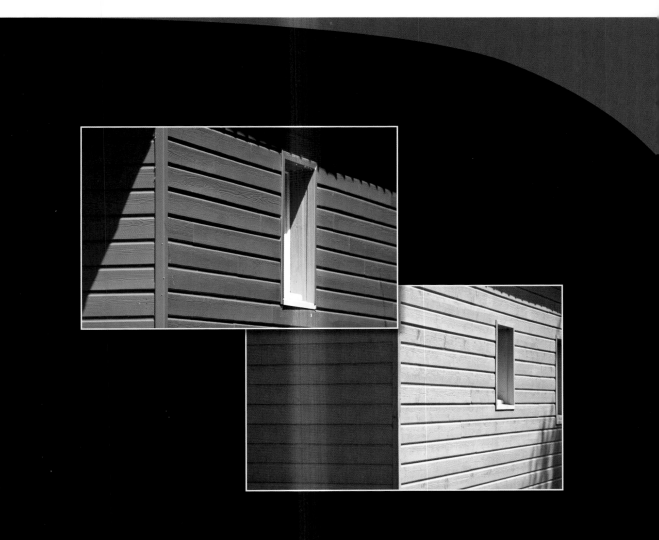

Lightroom starts helping you to organize and manage your growing photo library from the moment you click the Import button; you can make backups, create and organize folders, inspect images at high magnification, add keyword tags and other metadata that will save you hours sorting and searching your image library later—and all before your photos even reach your catalog!

Getting started

Before you start on this lesson, make sure you've set up the LR5CIB folder for your lesson files and created the LR5CIB Catalog file to manage them, as described in "Setting up a work folder" and "Creating a catalog file for working with this book" in the Getting Started chapter at the start of this book. Download the Lesson 3 folder from your Account page at www.peachpit.com to the LR5CIB/Lessons folder, if you haven't already done so, as detailed in the "Accessing the Classroom in a Book files" section in the chapter "Getting Started."

1   Start Lightroom. In the Adobe Photoshop Lightroom - Select Catalog dialog box, make sure the file LR5CIB Catalog.lrcat is selected under Select A Recent Catalog To Open, and then click Open.

▶ **Tip:** If you can't see the Module Picker, choose Window > Panels > Show Module Picker, or press the F5 key. If you're working on Mac OS, you may need to press the fn key together with the F5 key, or change the function key behavior in the system preferences.

2   Lightroom will open in the screen mode and workspace module that were active when you last quit. If necessary, switch to the Library module by clicking Library in the Module Picker at the top of the workspace.

The import process

Lightroom allows a great deal of flexibility in the import process. You can download images directly from a digital camera or card reader, import them from your hard disk or external storage media, and transfer them from another Lightroom catalog or from other applications. Import at the click of a button, use a menu command, or simply drag and drop. You can have Lightroom launch the import process when you connect your camera or import automatically when you move files into a watched folder. Wherever you're acquiring photos from, you'll be working with the Import dialog box, so we'll begin there.

You have the option to use the Import dialog box in either a compact or expanded mode, providing flexibility in the process from the very beginning. The top panel of the Import dialog box, common to both modes, presents the basic steps in the import process, arranged from left to right: choose an import source, specify how Lightroom is to handle the files you're importing, and then—if you choose to copy or move the source files—set up an import destination.

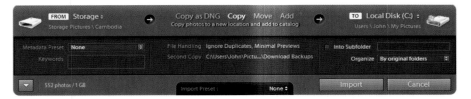

In expanded mode, the Import dialog box looks and works like the Lightroom workspace modules. The Source panel at the left provides easy access to your files on any available drive. The Preview pane displays images from the source selection as thumbnails in Grid view or enlarged in Loupe view. Depending on the type of import, the right panel group offers a Destination panel that mirrors the Source panel, and a suite of controls for processing your images as they're imported.

Importing photos from a digital camera

If you have a digital camera or a memory card reader at hand, you can step through this exercise using your own photos. If not, you can simply read through the steps and study the illustrations—most of the information in this exercise is equally applicable to importing from other sources.

To begin with, you'll configure the Lightroom preferences so that the import process is triggered automatically whenever you connect your camera or a memory card to your computer.

1   Choose Edit > Preferences (Windows) / Lightroom > Preferences (Mac OS). In the Preferences dialog box, click the General tab. Under Import Options, activate the option Show Import Dialog When A Memory Card Is Detected by clicking the checkbox.

Some cameras generate folder names on the memory card. If you don't find these folder names helpful for organizing your images, activate the option Ignore Camera-Generated Folder Names When Naming Folders. You'll learn more about folder naming options later in this lesson.

● **Note:** You'll find more options relating to the creation of DNG files during import on the File Handling preferences tab, but for the purposes of this exercise, you can ignore those settings. For more detailed information on DNG files, see the section "About file formats," later in this lesson.

If your camera records Raw images, it may also generate a JPEG version of each photo. If you wish to import both files, activate the option Treat JPEG Files Next To Raw Files As Separate Photos; otherwise, Lightroom will display only the Raw images in the Import Photos dialog box.

2   Click OK / the Close button (⊖) to close the Preferences dialog box.

3   Connect your digital camera or card reader to your computer, following the manufacturer's instructions.

4   This step may vary depending on your operating system and the image management software on your computer:

- On Windows, if the AutoPlay dialog box shown in the illustration at the right appears, double-click Import Photos Using Photoshop Lightroom. If you wish, you can set this option as the default.

- If you have more than one Adobe image management application—such as Adobe Bridge—installed on your computer and the Adobe Downloader dialog box appears, click Cancel.

- If the Import dialog box appears, continue to step 5.

- If the Import dialog box does not appear, choose File > Import Photos And Video, or click the Import button below the left panel group.

5 If the Import dialog box appears in compact mode, click the Show More Options button at the lower left of the dialog box to see all the options in the expanded Import dialog box.

The top panel of the Import dialog box—which is visible in both the compact and expanded modes—presents the three basic steps in the import process, arranged from left to right:

- Select the source location of the images you wish to add to your catalog.

- Specify the way you want Lightroom to handle the files you're importing.

- Choose the destination to which the image files will be copied and any develop presets, keywords, or other metadata that you would like applied to your photos as they are added to your catalog.

Your camera or memory card is now shown as the import source in the FROM area at the left of the top panel and under Devices in the Source panel at the left of the Import dialog box.

Depending on your computer setup, it's possible that your camera's memory card will be recognized as a removable storage disk. If this is the case, you may see some differences in the options available in the Import dialog box, but these differences will not affect the actions you'll take in the remainder of this exercise.

6 If your memory card is listed as a removable disk—rather than a device—in the Source panel, click to select it from the Files list and make sure that the Include Subfolders option is activated.

7 From the import type options in the center of the top panel, choose Copy, so that the photos will be copied from your camera to your hard disk, and then added to your catalog, leaving the original files on your camera's memory card.

Lightroom displays a brief description of the action that will be taken for whichever option is currently selected, as shown in the illustration below.

8 Move your pointer over each of the options shown in the bar across the top of the Preview pane to see a tool tip describing the option. For this exercise, leave the default All Photos option selected. Don't click the Import button yet.

A check mark in the top left corner of an image cell indicates that the photo will be imported. By default, all the photos on your memory card will be check-marked for import; you can exclude an image from the selection to be imported by clicking its checkbox to remove the check mark.

You can select multiple images, and then change all of their check marks simultaneously. To select a contiguous range of images, select the first image in the range by clicking the thumbnail or the surrounding image cell, then hold down the Shift key and select the last image in the series. To select individual additional photos, Ctrl-click / Command-click their thumbnails. Click the check mark of any image in a multiple selection to change the import status for the entire selection.

When you import photos from your hard disk or from external storage media, the Import dialog box offers you the option to add them to your catalog without moving them from their current locations. This is possible because Lightroom does not actually import the image files themselves; it only adds entries to the library catalog to record their locations. However, because memory cards are expected to be erased and reused, images on your camera don't have very permanent addresses. For this reason, you're not offered the Add or Move options when you import from a camera—Lightroom expects to copy your photos from your camera to a more permanent location before it adds their addresses to the library catalog.

Therefore, the next step in the process of importing from a camera is to specify a destination folder to which your photos should be copied. This is the time to give some thought to how you are going to organize your photos on your computer hard disk. For now, leave the Import Photos dialog box open; you'll choose a destination folder and deal with the rest of the import options in the following exercises.

Organizing your copied photos in folders

Although there's no technical reason why you can't choose a different destination folder for each import, it will be much easier to keep your hard disk organized if you create a single folder to contain all the images that are associated with a particular catalog. Within this folder you can create a new subfolder for each batch of images downloaded from your camera or copied from other external media.

Before beginning the lessons in this book, you created a folder named LR5CIB inside your *[username]*/My Documents (Windows) or *[username]*/Documents (Mac OS) folder on your computer. This folder already contains subfolders for your LR5CIB Catalog file and for the image files used for the lessons in this book. For the purposes of this exercise, you'll create a subfolder inside the LR5CIB folder as the destination for the images that you import from your camera's memory card:

1   In the right panel group of the Import dialog box, collapse the File Handling, File Renaming, and Apply During Import panels; then, expand the Destination panel.

2   In the Destination panel, navigate to your LR5CIB folder. With the LR5CIB folder selected, click the Create New Folder button (⊕) at the left of the Destination panel header and choose Create New Folder from the menu.

3 In the Browse For Folder / Create New Folder dialog box, navigate to and select your LR5CIB folder, if it's not already selected. Click the Make New Folder / New Folder button, type **Imported From Camera** as the name for your new folder, and then press Enter (Windows) / click Create (Mac OS).

4 Make sure the new Imported From Camera folder is selected in the Browse For Folder / Create New Folder dialog box, and then click OK / Choose. Note that the new folder is now listed, and already selected, in the Destination panel.

The name of the new destination folder also appears in the TO area at the right of the top panel of the Import dialog box.

The Organize menu, near the top of the Destination panel, offers various options to help you organize your photos into folders as you copy them onto your hard disk:

- **Into One Folder** With the current settings, the images would be copied into the new Imported From Camera folder. You could then use the Into Subfolder option to create a new subfolder for each import.

Note: If your memory card has been recognized as a removable disk, you may also see the Organize option By Original Folders; this option will be discussed later in this lesson.

- **By Date:** *[Date Format]* The remaining options are all variations on organizing your photos by capture date. Your images would be copied into the Imported From Camera folder and placed into one or more subfolders, depending on your choice of date format. Choosing the date format "2013/04/27," for example, would result in one folder per year, containing one folder per month, containing one folder per day for each capture date, as shown in the illustration at the right.

You should think about which system of folder organization best suits your needs before you begin to import photos from your camera for your own purposes and maintain that system for all your camera imports.

5 For the purposes of this exercise, choose the option Into One Folder from the Organize menu.

6 Click the Into Subfolder checkbox and type **Lesson 3 Import** in the adjacent text box as the name for the new subfolder.

About file formats

Camera raw formats Camera raw file formats contain unprocessed data from a digital camera's sensor. Most camera manufacturers save image data in a proprietary camera format. Lightroom reads the data from most cameras and processes it into a full-color photo. You can use the controls in the Develop module to process and interpret the raw image data for your photo. For a list of supported cameras and camera raw formats, see http://www.adobe.com/products/photoshop/extend.html.

Digital Negative format (DNG) The Digital Negative (DNG) file format is a publicly available archival format for raw files generated by digital cameras. DNG addresses the lack of an open standard for the raw files created by individual camera models, helping ensure that photographers will be able to access their files in the future. You can convert proprietary raw files to DNG from within Lightroom. For more information about the Digital Negative (DNG) file format, visit www.adobe.com/dng.

TIFF format Tagged-Image File Format (TIFF, TIF) is used to exchange files between applications and computer platforms. TIFF is a flexible bitmap image format supported by virtually all paint, image-editing, and page-layout applications. Also, virtually all desktop scanners can produce TIFF images. Lightroom supports large documents saved in TIFF format (up to 65,000 pixels per side). However, most other applications, including older versions of Photoshop (pre-Photoshop CS), do not support documents with file sizes greater than 2 GB. The TIFF format provides greater compression and industry compatibility than Photoshop format (PSD), and is the recommended format for exchanging files between Lightroom and Photoshop. In Lightroom, you can export TIFF image files with a bit depth of 8 bits or 16 bits per channel.

JPEG format Joint Photographic Experts Group (JPEG) format is commonly used to display photographs and other continuous-tone images in web photo galleries, slide shows, presentations, and other online services. JPEG retains all color information in an RGB image but compresses file size by selectively discarding data. A JPEG image is automatically decompressed when opened. In most cases, the Best Quality setting produces a result indistinguishable from the original.

Photoshop format (PSD) Photoshop format (PSD) is the standard Photoshop file format. To import and work with a multi-layered PSD file in Lightroom, the file must be saved in Photoshop with the Maximize PSD and PSB File Compatibility option activated. You'll find this option in the Photoshop file handling preferences. Lightroom saves PSD files with a bit depth or 8 bits or 16 bits per channel.

PNG files Lightroom imports PNG files but transparency is not supported; it will appear white.

CMYK files Lightroom imports CMYK files but edits and output are performed in the RGB color space.

Video files Lightroom 3 will import video files from most digital cameras. You can tag, rate, filter and include video files in collections and slideshows, but editing is not supported. Click the camera icon on the video file's thumbnail to launch an external viewer such as QuickTime or Windows Media Player.

File format exceptions Lightroom does not support the following types of files: Adobe Illustrator® files; Nikon scanner NEF files; files with dimensions greater than 65,000 pixels per side or larger than 512 megapixels.

Note: To import photos from a scanner, use your scanner's software to scan to TIFF or DNG format.

Creating import presets

When you import photos on a regular basis, you'll probably find that you're setting up the same configurations of options over and over. Lightroom enables you to streamline your import workflow by saving your preferred settings as import presets. To create an import preset, set up your import in the expanded Import dialog box, and then choose Save Current Settings As New Preset from the Import Preset menu below the Preview pane.

Type a descriptive name for your new preset, and then click Create.

Your new preset will include all of your current settings: the source, import type (Copy as DNG, Copy, Move, or Add), file handling and renaming options, develop and metadata presets, keywords, and destination. You might set up one preset to move photos from a single folder on your hard disk into dated subfolders, and another to create a single folder of renamed black-and-white copies. Create separate import presets tailored to the characteristics of different cameras, so you can quickly apply your favorite noise reduction, lens correction and camera calibration settings during the import process, saving yourself time in the Develop module later.

Using the Import dialog box in compact mode

Once you've created the presets you need, you can speed up the process even more by using the Import dialog box in compact mode, where you can use your import preset as a starting point, and then change the source, metadata, keywords, and destination settings as required.

Backup strategies

Your next choice is whether or not to make backup copies of the images from your camera at the same time as Lightroom creates primary copies in the location you've just specified and adds them to the library catalog. It's a good idea to create backup copies on a separate hard disk or on external storage media so you don't lose your images should your hard disk fail or in case you accidentally delete them.

1 In the right panel group of the Import Photos dialog box, expand the File Handling panel and activate the option Make A Second Copy To by clicking the checkbox.

2 Click the small triangle to the right and select Choose Folder to specify a destination for your backup copies.

3 In the Browse For Folder / Choose Folder dialog box, navigate to the folder in which you wish to store the backup copies of your images, and then click OK / Choose.

The purpose of this backup is mainly as a precaution against loss of data due to disk failure or human error during the import process; it's not meant to replace the standard backup procedure you have in place—or should have in place—for the files on your hard disk.

It's worthwhile to archive each photo shoot by burning your images to a DVD, which you can store separately. This will also help you organize your image library in Lightroom because you'll feel more secure trimming your collection down to the best images knowing that you have a backup before you press the Delete key.

Renaming files as they are imported

The cryptic file names created by digital cameras are not particularly helpful when it comes to sorting and searching your photo library. Lightroom can help by renaming your images for you as they are imported. You can choose from a list of predefined naming options, or create your own customized naming templates.

1 In the right panel group of the Import dialog box, expand the File Renaming panel and activate Rename Files. Choose Custom Name - Sequence from the Template menu and type a descriptive name in the Custom Text box, and then press the Tab key on your keyboard. A sample name at the bottom of the File Renaming panel shows how your settings will be applied for the first image imported.

▶ Tip: An option you should consider, if it's supported by your camera, is to set the camera to generate file names with unique sequence numbers. When you clear your memory card, or change memory cards, your camera will continue to generate unique sequence numbers rather than start counting from one again. This way, the images you import into your library will always have unique file names.

You can enter a number other than 1 in the Start Number text box; this is useful if you're importing more than one batch of images from the same series.

2 Click the small triangle to the right of the Custom Text box; your new text has been added to a list of recently entered names. You can choose from this list if you import another batch of files that belong in the same series. This not only saves time and effort but helps you ensure that subsequent batches are named identically. Should you wish to clear the list, choose Clear List from the menu.

3 Choose Custom Name (x of y) from the Template menu. Note that the sample name at the bottom of the File Renaming panel is updated to reflect the change.

4 Choose Edit from the Template menu to open the Filename Template Editor.

In the Filename Template Editor dialog box you can set up a filename template that makes use of metadata information stored in your image files—such as file names, capture dates, or ISO settings—adding automatically generated sequence numbers and any custom text you specify. A filename template includes placeholders—or *tokens*—that will be replaced by actual values during the renaming process. A token is framed by curly brackets on Windows and enclosed by a blue outline on Mac OS.

You could rename your photos Resort_Village-April 27, 2013-01, and so on, by setting up a filename template with a custom text token, a date token, and a 2-digit sequence number token, separated by typed hyphens, as shown in the illustration at the right. After closing the Filename Template Editor you could type **Cottages** over the words Resort_Village in the Custom Text box; the word "Cottages" would then replace the custom text token in the filename. The capture date from the images' metadata and the sequence number will be added automatically.

▶ Tip: For more information on using the Filename Template Editor please refer to Lightroom Help.

5 Click Cancel to close the Filename Template Editor without making any changes.

Despite all of the options available for renaming your images during the import process, there's only so much information you can squeeze into a single file name. It might be better to take a minimal approach to renaming your photos and instead take advantage of the other file management capabilities of Lightroom. Metadata and keyword tags are far more powerful and versatile tools for organizing and searching your image library.

You'll learn about using metadata and keyword tags in the following exercises and in Lesson 5, "Organizing and Selecting."

You have now completed this exercise on importing photos from a digital camera or a memory card. You'll learn about the other options that are available in the Import dialog box in the exercises to follow.

6   For now, click Import if you wish to bring your photos into the LR5CIB catalog, or Cancel to close the Import dialog box without actually importing any images.

Importing images from a hard disk

When you import photos from your hard disk or from external storage media, Lightroom offers you more options for organizing your image files than are available when importing from a camera.

If you wish, you can still choose to copy your images to a new location during the import process as you did in the previous exercise, but you also have the option to add them to your catalog without moving them from their current locations. You might choose to do this if the images you wish to import are already well organized in a folder hierarchy.

For images that are already located on your hard disk you have an extra option: to *move* them to a new location, removing them from the original location at the same time. This option might appeal if the images on your hard disk are not already organized in a satisfactory manner.

1   To import images from your computer hard disk—or from a CD, DVD, or other external storage media—either choose File > Import Photos And Video, press Ctrl+Shift+I / Command+Shift+I, or simply click the Import button below the left panel group in the Library module.

2   In the Source panel at the left of the Import dialog box, navigate to the Lessons folder you've already copied into the LR5CIB folder on your hard disk. Select the Lesson 3 folder and click the checkbox at the top right of the Source panel to activate the Include Subfolders option.

An image count in the lower left corner of the Import dialog box shows that the Lesson 3 folder and its subfolders contain a total of 28 photos with a combined file size of 54 MB.

3   From the import type options in the center of the top panel, choose Add so that your photos will be added to your catalog without being moved—an option that is not available when importing images from a camera. Do not click Import yet!

4   Use the scrollbar at the right of the Preview pane to view all of the images in the Lesson 3 folder and its subfolders. Drag the Thumbnail slider below the Preview pane to the left to reduce the size of the thumbnails so that you can see as many of the images as possible in the Preview pane.

5   In the Source panel, disable the Include Subfolders option. The Preview pane now displays only the nine images in the Lesson 3 folder and the image count in the lower left corner of the Import dialog box reads: 9 photos / 16 MB.

In the next exercise, you'll apply keywords and other metadata to these images to make them easier to organize once you've added them to your catalog. For now, you can review the import type options above the Preview pane.

6   Click each of the import type options in turn, from left to right:

   •   Choose the option Copy As DNG to have Lightroom make copies of your images in DNG (Digital Negative) file format, which will be stored in a new location, and then added to your catalog. Collapse all of the panels in the right panel group. For the Copy As DNG, Copy, and Move options, the right panel group offers the same suite of panels—File Handling, File Renaming, Apply During Import, and Destination.

   •   Choose the option Copy to have Lightroom create copies of your images in a new location, and then add them to your catalog, leaving the originals in their current locations. You can set a destination for your copies in the Destination panel, as you did in the previous exercise. Expand the Destination panel and click the Organize menu. When you use either the Copy As DNG, Copy, or Move options to import images from your hard disk or from external storage media, the Organize menu offers you the option to copy your photos into a single folder, into subfolders based on the capture dates, or into a folder structure that replicates the original arrangement.

- Choose the option Move to have the images moved to a new location on your hard disk, arranged in whatever folder structure you choose from the Organize menu, and then deleted from their original locations.

- Choose Add to have Lightroom add the images to your catalog without moving or copying them from their current locations, or altering the folder structure in which they are stored. Note that for the Add option, the right panel group offers only the File Handling and Apply During Import panels; you cannot rename the original source images during import, and there's no need to specify a destination because the files will remain where they are. Expand the File Handling and Apply During Import panels to see the options available.

Applying metadata

Lightroom uses the metadata information attached to image files to enable you to quickly find and organize your photos. You can search your image library and filter the results by keyword, creation date, flag status, color label, shooting settings, or any combination of a wide range of other criteria. You can also choose specific information about your images from this metadata and have Lightroom display it as a text overlay applied to each image in a slideshow, web gallery, or print layout. Some metadata is automatically generated by your camera when you take a photo. You can also add your own information as part of the import process, making it even easier to locate and organize your images on your own terms.

1   In the Apply During Import panel, choose New from the Metadata menu.

2   In the New Metadata Preset dialog box, type a descriptive name for these nine photos in the Preset Name box (we used the place name "Valsanzibio"); then, enter metadata information that is applicable to the images as a group, such as labels or copyright information. You can customize the metadata for each individual image after import, adding information such as titles and captions.

3   Click Create to close the New Metadata Preset dialog box, and then confirm that your new metadata preset is selected in the Metadata menu.

You can edit your metadata presets by choosing Edit Presets from the Metadata menu in the Apply During Import panel. In the Edit Metadata Presets dialog box you can edit, rename, or delete presets, or save modified settings as a new preset.

4   In the Apply During Import panel, choose None from the Develop Settings menu and type **Lesson 3, Travel, Valsanzibio, Garden** in the Keywords text box.

5   In the File Handling panel, choose Minimal from the Render Previews menu. Check that your settings are the same as those shown in the illustration below, and then click Import.

The nine photos from the Lesson 3 folder are imported into your library catalog and thumbnails of the images appear in the Grid view and the Filmstrip in the Library module.

6   Right-click / Control-click any of the images in the Grid view and choose Go To Folder In Library from the context menu. In the Folders panel in the left panel group, the Lesson 3 folder is highlighted and the image count indicates that it contains 9 photos.

7   Right-click / Control-click the Lesson 3 folder in the Folders panel, and then choose Show In Explorer / Show In Finder from the context menu.

8   The Lessons folder opens in a Windows Explorer / Finder window, with the Lesson 3 folder highlighted. Leave the Windows Explorer / Finder window open for use in the next exercise.

Importing via drag and drop

Perhaps the easiest way to add photos to your image library is to simply drag a selection of files—or even an entire folder—directly into Lightroom.

1 The Windows Explorer / Finder window showing your Lesson 3 folder should still be open from the previous exercise. Position the window so that you can see the Grid view in the Lightroom workspace behind it.

2 Open your Lesson 3 folder, if necessary, and drag the Batch1 folder from the Windows Explorer / Finder window onto the Grid view.

In the Import dialog box, the Batch1 subfolder is now selected in the Source panel and the seven photos it contains are displayed in the Preview pane.

3 In the Apply During Import panel, choose None from the Metadata menu and type **Lesson 3, Spiral** in the Keywords box. Don't click Import just yet.

Evaluating photos before importing

Lightroom makes it easier to decide which of your photos you wish to import by providing an enlarged Loupe view in the Import dialog box; you can examine each image in detail so that you can choose between similar images or exclude a photo that is out of focus.

1   Double-click any of the thumbnails to see the photo in Loupe view, or select the thumbnail and click the Loupe view button ( ) below the preview pane; the image is enlarged to fit the preview area and the pointer becomes a magnifying glass cursor ( ).

2   Click the image again to further magnify the image to a zoom ratio of 1:1. Use the Zoom slider below the preview pane to see even more detail. Drag the enlarged image in the preview pane to inspect portions of the photo that are not currently visible.

While you're examining the photo in Loupe view, you can check mark the image for import or un-check it to exclude it by clicking the Include In Import check box below the preview pane. Alternatively, press the P key to check-mark the photo, the X key to un-check it, or the Tilde key (~) to toggle between the two states.

● **Note:** The P, X, and Tilde (~) keyboard shortcuts are disabled at magnification levels higher than 1:1.

3   Click the enlarged preview to return to the Fit view where the entire image is visible. Double-click the image, or click either the Loupe view button or the Grid view button beside it to return to the thumbnail display.

4   For the purposes of this exercise, un-check one of the images to exclude it, and then click Import.

5 In the Folders panel, click the triangle beside the Lesson 3 folder, if necessary, to see the listing for the Batch1 subfolder inside it.

Both the Batch1 subfolder and the Previous Import listing in the Catalog panel show an image count of 6 and the six recently imported photos are displayed in the Grid view and the Filmstrip.

6 Switch back to Windows Explorer / the Finder and drag the Batch1 folder onto the Grid view in the Library module again.

In the Import dialog box, the six photos that are already registered in the catalog are dimmed and unavailable for import. Clicking New Photos above the Preview pane would remove them from view entirely.

7 Type **Lesson 3, Spiral** in the Keywords box, and then click Import to add the remaining Batch1 photo to your library catalog.

8 In the Folders panel, the Batch1 folder now shows an image count of 7; click the Batch1 folder to see all seven photos in the Grid view and the Filmstrip.

Importing and viewing video

Lightroom will import many common digital video files from digital still cameras, including AVI, MOV, MP4, and AVCHD. Choose File > Import Photos And Video or click the Import button in the Library module; then, set up your import in the Import dialog box, just as you would for photos.

In the Library module Grid view, you can scrub backwards and forwards in your video clips by simply moving the mouse over the thumbnails, making it easy to select the clip you want. Double-click a thumbnail to preview the video in Loupe view; drag the circular current time indicator in the playback control bar to scrub through the video manually.

Setting distinctive thumbnail images (poster frames) for your videos can make it easier to find the clip you want in the Grid view. Move the current time indicator to the frame you want; then, click the Frame button (⬛) in the control bar and choose Set Poster Frame. Choose Capture Frame from the same menu to convert the current frame to a JPEG image that will be stacked with the clip.

To shorten a video clip, click the Trim Video button (⚙). The playback control bar expands to display a time-line view of the clip where you can drag the start and end markers to trim the clip as desired.

Importing to a specific folder

From within the Library module, you can import photos directly to a folder in the Folders panel without needing to specify a destination in the Import dialog box.

1   In the Folders panel, right-click / Control-click the Batch1 folder and choose Import To This Folder from the context menu.

2   In the Import dialog box, click Select A Source at the left of the top panel, just above the Source panel, and then choose the path to the Lesson 3 folder from the list of recent sources in the menu.

3 Expand the Source panel; then expand the Lesson 3 folder so that you can see the subfolders inside it. Select the folder Extras, which contains two photos. In the top panel, choose Move from the import type options to move the photos from the Extras folder to the destination folder and add them to your catalog. Check that your previous settings are still active in the Apply During Import panel. You may need to re-type **Lesson 3, Spiral** in the Keywords box.

4 Expand the Destination panel, if necessary. You can see that the Batch1 folder has been automatically selected as the destination to which the photos will be moved from the Extras folder. At the top of the Destination panel, choose Into One Folder from the Organize menu; then, click Import. Thumbnails of the two new images appear in the Grid view and the Filmstrip in the Library module.

5 In the Folders panel, the Batch1 folder now shows an image count of 9. Click the Batch1 folder to see all nine images together in the Grid view and the Filmstrip.

6 In the Folders panel, right-click / Control-click the Lesson 3 folder and choose Show In Explorer / Show In Finder from the context menu. In the Windows Explorer / Finder window, open the Extras folder inside the Lesson 3 folder; the two image files have been removed and the Extras folder is now empty.

Importing from other catalogs

If you work on a laptop while you're on location and need to merge your new photos with the Lightroom library on your desktop computer, or if you work in a situation where more than one person will be using the same images in Lightroom on different computers, you can move photos from one computer to another using the Export As Catalog and Import From Catalog commands. Your images will be transferred with all of your edits, adjustments, and settings in place—including any keywords or other metadata you may have added.

Lesson 11, "Making Backups and Exporting Photos," will discuss exporting photos as a catalog; for this lesson you'll import photos from a catalog you'll find in the Batch2 subfolder inside the Lesson 3 folder on your hard disk.

1   Choose File > Import From Another Catalog.

2   In the Import From Lightroom Catalog dialog box, navigate to and open your Lessons > Lesson 3 > Batch2 folder, select the file Batch2Catalog.lrcat, and then click Open / Choose.

3   In the Import From Catalog dialog box, click the Show Preview check box in the lower left corner. Choose Add New Photos To Catalog Without Moving from the File Handling menu, and then click Import.

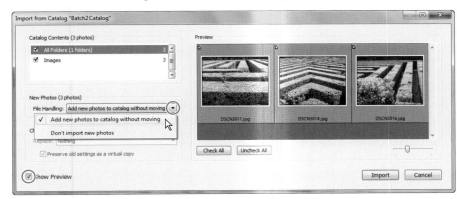

► **Tip:** The option Don't Import New Photos in the File Handling menu is useful when you've exported images from one computer, modified the files on a different computer, and then wish to re-import them without importing any new images.

4   The Batch2 subfolder is now listed in the Folders panel and three newly imported photos are displayed in the Grid view and the Filmstrip.

5   In the Grid view, all three image cells are marked with the Photo Is Missing badge (![]). Select the first image; the photo's missing status is also indicated in the Histogram panel. Click the badge on the image cell; then, click Locate in the Confirm dialog box. Navigate to the folder Lesson 3 > Batch2 > Images, select the missing photo, activate Find Nearby Missing Photos, and then click Select.

When you import images from a Lightroom catalog, you don't have the option to apply develop settings or to add keywords and other metadata during the import process as you do when you import from your camera or hard disk. Lightroom preserves and imports the keywords and other metadata that were exported in the catalog with the images.

6 Select one of the images in the Grid view.

In the Keywording panel in the right panel group, you can see that the keyword tags Lesson 3, Travel, Valsanzibio, and Garden have already been applied. If you wished, you could add more keywords to the images individually.

7 Expand the Metadata panel in the right panel group. If necessary, collapse the other panels in the group or scroll down so that you can see the contents of the Metadata panel. Note that these images already include the metadata from the Valsanzibio preset. You can edit the metadata to your liking.

The imported images have also been edited. Lightroom records every editing operation performed on an image in the library catalog file. When images are exported in a catalog their entire edit history is exported with them.

8 Select one of the images in the Grid view, and then switch to the Develop module. If necessary, scroll down in the left panel group so that you can see the contents of the History panel. Click the Import entry at the bottom of the History panel to see how the image looked originally. Then, choose Edit > Undo to return to the edited version.

9 Switch back to the Library module in readiness for the next exercise.

Importing photos from Photoshop Elements

Lightroom makes it easy to import photographs and video from Photoshop Elements. The media files from your Photoshop Elements catalog are imported complete with keyword tags, ratings, and labels—even your stacks are preserved. Version sets from Photoshop Elements are converted to stacks in Lightroom, and your albums become collections.

If you're migrating from Photoshop Elements to Lightroom, or if you intend to work with both applications, you might like to watch to the tutorial videos in "Going from Photoshop Elements to Lightroom" on Adobe TV (http://tv.adobe.com/show/going-from-photoshop-elements-to-lightroom/) for tips on making the transition, understanding the differences between the way Lightroom and Photoshop Elements work, and using the two applications together.

Upgrading a Photoshop Elements catalog

Lightroom 5 can import photos and library catalog information from Photoshop Elements 6 through Elements 11 on Windows, and from Photoshop Elements 9 to 11 on Mac OS, but first you'll need to upgrade your Photoshop Elements catalog.

1   In the Library module, choose File > Upgrade Photoshop Elements Catalog.

Lightroom searches your computer for Photoshop Elements catalogs and displays the most recently opened catalog in the Upgrade Photoshop Elements Catalog dialog box.

2   To choose a different Photoshop Elements catalog, click the Photoshop Elements menu. To specify a different destination for the new Lightroom catalog, click Change at the right of the Lightroom Catalog Destination path and navigate to the desired folder.

3   Click Upgrade to import the photos and catalog information from your Photoshop Elements library catalog into a new Lightroom catalog.

4   To combine a converted Photoshop Elements library with an existing Lightroom catalog, open the destination catalog and use the File > Import From Another Catalog command.

Importing from a watched folder

Designating a folder on your hard disk as a *watched folder* can be a very convenient way to automate the import process. Once you've nominated a folder that is to be watched, Lightroom will detect any photos that are placed or saved into it, then automatically move them to a specified location and add them to the catalog. You can even have Lightroom rename the files and add metadata in the process.

1   Choose File > Auto Import > Auto Import Settings.

2   In the Auto Import Settings dialog box, click the first Choose button to designate a watched folder.

3   In the Auto-Import From Folder dialog box, navigate to the Lesson 3 folder. Open the Auto Import folder and select the subfolder named Watched Folder; then, click Select Folder / Choose.

4   Now that you have designated a watched folder, you can click the checkbox at the top of the Auto Import Settings dialog box to enable Auto Import.

5   Click the second Choose button under Destination to specify a folder to which Lightroom will move your photos in the process of adding them to the library catalog.

6   In the Choose Folder dialog box, navigate to the Lessons folder. Select the Lesson 3 folder (you'll set up a subfolder inside the Lesson 3 folder in the next step), and then click Select Folder / Choose.

7   Still in the Destination section in the Auto Import Settings dialog box, type **Batch3** in the Subfolder Name text box. Lightroom will create this subfolder inside the Lesson 3 folder.

8   Choose Filename from the File Naming menu.

9   Under Information, choose the metadata preset you created earlier in this lesson from the Metadata menu and type **Lesson 3, Birds** in the Keywords text box. Choose None from the Develop Settings menu and Minimal from the Initial Previews menu. Click OK to close the Auto Import Settings dialog box.

10 Switch to Windows Explorer / the Finder and navigate to the Lesson 3 folder. Note that as yet there is no Batch3 folder inside the Lesson 3 folder. Open the folder Auto Import and drag the seven image files inside it to the Watched Folder. When Lightroom has finished importing, you'll see the newly created Batch3 folder inside the Lesson 3 folder. The Watched Folder is empty once more and the seven lesson images have been moved into the Batch3 folder.

▶ **Tip:** Once you've set a watched folder, you can activate or disable Auto Import at any time, without opening the Auto Import Settings dialog box, by choosing File > Auto Import > Enable Auto Import. A check mark beside this menu command indicates that the Auto Import feature is currently enabled.

11 Return to Lightroom; the Batch3 folder is now listed in the Folders panel and the newly imported photos are displayed in the Grid view and the Filmstrip.

You can now import images into your Lightroom library by simply dragging them onto the watched folder. This makes importing photos directly from a camera or memory card reader even easier; there's no need to attend to a dialog box and yet your images can be renamed and have custom metadata added automatically.

Specifying initial previews when importing

As photos are imported, Lightroom can immediately display a photo's embedded preview, or display higher-quality previews as the program renders them. You can choose the rendered size and quality for previews using the Standard Preview Size and Preview Quality menus on the File Handling tab of the Catalog Settings (choose Edit > Catalog Settings / Lightroom > Catalog Settings). Please keep in mind that embedded previews are created on-the-fly by cameras and are not color managed therefore they don't match the interpretation of the camera raw files made by Lightroom. Previews rendered by Lightroom are color managed.

In the Import Photos dialog box, do one of the following:

- To immediately display images using the smallest previews embedded in the photos, choose Render Previews > Minimal. Lightroom renders standard-size previews when needed.

- To display the largest possible preview available from the camera, choose Render Previews > Embedded & Sidecar. This may take longer to display than a Minimal preview but is still faster than rendering a standard-size preview.

- To display previews as Lightroom renders them, choose Render Previews > Standard. Standard-size previews use the ProPhoto RGB color space.

- To display previews that are a 1 to 1 view of the actual pixels, as in the Develop module, choose Render Previews > 1:1.

—From Lightroom Help

Tethered shooting

Many modern digital cameras support tethered shooting, a process where you connect—or tether—your digital camera to your computer and save images to the computer's hard disk rather than to the camera's memory card. With tethered shooting you can view a photo on your computer screen immediately after you shoot it—a vastly different experience from seeing it on your camera's LCD screen.

Tip: To see a list of cameras for which integrated tethered shooting is currently supported, please refer to Lightroom Help.

For a range of DSLR cameras including many models from Canon and Nikon, you can capture photographs directly into Lightroom without the need for any third-party software. If your camera allows tethered shooting, but is not on the list of models supported by Lightroom, you can still capture images into your Lightroom library using either the image capture software associated with the camera or any of a number of third-party software solutions.

You can have Lightroom name the photos, add metadata, apply developing settings, and organize them in your library then and there. If necessary, you can adjust your camera settings (white balance, exposure, focus, depth of field, and others), or even change cameras, before taking the next shot. The better the quality of the captured image the less time you'll need to spend adjusting it later.

Tethered shooting with a supported camera

Note: Depending on your camera model and the operating system your computer uses, you may also need to install the necessary drivers for your camera.

1 Connect your camera to the computer.

2 In the Library module, choose File > Tethered Capture > Start Tethered Capture.

3 In the Tethered Capture Settings dialog box, type a name for your shooting session. Lightroom will create a folder with this name inside the destination folder of your choice; this session folder will appear in the Folders panel.

4 Chose a naming scheme for your shots, select a destination folder, and specify any metadata or keywords that you want Lightroom to apply as the newly captured images are imported.

5 Click OK to close the Tethered Capture Settings dialog box. The tethered capture control bar appears.

The control bar displays the model name of the connected camera, the name you entered for the shooting session, and the current camera settings. You can choose from a wide range of Develop presets in the Develop Settings menu at the right. You can trigger the shot with your camera's shutter button, by clicking the large circular button at the right of the control bar, or by pressing F12 on your keyboard.

As you shoot, the images captured will appear in both the Grid view and the Filmstrip. To see each captured photo as large as possible, use the Loupe view and hide unwanted panels—as shown in the illustration below—or chose Window > Screen Mode > Full Screen And Hide Panels.

▶ **Tip:** To collapse the control bar to just the shutter button, hold down the Alt / Option key and click the close button at the upper right. Repeat to expand the control bar again.

Tethered shooting with other cameras

▶ **Tip:** To find out about third-party image capture software compatible with your camera, search "tethered shooting" on the Internet or in Adobe Community Help.

If your camera allows tethered shooting, but is not on the list of models for which the process is integrated in Lightroom, you can still capture images into your Lightroom library by using the image capture software associated with your camera—or a third-party software solution—to save your photos to a watched folder. Lightroom will remove the images from the watched folder and add them to your catalog as soon as it detects them.

1 Choose File > Auto Import > Auto Import Settings. In the Auto Import Settings dialog box, click the first Choose button to choose a watched folder. Once you've designated a folder to be watched, you can click the checkbox at the top of the Auto Import Settings dialog box to enable Auto Import.

2 Click the second Choose button under Destination to specify a folder to which Lightroom will save your photos in the process of adding them to the library catalog. Type a name for your photo shoot in the Subfolder Name text box; Lightroom will create this subfolder inside the designated destination folder.

3 Choose a naming option for your images from the File Naming menu. Under Information, you can choose a metadata preset and enter any keywords that you wish Lightroom to apply as your newly captured images are imported. If you wish, you can also choose a developing preset and specify a preview option. Click OK to close the Auto Import Settings dialog box.

4 Use your camera's image capture software to designate your new watched folder as the destination to which the camera will save your photos.

By way of an example, this illustration shows the download and metadata options from the Camera Control component of Nikon's Capture NX software.

5 Before you begin shooting, make sure that you are in the Library module. In the Folders panel, select the subfolder you created for your tethered shoot in step 2, so that your newly captured photos will be displayed as they are imported.

Review questions

1 When would you choose to copy imported images to a new location on your hard disk and when would you want to add them to your library catalog without moving them?

2 Which file formats are supported by Lightroom?

3 What is DNG?

4 When would you use the Import dialog box in compact mode?

5 How can you transfer photos between Lightroom libraries on separate computers?

Review answers

1 You don't have the option to import photos from a camera at their current location; Lightroom needs to record a location for each file in the library catalog, and as memory cards are expected to be erased and reused the images need first to be copied to a more permanent location. Copying or moving images might also be useful when you want Lightroom to organize the files into a more ordered folder hierarchy during the import process. Images that are already arranged in a useful way on the hard disk or removable media can be added to the library catalog in their current locations.

2 Lightroom supports the following file formats: most camera raw formats, Digital Negative (DNG), TIFF, JPEG, Photoshop PSD, PNG, and CMYK files. Lightroom does not support files in Adobe Illustrator format, Nikon scanner NEF files, or files with dimensions greater than 65,000 pixels per side or larger than 512 megapixels.

3 The Digital Negative (DNG) file format is a publicly available archival format intended to address the lack of an open standard for raw files generated by cameras. Converting raw files to DNG in Lightroom will help ensure that you'll be able to access your raw files in the future even if the original proprietary format is no longer supported.

4 Once you've created import presets to suit your workflow, you can speed up the import process by using the Import dialog box in compact mode. Use your import preset as a starting point, and then modify the settings as required.

5 On one computer, export the images from Lightroom as a catalog file. On the other computer, choose File > Import From Another Catalog to import the photos into the Lightroom library together with their develop settings and metadata.

PHOTOGRAPHY SHOWCASE
SETH RESNICK

"I am stimulated by color design, light, texture, spontaneity and gesture. I try to bring back images that another photographer would not visualize from my minds eye."

My visual philosophy is to produce images nobody else envisions. I try to bring back images that another photographer would not visualize from my "minds eye". Ideally, someone standing next to me won't see what I see.

I am stimulated by color, design, light, texture, spontaneity and gesture. These qualities make photography spectacularly rewarding for me. Like anything in life practice helps to make perfection and photography requires practice, which brings me to one of the reasons for my success. I always carry a camera because without the camera there can be no perfection. Photography is an expression of what I see around me, and how it makes me feel. I want to re-create the beauty that I see, and ignite an emotional response in my audience.

Photography is a highly creative art form of art and communication that draws me to it's challenges. I photograph because it is like capturing a moment in time you know you will never be able to go back to. And capturing strong graphic images of those moments in time gives me a feeling of fulfillment and a passion to continue learning and sharing. I hope that my images foster a sense of intellectual curiosity and spark imagination.

http://www.sethresnick.com
http://www.d65.com
http://www.digitalphotodestinations.com

SALINAS GRANDE

RED & GREEN WALL- RWANDA

GOING TO WORK- RWANDA

SOUSSUSVIEI- NAMIBIA

CIERVA COVE- ANTARCTICA

NEKO HARBOR

4 REVIEWING

Lesson overview

It's a good policy to spend some time reviewing, sorting, and marking your newly imported images. A little time spent organizing and grouping photos at this stage will make it much easier to find exactly the images you want when you need them.

In this lesson you'll become familiar with using a variety of viewing modes, tools, and techniques for reviewing your images and navigating through your Lightroom catalog:

- Working in the different Library module views
- Navigating through your catalog
- Using the Navigator panel
- Comparing photos
- Flagging rejects and deleting images
- Using the Quick Collection
- Designating a target collection
- Hiding the Filmstrip and adjusting its size
- Applying the Filmstrip Source Filters
- Rearranging photos in the Grid view or the Filmstrip

 You'll probably need between one and two hours to complete this lesson. If you haven't already done so, download the Lesson 4 work files from the Lesson & Update Files tab on your Account page at www.peachpit.com.

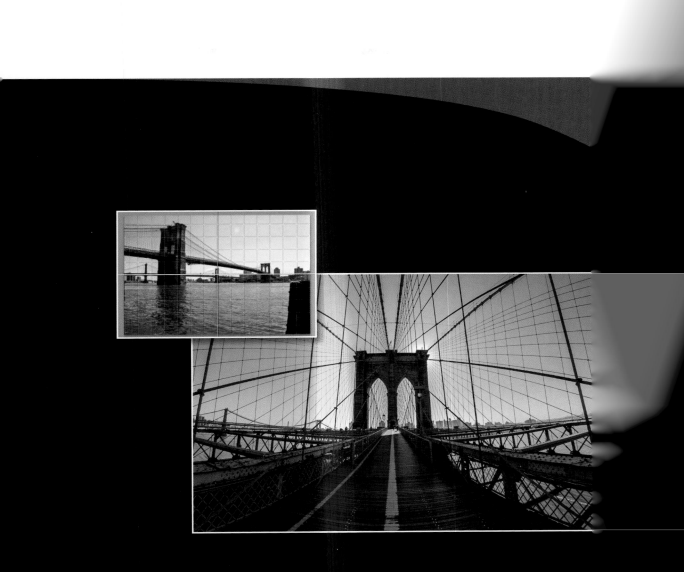

The Lightroom Library module offers you a variety of ways to review, evaluate, mark, and label your photos after you import them, making it easier to organize and manage your growing image library. You can sort and group thumbnails in the Grid view, examine a single photo up close in Loupe view, assess images side by side in Compare view, or refine a multiple selection of shots in Survey view.

Getting started

● **Note:** This lesson assumes that you already have a basic working familiarity with the Lightroom workspace. If you find that you need more background informa- tion, refer to Lightroom Help, or review the previous lessons.

Before you start on this lesson, make sure you've set up the LR5CIB folder for your lesson files and created the LR5CIB Catalog file to manage them, as described in "Setting up a work folder" and "Creating a catalog file for working with this book" in the Getting Started chapter at the beginning of this book.

If you haven't already done so, download the Lesson 4 folder from your Account page at www.peachpit.com to the LR5CIB/Lessons folder, as detailed in the section "Accessing the Classroom in a Book files" in the chapter "Getting Started."

1   Start Lightroom.

2   In the Adobe Photoshop Lightroom - Select Catalog dialog box, make sure that the file LR5CIB Catalog.lrcat is selected under Select A Recent Catalog To Open, and then click Open.

Adobe Photoshop Lightroom – Select Catalog

Select a recent catalog to open

Lr LR5CIB Catalog.lrcat	/Users/John/Documents/LR5CIB/LR5CIB Catalog
Lightroom 5 Catalog.lrcat	/Users/John/Pictures/Lightroom/Lightroom 5 Catalog

☐ Always load this catalog on startup   ☐ Test integrity of this catalog

Note: Lightroom Catalogs cannot be on network volumes or in read-only folders.

[Choose a Different Catalog...] [Create a New Catalog...]   [Quit] [Open]

▶ **Tip:** If you can't see the Module Picker, choose Window > Panels > Show Module Picker, or press the F5 key. If you're working on Mac OS, you may need to press the fn key together with the F5 key, or change the function key behavior in the system preferences.

3   Lightroom will open in the screen mode and workspace module that were active when you last quit. If necessary, switch to the Library module by clicking Library in the Module Picker at the top of the workspace.

 Lightroom   File   Edit   Library   Photo   Metadata   View   Window   Help

LR5CIB Catalog.lrcat - Adobe Photoshop Lightroom - Library

Lr Adobe Photoshop Lightroom 5   (**Library**) Develop | Map | Book | Slideshow | Print | Web

---

Importing images into the library

The first step is to import the images for this lesson into the Lightroom library.

1   In the Library module, click the Import button below the left panel group.

2 If the Import dialog box appears in compact mode, click the Show More Options button at the lower left of the dialog box to see all the options in the expanded Import dialog box.

3 Under Source at the left of the expanded Import dialog box, navigate to and select the LR5CIB > Lessons > Lesson 4 folder. Ensure that all twelve images in the Lesson 4 folder are checked for import.

4 In the import options above the thumbnail previews, select Add so that the imported photos will be added to your catalog without being moved or copied. Under File Handling at the right of the expanded Import dialog box, choose Minimal from the Render Previews menu and ensure that the Don't Import Suspected Duplicates option is activated. Under Apply During Import, choose None from both the Develop Settings menu and the Metadata menu and type **Lesson 4, New York** in the Keywords text box. Make sure that your import is set up as shown in the illustration below, and then click Import.

The twelve images are imported from the Lesson 4 folder and now appear in both the Grid view of the Library module and in the Filmstrip across the bottom of the Lightroom workspace.

Viewing and managing your images

The Library module offers a range of viewing modes and a variety of tools and controls to help you evaluate, compare, sort, mark, and group your images. During the import process you applied common metadata in the form of keyword tags to the selection of images as a whole. As you review your photos in the Library module you can add another layer of organization to your catalog, flagging images as picks or rejects, assigning ratings, and applying tags and labels.

The Library module also provides sophisticated search functions and customizable filters that enable you to leverage the metadata you attach to your photos. You can search and sort the images in your library by category, subject, or any other association, and then create Collections to group them—making it easy to retrieve exactly the photos you want quickly, no matter how extensive your catalog.

In the left panel group of the Library module are panels where you can access and work with the folders and collections containing your photos. The right panel group contains panels for adjusting your images and working with keywords and metadata. At the top of the work area is the Filter bar, where you can set the criteria for a customized search of your catalog. The Toolbar, immediately below the work area, provides easy access to your choice of tools and controls.

Switching views

In the Library module you can move between four viewing modes to suit different phases of your workflow. Press the G key or click the Grid view button (▦) in the Toolbar to see thumbnails of your images while you search, apply flags, ratings and labels, or create collections. Use the keyboard shortcut E or click the Loupe view button (�ⁿ) to inspect a single photo at a range of magnifications. Press C or click the Compare view button (⊠⊻) to see two images side by side. Click the Survey view button (▤▥) in the Toolbar or use the keyboard shortcut N to evaluate several images at once. The Toolbar displays a different set of controls for each view mode.

The Grid view

By default your images will be displayed in Grid view after they've been imported.

1   Click the triangle at the right end of the Toolbar and ensure that View Modes is activated in the tools menu. If you're working on a small screen, you can disable all the other options except Thumbnail size for this lesson.

Tools and controls that are currently visible in the Toolbar have a check mark beside their names in the menu. The order of the tools and controls from top to bottom in the menu corresponds to their order from left to right in the Toolbar.

2   If Grid view is not already selected, click the Grid view button (▦). Adjust the size of the thumbnails by dragging the Thumbnails slider so that you can see at least two rows of thumbnails in the Grid view without having to scroll down.

3   To specify how your photos will be displayed in the Grid view image cells, choose View > View Options. The Library View Options dialog box appears.

4   Activate the Show Grid Extras option and choose Compact Cells from the menu beside it. Customize the Options, Cell Icons, Compact Cell Extras, and Expanded Cell Extras settings to your liking. As a guide to the options available, please refer to "View Options for the Grid view" on the facing page.

5   From the Show Grid Extras menu at the top of the Library View Options dialog box, choose Expanded Cells. Examine the options available and make whatever changes you wish. When you're done, choose Compact Cells from the Show Grid Extras menu and close the Library View Options dialog box.

To switch quickly between the two groups of options that you just set in the Library View Options dialog box, choose from the Grid View Style options on the View menu.

6   Switch to the Expanded Cell mode by choosing the Expanded Cells option from the View > Grid View Style menu. Make sure that the Show Extras option is activated in the same menu.

7   To conveniently cycle through the different Grid view styles, press the J key on your keyboard repeatedly, or choose View > Grid View Style > Cycle View Style.

View options for the Grid view

Depending on the way you like to work, you can choose from a wide range of options that affect the way your photos are displayed in the Grid view image cells—from simplified cells containing nothing but the image thumbnails to expanded cells that display your choice of image information, status indicators, labels, and clickable (interactive) controls.

Show Grid Extras Displays your choice of labels, markers, and controls in each image cell. If this option is disabled, most of the other Grid view options are unavailable.

Compact Cells Shows simple cells with less information so more thumbnails are visible in the grid.

Expanded Cells Expands the image cells to include more information in cell headers and footers.

Show Clickable Items On Mouse Over Only Displays rotation controls, flags, and labels only when you move the pointer over an image cell. Disable this option to show these controls at all times.

Tint Grid Cells With Color Labels Tints the image cell around a photo to indicate its color label.

Show Image Info Tooltips Displays a brief description of an item when you hold the pointer over it, including image info and the names of the controls, status badges, and indicators in the image cell.

Flags Activates clickable flag status indicators in the upper left corner of the image cells. Click the indictor to change the flag status.

Quick Collection Markers Shows a clickable Quick Collection marker in the upper right corner of each thumbnail. Images with a solid grey dot are part of the Quick Collection. Click the marker to add an image to, or remove it from, the Quick Collection.

Thumbnail Badges Displays indicator badges on the thumbnail images indicating which photos have keywords attached and which have been adjusted or cropped.

Unsaved Metadata An icon with a down arrow in the upper right of a cell indicates that an image has changes in its metadata that have not yet been saved to file. An up arrow icon shows that the image file's metadata has been changed in an external application and an exclamation mark icon indicates that a photo's metadata has unsaved changes made in both Lightroom and an external application.

Index Number Shows image cell numbers indicating the order of the photos in the Grid view.

Rotation Displays Rotation buttons in the lower corners of the image cells.

Top Label and **Bottom Label** Displays your choice of image information and attributes above and below the thumbnail in a compact image cell.

Show Header With Labels Displays up to four labels in the headers of expanded image cells, showing whatever information you specify. For each label, you can choose from a menu of image information and attributes.

Use Defaults Restores the Header Label options to their default settings.

Show Rating Footer Shows the rating stars, and optionally the color label and rotation buttons, below the thumbnail in expanded image cells.

Working in Loupe view

In Loupe view you can look closely at one photo at a time at a wide range of zoom levels. Use the Loupe view to help you evaluate your images as you sort them in the Library module and to inspect and edit them in detail in the Develop module.

In the Navigator panel you can set the level of magnification for the Loupe view and find your way around a zoomed image with ease. Like the Loupe view, the Navigator is common to both the Library and Develop modules.

1   In the Grid view or the Filmstrip, select the image NY_Details_1.jpg, and then click the Loupe view button (⬜) in the Toolbar. Alternatively, double-click the thumbnail in the Grid view or the Filmstrip, or press the E key.

▶ **Tip:** The Show Grid Extras option on the Grid View tab of the Library View Options dialog box enables you to display a range of information about your photos in their image cells. In the Loupe View options, activate Show Info Overlay to display the same kind of information overlaid on your enlarged image in the Loupe view. By default, the Loupe view info overlay in disabled.

2   If necessary, expand the Navigator panel at the top of the left panel group. The zoom controls for the Loupe view are in upper right corner of the Navigator panel. Click 1:1 to see this photo at 100% (or "actual pixels") magnification.

3   Click the small triangle at the right of the Navigator panel header and choose
    the zoom ratio 3:1 from the menu.

4   When you're working at such a high level of magnification, the Navigator helps
    you to move around in the image quickly and easily. Click anywhere in the
    Navigator preview and the zoomed view will be centered on that point. The
    white rectangle overlaid on the Navigator preview indicates the area currently
    displayed in the Loupe view. Drag the rectangle to pan the zoomed view.

5   Click in the Loupe view to move back and forth between the last two zoom
    levels; when zooming, the view will be centered on the point you click. Double-
    click the image to switch quickly back and forth between Loupe and Grid views.

6   In the header of the Navigator panel, click each of the four zoom levels in turn. Press the Ctrl key / Command key together with the Minus key (-) repeatedly to zoom out through the last four zoom levels and then switch to Grid view; press the Ctrl / Command key together with the Equal key (=) repeatedly to switch back to Loupe view and then zoom in. Finally, set the zoom level to Fit.

When you're working in Loupe view in the Library, the Develop module, or during a tethered capture session, you can choose to show configurable overlays that can be useful for setting up a layout, aligning elements, or making transformations.

7   Select any image in the Filmstrip, and then press Shift+Tab to hide all panels, making more space for the Loupe view. Choose View > Loupe Overlay > Show. Make sure the Grid and Guides options are both checked in the same submenu.

▶ **Tip:** Alternatively, You can show and hide the Loupe overlays as you work, by pressing Ctrl / Command +Alt / Option together with the 0 (zero) key.

8   Hold down the Ctrl / Command key to show controls for customizing the layout grid and guides. Drag over the Size and Opacity values at the top of the view to change the appearance of the Grid overlay. Drag the pin at the intersection of the Guides overlay to reposition it.

9   Press Shift+Tab to show all panels. Press Ctrl+Alt / Command+Option together with the O (for Oscar) key to hide the layout grid and guides.

Comparing photos

As the name suggests, the Compare view is ideal for examining and evaluating images side by side.

1   Press F5 and F7, or click the white arrows at the top and left edges of the workspace to hide the Module Picker and the left panels. In the Filmstrip, select the photo Architecture_3.jpg; then, Ctrl-click / Command-click its neighbor, Architecture_4.jpg. Click the Compare View button (⊠Ⓨ) in the Toolbar.

The first image selected becomes the *Select* image, which is displayed in the left pane of the Compare view; the image displayed in the right pane is the *Candidate*. In the Filmstrip, the Select image is marked with an white, or un-filled, diamond in the upper right corner of the image cell, and the Candidate image with a black diamond.

To use the Compare view to make a choice from a group of more than two photos, select your favored choice first to place it as the Select image, and then add the other photos to the selection. Click the Select Previous Photo and Select Next Photo buttons (⇦ ⇨) in the Toolbar or press the left and right arrow keys on your keyboard to move between the selected candidates. Should you decide that the current Candidate is better than the Select image, you can reverse their positions by clicking the Swap button (⊠Ⓨ) in the Toolbar.

2   To compare fine detail in the images, zoom in by dragging the Zoom slider in the Toolbar. You'll notice that the images are zoomed together. Drag either of the images in the Compare view and the images move in unison. The closed lock icon to the left of the Zoom slider indicates that the view focus of the two images is locked.

In some situations, this may prove to be inconvenient; In our example, for instance, the detail we are comparing was photographed at different zoom levels.

3   To zoom and move the Select and Candidate images independently, click the view focus lock icon to unlink them. Click the Select photo to make it the active image, increase the zoom ratio to 2:1, and then drag to match the views.

A thin white line surrounds whichever of the two images in the Compare view is currently the *active* image: the image that will be affected by the Zoom slider, the controls in the right panel group, and any menu command that you may apply.

4   Press Shift+Tab twice to show all panels. Click the lock icon to re-link the views, and then choose Fit from the zoom picker at the top of the Navigator.

5   Click the Select photo to make it the active image: the image to which your edits will be applied. Expand the Quick Develop panel; then, choose Lightroom B&W Toned Presets > Cyanotype from the Saved Preset menu at the top of the Quick Develop panel. In the Tone Control pane, click the third button to the right of the Exposure control (the right-facing single arrow) once, and then click the right-facing double arrow buttons for Shadows and Clarity twice each.

Using the controls in the Quick Develop panel while you're working in Compare view can be a helpful aid in making a choice between images. Although the candidate image in our example is sharper and better exposed, the Select image is more graphically striking and—with the Cyanotype effect—more atmospheric. Applying a develop preset or making Quick Develop adjustments can help you to assess how a candidate image will look once it's edited and adjusted. You can then either undo your Quick Develop operations and move to the Develop module to edit the image with greater precision, or keep the modifications you've made as a starting point.

Using Survey view to narrow a selection

The last of the four viewing modes in the Library module, the Survey View lets you see multiple images together on one screen, and then refine your selection by dropping one photo after another from the view.

1   In the Filmstrip, select the four images of the Brooklyn Bridge. Click the Survey view button (▦) in the Toolbar, or press the N key on your keyboard. Press F5, or click the arrow at the left edge of the workspace, to hide the Module Picker.

2   Navigate between the images by pressing the arrow keys on your keyboard or click the Select Previous Photo and Select Next Photo buttons (⬅ ➡) in the Toolbar. The active image is surrounded by a thin white border.

3   Position the pointer over the second photo; then, click the Deselect Photo icon (✖) in the lower right corner of the thumbnail to drop this image from the selection in the Survey view.

As you eliminate candidates, the remaining photos are progressively resized and shuffled to fill the space available in the work area.

▶ **Tip:** If you have eliminated a photo accidentally, choose Edit > Undo to return it to the selection, or simply Ctrl-click / Command-click its thumbnail in the Filmstrip. You can easily add a photo to the selection in the Survey view in the same way.

Dropping a photo from the Survey view doesn't delete it from its folder or remove it from the catalog; the dropped image is still visible in the Filmstrip—it has simply been deselected. You can see that the images that are still displayed in the Survey view are also the only ones that remain selected in the Filmstrip.

4   Continue to eliminate photos from the Survey view. For the purposes of this exercise, deselect all but one favorite (we chose the active image—the photo at the left, framed with a white border—in the illustration above).

Flagging and deleting images

Now that you've narrowed down a selection of images to one favorite in the Survey view, you can mark your choice with a flag.

Flagging images as either picks or rejects as you review them is an effective way to quickly sort your work; flag status is one of the criteria by which you can filter your photo library. You can also quickly remove images flagged as rejects from your catalog using a menu command or keyboard shortcut.

A white flag denotes a pick (⚐), a black one with an x marks a reject (⚑), and a neutral grey flag indicates that an image has not been flagged (⚐).

1 Still in the Survey view, move the pointer over the remaining photo to see the flag icons just below the lower left corner. The grayed icons indicate that the image is not yet flagged. Click the flag to the left. The flag turns white, which marks this image as a pick. In the Filmstrip, you can see that the thumbnail now displays a white flag in the upper left of the image cell.

▶ **Tip:** Press the P key on your keyboard to flag a selected image as a pick (⚑), the X key to flag it as a reject (⚑), or the U key to remove any flags.

2 Select a different image in the Filmstrip, and then press the X key. The black reject flag icon appears at the lower left corner of the image in the Survey view and at the upper left of the thumbnail in the Filmstrip. The thumbnail of the rejected image is dimmed in the Filmstrip.

3 Choose Photo > Delete Rejected Photos or press Ctrl+Backspace / Command+Delete; then, click Remove to remove the rejected photo from your catalog without also deleting the master file from your hard disk.

Having been removed from the Lightroom library catalog file, the rejected image is no longer visible in the Filmstrip.

4 Press the G key or click the Grid view icon in the Toolbar to see all the remaining images as thumbnails in the Grid view.

Grouping images in the Quick Collection

A collection is a convenient way to keep a group of photos together in your catalog, even when the image files are actually located in different folders on your hard disk. You can create a new collection for a particular presentation or use collections to group your images by category or any other association. Your collections are always available from the Collections panel where you can access them quickly.

The Quick Collection is a temporary holding collection: a convenient place to group images as you review and sort your new imports, or while you assemble a selection of photos drawn from different folders in your catalog.

In the Grid view or the Filmstrip, you can add images to the Quick Collection with a single click—and remove them just as easily. Your images will stay in the Quick Collection until you're ready to convert it to a more permanent grouping that will be listed in the Collections panel. You can access the Quick Collection from the Catalog panel so that you can return to work with the same selection of images at any time.

Moving images into or out of the Quick Collection

1   Expand the Catalog panel in the left panel group, if necessary, to see the listing for the Quick Collection.

2   In the Grid view or the Filmstrip, select the image NY_Details_1.jpg, and then Shift-click the image NY_Details_4.jpg to select all four NY_Details photos.

3   To add the selected photos to the Quick Collection, press the B key or choose Photo > Add To Quick Collection.

The image count beside the Quick Collection in the Catalog panel indicates that the Quick Collection now contains four images. If you have activated the option Show Quick Collection Markers in the Library View Options dialog box, each image in the Quick Collection is marked with a gray dot in the upper right corner of its thumbnail in the Grid view. The same markers are also shown in the Filmstrip unless the thumbnail size is too small.

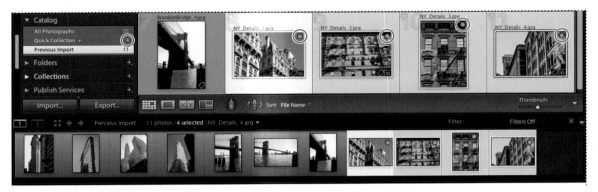

You can remove all of the selected photos from the Quick Collection by simply clicking the marker on one of the thumbnails or by pressing the B key.

4   For this exercise, you'll remove only the last image, NY_Details_4.jpg, from the Quick Collection. First, deselect the other three images; then, with only the image NY_Details_4.jpg selected, press the B key. The image count for your Quick Collection has been reduced to three.

Converting and clearing the Quick Collection

1   Click the Quick Collection entry in the Catalog panel. The Grid view now displays only three images. Until you clear the Quick Collection, you can easily return to this group of images to review your selection.

▶ **Tip:** If you don't see the Quick Collection marker when you move your pointer over a thumbnail, make sure that Show Extras is activated in the View > Grid View Style menu. Choose View > View Options and activate Quick Collection Markers under Cell Icons in the Library View Options dialog box.

Now that you've refined your selection you can move your grouped images to a more permanent Collection.

2   Choose File > Save Quick Collection.

3   In the Save Quick Collection dialog box, type **New York Collection** in the Collection Name box. Activate the option Clear Quick Collection After Saving, and then click Save.

4   In the Catalog panel, you can see that the Quick Collection has been cleared; it now has an image count of 0. If necessary, expand the Collections panel so that you can see the listing for your new collection, which displays an image count of 3.

5   In the Folders panel, click the Lesson 4 folder. The grid view once more shows all the lesson images, including those in your new collection.

Designating a target collection

By default, the Quick Collection is designated as the *target collection;* this status is indicated by the plus sign (+) that follows the Quick Collection's name in the Catalog panel. The target collection is that collection to which a selected image is moved when you press the B key or click the circular marker in the upper right corner of the thumbnail, as you did in the previous exercise.

You can designate a collection of your own as the target collection so that you can use the same convenient techniques to add and remove photos quickly and easily.

1   Right-click / Control-click the entry for your new New York Collection in the Collections panel, and then choose Set As Target Collection from the context menu. The name of your collection is now followed by a plus sign (+).

2   Click the Previous Import folder in the Catalog panel; then, Control-click / Command-click to select two or three images in the Grid view or the Filmstrip.

3   Open the Collections panel and watch as you press the B key on your keyboard; the image count for the New York Collection increases the selected images are added to the collection.

4   Right-click / Control-click the Quick Collection in the Catalog panel and choose Set As Target Collection from the context menu. The Quick Collection once again displays the plus sign (+).

Working with the Filmstrip

No matter which module or view you're working in, the Filmstrip across the bottom of the Lightroom workspace provides constant access to the images in your selected folder or collection.

As with the Grid view, you can quickly navigate through your images in the Filmstrip using the arrow keys on your keyboard. If there are more images than will fit in the Filmstrip you can either use the scroll bar below the thumbnails, drag the Filmstrip by the top edge of the thumbnail frame, or click the shaded thumbnails at either end to access photos that are currently out of view.

Across the top of the Filmstrip, Lightroom provides a convenient set of controls to help streamline your workflow.

At the far left you'll find buttons for working with two displays, with pop-up menus that enable you to set the viewing mode for each display independently.

To the right of these buttons is the Grid view button, and arrow buttons for navigating between the different folders and collections you've recently been viewing.

Next is the Filmstrip Source Indicator, where you can see at a glance which folder or collection you're viewing, how many photos it contains, which images are currently selected, and the name of the image currently under your pointer. Click the Source Indicator to see a menu with all the image sources you've recently accessed.

At the far right of the Filmstrip header are the Filter controls, which we'll look at later in this lesson.

Hiding the Filmstrip and adjusting its size

You can show and hide the Filmstrip and adjust its size, as you can with the side panel groups, to make more screen space available for the image you're working on.

1   Click the triangle in the lower border of the workspace window to hide and
     show the Filmstrip. Right-click / Control-click the triangle to set the automatic
     show and hide options.

2   Position the pointer over the top edge of the Filmstrip; the cursor becomes
     a double arrow. Drag the top edge of the Filmstrip up or down to enlarge
     or reduce the thumbnails. The narrower you make the Filmstrip the more
     thumbnails it can display.

Using filters in the Filmstrip

With so few photos in the Lesson 4 folder it's not difficult to see all the images at
once in the Filmstrip. However, when you're working with a folder containing many
images it can be inconvenient to scroll the Filmstrip looking for the photos you
want to work with.

You can use the Filmstrip filters to narrow down the images displayed in the
Filmstrip to only those that share a specified flag status, rating, color label, or any
combination of these attributes.

1   In the Filmstrip you can see that one of the images in the Lesson 4 folder
     displays the white Pick flag that you assigned in a previous exercise. If you don't
     see the flag, right-click / Control-click anywhere in the Filmstrip and activate
     the context menu option View Options > Show Ratings And Picks. Examine the
     other options available in the Filmstrip context menu. Many of the commands
     apply to the image or images currently selected; others affect the Filmstrip itself.

2   From the Filter menu at the top right of the Filmstrip, choose Flagged. Only the
     image with the white flag is displayed in the Filmstrip.

3 The white flag icon is now highlighted among the Filter controls in the top bar of the Filmstrip. Click the word Filter at the left of the flag icons to see the attribute filter options displayed as buttons in the Filmstrip header.

You can activate or disable any of the filters you saw in the Filter menu by clicking the respective Filter buttons. You can set up a combination of filters and save it as a custom preset by choosing Save Current Settings As New Preset from the menu.

4 Click the white flag button to deactivate the active filter or choose Filters Off from the menu to disable all filters. The Filmstrip once more displays all the images in the folder. Click the word Filter again to hide the filter buttons.

You'll learn more about using filters in Lesson 5, "Organizing and Selecting."

Changing the sorting order of the thumbnails

Use the Sort Direction control and the Sort Criteria menu in the Toolbar to change the display order of the thumbnails images in the Grid view and the Filmstrip.

1 If the sorting controls are not currently visible in the Toolbar, choose Sorting from the tools menu at the right of the Toolbar.

2 Choose Pick from the Sort Criteria menu.

The thumbnails are rearranged in both the Grid view and the Filmstrip to display the image with the white Pick flag first.

3 Click the Sort Direction control (![icon]) to reverse the sorting direction of the thumbnails. The image with the white Pick flag now appears last in the order.

When you've grouped images in a Collection, you can manually rearrange their order however you wish. This can be particularly useful when you're creating a presentation such as a slideshow or web gallery, or putting together a print layout, as the images will be placed in the template according to their sort order.

4 Expand the Collections panel and click the New York
   Collection that you created earlier in this lesson.
   Choose File Name from the Sort Criteria menu.

5 In the Filmstrip, drag the second image to the right and release the mouse
   button when you see a black insertion bar appear between the third and fourth
   thumbnails.

► **Tip:** You can also
change the order of
the photos in a collec-
tion by dragging the
thumbnail images in
the Grid view.

The image snaps to its new location in both the Filmstrip and the Grid view. The
new sorting order is also apparent in the Toolbar; your manual sorting order has
been saved and is now listed as User Order in the Sort Criteria menu.

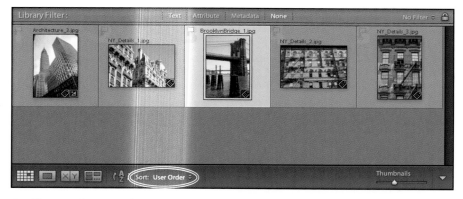

6 Choose File Name from the Sort menu; then return to your manual sorting by
   choosing User Order.

Congratulations; you've finished another lesson. You've gained confidence navigating through your library and learned techniques for reviewing, sorting, filtering,
and grouping your images as collections. You'll learn more about structuring and
organizing your photo library in the next lesson.

Review questions

1 Name the four working views in the Library module, and explain how they're used.

2 What is the Navigator?

3 How do you use the Quick Collection?

4 What is the target collection?

Review answers

1 Press the G key or click the Grid view button () in the Toolbar to see thumbnails of your images while you search, apply flags, ratings and labels, or create collections. Use the keyboard shortcut E or click the Loupe view button () to inspect a single photo at a range of magnifications. Press C or click the Compare view button () to see two images side by side. Click the Survey view button () in the Toolbar or use the keyboard shortcut N to evaluate several images at once or refine a selection.

2 The Navigator is an interactive full image preview that helps you move around easily within a zoomed image in Loupe view. Click or drag in the Navigator preview to reposition the view while a white rectangle indicates the portion of the magnified image that is currently visible in the workspace. The Navigator panel also contains controls for setting the zoom levels for the Loupe view. Click the image in Loupe view to switch between the last two zoom levels set in the Navigator panel.

3 To create a Quick Collection, select one or more images and then press the B key or choose Photo > Add To Quick Collection. The Quick Collection is a temporary holding area; you can continue to add—or remove—images until you are ready to save the grouping as a more permanent Collection. You'll find the Quick Collection listed in the Catalog panel.

4 The target collection is the collection to which a selected image will be moved when you press the B key or click the circular marker in the upper right corner of the thumbnail. By default, the Quick Collection is designated as the target collection; this status is indicated by the plus sign (+) that follows the Quick Collection's name in the Catalog panel. You can designate a collection of your own as the target collection so that you can use the same convenient techniques to add and remove photos quickly.

PHOTOGRAPHY SHOWCASE
CHRIS ORWIG

"Photography is a means to express deeper ideas, to convey quiet moments, and to savor life before it slips away."

I became a photographer because I was in a major slump. I was wrestling with some significant identity and health issues, and I was losing my grip. Then, suddenly, my father gave me a camera. And that camera was my ticket to a new life.

By holding the camera up to my eye, the world no longer revolved in the same way. My own pain and sorrows drifted away. The camera slowed time down and taught me about the value of life. Soon it became a passport to a whole new way to live.

Photography enriches, enlivens, and expands how we think. It heightens what we see and deepens who we are. It's so easy to drift through life and to neglect the small details. Photography is a wake up call to not let any of it pass us by.

While I enjoy and appreciate many types of photography, I like to photograph people who excel in life and are intensely committed to what they do.

In this set of photographs, you will find some legends in the surfing world. And rather than photograph their mythic stature, my aim was to capture something more real. These pictures have a quiet, subtle, and maybe a poetic voice. Photography is similar to poetry in many ways. What the novelist says in 10,000 words a poet says in 10. The poet not only says less, but sometimes uses less to even say more.

www. chrisorwig.com

TOM

ROB

ANTON

SHAUN

KELLY

TAYLOR

5 ORGANIZING AND SELECTING

Lesson overview

As your photo library grows larger, organizing your files so that they can be easily found will become increasingly important. Lightroom offers options for organizing your images before you even click the Import button—and even more once they're in your catalog. Manage your folders and files without leaving the Library module; then apply keyword tags, flags, ratings, and labels, and group your photos in convenient collections, regardless of where they're stored.

This lesson will familiarize you with the tools and techniques you'll use to organize, manage, and search your photo library:

- Creating a folder structure
- Moving files and synchronizing folders
- Understanding Collections
- Working with keywords, flags, ratings, and labels
- Organizing images by location in the Map module
- Editing Metadata and using the Painter tool
- Finding and filtering files
- Reconnecting renamed and missing files

You'll probably need between one and two hours to complete this lesson. If you haven't already done so, download the Lesson 5 work files from the Lesson & Update Files tab on your Account page at www.peachpit.com.

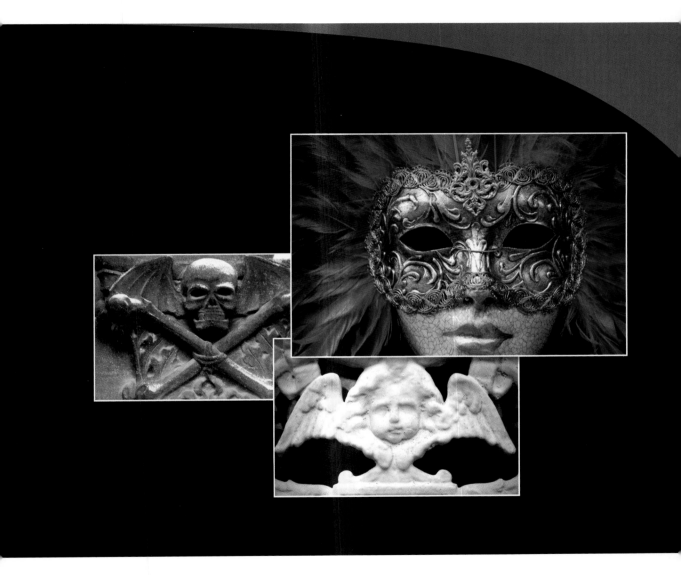

Lightroom delivers powerful, versatile tools to help you organize your image library. Use keywords, flags, labels, ratings—even GPS information—to sort your images, and group them into virtual collections by any association you choose. You can easily make fast, sophisticated searches, based on practically limitless combinations of criteria, that will put the photos you want at your fingertips, right when you need them.

Getting started

● **Note:** This lesson assumes that you already have a basic working familiarity with the Lightroom workspace. If you find that you need more background informa-tion, refer to Lightroom Help, or review the previous lessons.

Before you start on this lesson, make sure you've set up the LR5CIB folder for your lesson files and created the LR5CIB Catalog file to manage them, as described in "Setting up a work folder" and "Creating a catalog file for working with this book" in the Getting Started chapter at the beginning of this book.

If you haven't already done so, download the Lesson 5 folder and the Lesson 5 GPS folder from your Account page at www.peachpit.com to the LR5CIB/Lessons folder, as detailed in the section "Accessing the Classroom in a Book files" in the chapter "Getting Started."

1 Start Lightroom.

2 In the Adobe Photoshop Lightroom - Select Catalog dialog box, make sure the file LR5CIB Catalog.lrcat is selected under Select A Recent Catalog To Open, and then click Open.

▶ **Tip:** The first time you enter any of the Lightroom modules, you'll see module tips that will help you get started by identifying the components of the Lightroom workspace and stepping you through the workflow. Dismiss the tips by click-ing the Close button. To reactivate the tips for any module, choose [Module name] Tips from the Help menu.

3 Lightroom will open in the screen mode and workspace module that were active when you last quit. If necessary, switch to the Library module by clicking Library in the Module Picker at the top of the workspace.

Importing images into the library

The first step is to import the images for this lesson into the Lightroom library.

1 In the Library module, click the Import button below the left panel group.

2   If the Import dialog box appears in compact mode, click the Show More Options button at the lower left of the dialog box to see all the options in the expanded Import dialog box.

3   Under Source at the left of the expanded Import dialog box, navigate to and select the LR5CIB > Lessons > Lesson 5 folder. Ensure that all twelve images in the Lesson 5 folder are checked for import.

4   In the import options picker above the thumbnail previews, select Add so that the imported photos will be added to your catalog without being moved or copied. Under File Handling at the right of the Import dialog box, choose Minimal from the Render Previews menu and ensure that the Don't Import Suspected Duplicates option is activated. Under Apply During Import, choose None from both the Develop Settings menu and the Metadata menu, and type **Lesson 5, Europe** in the Keywords text box. Make sure that your import is set up as shown in the illustration below, and then click Import.

The twelve images are imported from the Lesson 5 folder and now appear in both the Grid view of the Library module and in the Filmstrip across the bottom of the Lightroom workspace.

Organizing folders

Each time you import an image, Lightroom creates a new catalog entry to record the file's address and lists the folder in which it is stored—and the volume that contains that folder—in the Folders panel in the left panel group.

In the Folders panel, you can organize your photo library at the most basic level by rearranging files and folders on your hard disk without ever leaving the Lightroom workspace; you can create or delete folders at the click of a button and move files and folders by simply dragging them.

When you use the Folders panel to move a photo between folders, Lightroom will delete the image file from its original location and update the library catalog with the file's new address. Lightroom maintains a single catalog entry for each photo you import, so a master image cannot be duplicated in separate folders or added to the catalog twice.

Creating subfolders

In this exercise you'll use the Folders panel to begin organizing the photos in the Lesson 5 folder into categories by separating them into subfolders. You'll use two methods of creating a subfolder.

1   Click the Lesson 5 folder in the Folders panel; then, Ctrl-click / Command-click to select the four images of masks in the Grid view.

2   In the Folders panel header, click the Create New Folder button (⊕) and choose Add Subfolder from the menu. Make sure the Show Photos In Subfolders option is activated.

3   In the Create Folder dialog box, type **Masks** as the name for the new subfolder, activate the option Include Selected Photos, and then click Create.

4 In the Folders panel, expand the Lesson 5 folder to see the Masks folder nested inside it. The image count for the new subfolder shows that it contains the four images that you selected in step 1.

5 With the Lesson 5 folder still selected in the Folders panel, select the remaining eight images.

6 Right-click / Control-click the Lesson 5 folder and choose Create Folder inside "Lesson 5" from the context menu. Type **Architecture** as the folder name, activate the Include Selected Photos option, and then click Create. Click the Architecture subfolder to see the eight images you selected in step 5.

Making changes to a folder's content

When you rearrange files and folders in the Folders panel the changes are also made on your hard disk. Inversely, the Folders panel needs to be updated to reflect any changes you make to the location, name, or contents of a folder from outside the Lightroom workspace. In this exercise you'll experience this first hand by deleting an image in Windows Explorer / the Finder.

1 Click the Lesson 5 folder in the Folders panel. Right-click / Ctrl-click any of the photos of masks in the Grid view or the Filmstrip and choose Show In Explorer / Show In Finder from the context menu.

▶ **Tip:** To rename a folder in the Folders panel, right-click / Control-click its name and choose Rename from the context menu. Be aware that when you rename a folder in the Folders panel, the change affects the folder on the hard disk.

2   The Explorer / Finder window opens. Note the Architecture and Masks subfolders inside the Lesson 5 folder. Right-click / Ctrl-click the image file DSC_0249.jpg inside the Lesson 5 folder and choose Delete / Move To Trash from the context menu.

3   Switch back to Lightroom. In the Grid view, note that the thumbnail of the image that you deleted in the Explorer / Finder window now has an alert badge in the upper right corner of its grid cell. This indicates that there is still an entry for the image in the library catalog but the link to the original file is broken. When the image is selected, the missing photo alert also appears below the Histogram.

4   Click the missing photo badge. A dialog box opens offering you the option to locate the missing file and reestablish its link to the catalog. Click Cancel.

As you deleted the file intentionally you should now remove it from the library catalog. You can remove a missing photo from your catalog by selecting its thumbnail in the Grid view or the Filmstrip and pressing Alt+Backspace / Option+Delete or by choosing Photo > Remove Photo From Catalog. Don't remove the photo from the catalog yet—if you've done so already, choose Edit > Undo Remove Images. In the next exercise you'll learn a different technique for updating the catalog by synchronizing folders.

Synchronizing folders

When you synchronize the folders in the Lightroom catalog with the folders on your hard disk you have the option to remove catalog entries for files that have been deleted, import photos that have been added to your folders, or scan for files with updated metadata.

You can specify which folders and subfolders will be synchronized and which new images you want added to your library.

1 Make sure that the Lesson 5 folder is still selected in the Folders panel.

2 Choose Library > Synchronize Folder.

3 In the Synchronize Folder "Lesson 5" dialog box, the import options are unavailable, indicating that there have been no new photos added to the Lesson 5 folder. Activate the option Remove Missing Photos From Catalog (1), disable Scan For Metadata Updates, and then click Synchronize.

▶ **Tip:** The Import New Photos option in the Synchronize Folders dialog box automatically imports any files that have been added to a folder without yet having been added to your image library. Optionally, activate Show Import Dialog Before Importing to choose which of those files you wish to import. Activate the Scan For Metadata Updates option to check for files with metadata modified in another application.

The missing image is removed from your catalog and its thumbnail is no longer displayed in the Grid view; all the remaining links between your library catalog and the Lesson 5 folder on your hard disk have been restored.

Using collections to organize images

Although an organized system of folders provides a good foundation for your photo library, grouping images into collections is a far more efficient and flexible way to classify your images—and offers many more options when you need to access them.

A collection is like a virtual folder: a grouping of photos from your library based on your own associations rather than on the actual location of the files. A collection may contain images drawn from any number of separate folders on your hard disk. Inversely, a single master image can be included in any number of collections; the same photo might appear in a collection of images with architectural content and also in a compilation of shots with an Autumn theme; it may be part of a collection you've assembled for a client presentation and in another created for a family vacation slideshow. Grouping images as collections in your library doesn't affect the arrangement of the files and folders on your hard disk, and removing a photo from a collection won't remove it from the library catalog or delete it from the hard disk.

● **Note:** Once you've grouped a selection of photos as a collection you can rearrange them in the Grid view or the Filmstrip, changing the order in which they will appear in a presentation or a print layout. Your customized sorting order will be saved with the collection.

There are three basic types of collection: Collections, Smart Collections and the Quick Collection. Any collection can also be part of an Output Collection—a listing in the Collections that is created automatically when you save a print layout or a creative project such as a photo book or web gallery. An Output Collection links a set of images to a particular project template and records all of your customized settings. Any collection or selection of images can also become a Publish collection, which automatically keeps track of images that you've shared online.

▶ **Tip:** You'll learn more about Publish collections in Lesson 10, "Publishing Your Photos."

The Quick Collection

● **Note:** If the Thumbnail Badges option is activated in the Library View Options, a photo that is included in a collection of any kind displays the collection badge () in the lower right of its thumbnail.

The Quick Collection is a temporary holding collection; a convenient place to group images while you gather photos from different folders. You can access the Quick Collection from the Catalog panel so that you can easily return to work with the same selection of images at any time. Your images will stay in the Quick Collection until you are ready to convert your selection to a permanent collection that will then be listed in the Collections panel.

You can create as many collections and smart collections as you wish, but there is only one Quick Collection; if there is already a selection of images in the Quick Collection, you'll need to convert it to a standard collection, and then clear the Quick Collection before you can use it to assemble a new a new grouping. To create a new collection for images that are currently in the Quick Collection, right-click / Control-click the Quick Collection folder in the Catalog panel and choose Save Quick Collection from the context menu.

Photo is in collection

Click the badge to see a menu listing the collections in which the image is included. Select a collection from the list to switch to that collection as the image source folder.

If the Quick Collection Markers option is enabled in the View Options for the Grid view, a circular marker appears in the top right corner of a thumbnail in the Grid view or the Filmstrip when you move your pointer over the image cell. You can add the image to the Quick Collection by clicking this marker.

Once the photo is added to the Quick Collection the marker becomes a solid grey circle. Click the solid marker to remove the image from the Quick Collection. You can select multiple images and perform the same operations for the whole group by clicking the Quick Collection marker on any of the selected thumbnails.

You can also add a selected image or group of images to the Quick Collection by pressing the B key or choosing Photo > Add To Quick Collection, or remove a selected image or group of images from the Quick Collection by pressing the B key again or choosing Photo > Remove From Quick Collection.

Collections

You can create as many permanent collections as you wish. Use a collection to collate the images you need for a particular project or to group photos by subject or any other association.

When you create a collection of images for a slideshow or a web page, all the work you do on your presentation will be saved with the collection in the catalog file. In fact, the catalog entry for a single collection can incorporate your settings from the Develop module, a slide layout and playback options from the Slideshow module, designs you set up in the Book and Web modules, and a page layout modified in the Print module. Output collections for print jobs will also include your color management and printer settings.

To create a collection, choose Library > New Collection. Alternatively, click the New Collection button (⊕) in the header of the Collections panel and choose Create Collection from the menu. Enter a name for the collection and click Create. Your new collection will be listed in the Collections panel; you can then simply drag photos onto the listing in the Collections panel to add them to the collection.

● **Note:** Remember that a single photo can be included in any number of collections, although the master image file is located in only one folder in your library. For this reason, grouping your images in collections is a far more versatile organizational method than sorting them into categorized folders.

Smart collections

A smart collection searches the metadata attached to your photos and gathers together all those images in your library that meet a specified set of criteria. Any newly imported photo that matches the criteria you've set up for a smart collection will be added to that collection automatically.

You can create a Smart Collection by choosing Library > New Smart Collection, and then specify the search criteria for your smart collection by choosing options from the menus in the Create Smart Collection dialog box.

You can add more search criteria by clicking the + button to the right of any of the rules. Hold down the Alt / Option key and click the Plus button (+) to refine a rule. In the illustration below a second rule has been added to search for images containing "Europe" in any searchable text, and then a refined rule has been added to search for images which were either captured or edited this year.

Stacking images

Another effective way of organizing images within a folder or collection is by creating stacks.

Stacks are ideal for reducing clutter in the Grid view—and the number of thumbnails you need to scroll through in the Filmstrip—by grouping similar or related photos so that only the top image in each stack is displayed. You can stack a selection of images of the same subject, a series of photos shot to test different camera settings, or action shots taken using burst mode or auto-bracketing.

A stack can be identified in the Grid view and the Filmstrip by an icon representing a stack of photos, together with an image count, in the upper left corner of the thumbnail.

You can expand or collapse the stack by clicking the stack icon; rearrange the order of the photos within the stack or specify which image appears at the top either by choosing commands from the Photo > Stacking menu or by using keyboard shortcuts.

When you're working with a folder containing hundreds of photos from the same shoot, you can have Lightroom stack the images automatically based on capture time; you can specify the time interval between stacks so that your shots are grouped in a way that reflects the flow of the shoot.

To create a stack, select two or more images in the Grid view or the Filmstrip, and then choose Photo > Stacking > Group Into Stack.

Photo		
Toggle Quick Collection	B	
Open in Loupe	Enter	
Show in Explorer	Ctrl+R	
Go to Folder in Library		
Lock to Second Window	Ctrl+Shift+Enter	
Edit In	▶	
Stacking	▶	**Group into Stack** — Ctrl+G
Create Virtual Copies	Ctrl+'	Unstack — Ctrl+Shift+G
Set Copy as Master		Remove from Stack
Rotate Left (CCW)	Ctrl+[	Split Stack
Rotate Right (CW)	Ctrl+]	Toggle Stack — S
Flip Horizontal		
Flip Vertical		Collapse All Stacks
		Expand All Stacks
Set Flag	▶	Move to Top of Stack — Shift+S
Set Rating	▶	Move Up in Stack — Shift+[
Set Color Label	▶	Move Down in Stack — Shift+]
Auto Advance		
		Auto-Stack by Capture Time...

To learn more about Stacks, please refer to Lightroom Help.

Applying keyword tags

Perhaps the most direct way to mark your photos so that they're easier to find later is by tagging them with keywords—text metadata attached to the image files to categorize them by subject or association.

For example, the image in the illustration at the right could be tagged with the keywords Architecture and Paris, and could therefore be located by searching for either or both of those tags. If the Thumbnail Badges option is activated in the Library View Options dialog box, photos with keyword tags are identified by a keywords badge () in the lower right corner of the thumbnail.

Photo has keywords

You can apply keywords to your photos individually or tag an entire series of images with shared metadata in one operation, thereby linking them by association and making them easier to access amongst all the photos that make up your library. Keywords added to images in Lightroom can be read by Adobe applications such as Bridge, Photoshop, and Photoshop Elements, and by other applications that support XMP metadata.

Viewing keyword tags

Because you applied keyword tags to the images for this lesson during the import process, the thumbnails in the Grid view and the Filmstrip are all marked with the keywords badge. Let's review the keywords you already attached to these photos.

1   Make sure that you are still in the Grid view, and then select the Lesson 5 folder in the Folders panel.

2   Show the right panel group, if necessary; then, expand the Keywording panel. Expand the Keyword Tags pane at the top of the panel. By selecting each thumbnail in the Grid view in turn you can confirm that all the images in the Lesson 5 folder share the keywords "Lesson 5" and "Europe."

► **Tip:** Clicking the keyword badge of an image in Grid view will automatically expand the Keywording panel.

3   Select any one of the photos in the Lesson 5 folder. In the Keyword Tags pane at the top of the Keywording pane, select the text "Lesson 5" and press the Backspace key on your keyboard to delete it.

4   Click anywhere in the Grid view, and then choose Edit > Select All or press Ctrl+A / Command+A to select all the Lesson 5 photos. In the Keyword Tags pane, the keyword "Lesson 5" is now marked with an asterisk to indicate that this tag is not shared by every image in the selection.

5   Expand the Keyword List panel.

▶ Tip: You can apply an existing keyword tag to selected images by clicking the tag in the Keyword Suggestions pane in the Keywording panel. To remove a tag from a selected photo or photos, either delete the word from the Keyword Tags pane in the Keywording panel, or click the checkbox to disable that keyword in the Keyword List panel.

In the Keyword List, a check mark in front of the keyword "Europe" indicates that this tag is shared by every image in the selection, while the tag "Lesson 5" is marked with a dash—indicating that it attached to some, but not all, of the selected images. The image count to the right of the Lesson 5 tag shows that it is shared by only ten of the eleven images.

6   With all eleven images still selected, click the dash mark in front of the Lesson 5 tag to reinstate the deleted tag; a check mark replaces the dash and the image count for the Lesson 5 keyword increases to 11.

Adding keyword tags

You already added keywords to your images during the process of importing them into your Lightroom library. Once the images have been added to your Lightroom library, you can add more keywords by using the Keywording panel.

1   In the Folders panel, select the Architecture subfolder inside the Lesson 5 folder, and then choose Edit > Select All or press Ctrl+A / Command+A.

2   In the Keywording panel, click the grey text "Click Here To Add Keywords" below the Keyword Tags pane and type **Paris, France**. Make sure to separate the words with a comma as shown in the illustration at the right, below.

Always use a comma to separate keywords. Using a space or period will not work; Lightroom would treat both "Paris France" and "Paris. France" as a single keyword.

3   Press Enter / Return. The new keywords are listed in alphabetical order in the Keyword Tags panel and in the Keyword List panel.

4   In the Folders panel, select the Lesson 5 folder, and then choose Edit > Invert Selection to select all the images other than the eight in the Architecture folder.

5   In the Keywording panel, click in the text box below the Keyword Tags pane and type **Italy**. Press Enter / Return.

6   Choose Edit > Select None or press Ctrl+D / Command+D on your keyboard.

Working with keyword sets and nesting keywords

You can use the Keyword Set pane of the Keywording panel to work with *keyword sets*; groups of keyword tags compiled for a particular purpose. You could create a set of keywords for a specific project, another set for a special occasion, and one for your friends and family. Lightroom provides three basic keyword set presets. You can use these sets as they are or as starting points for creating sets of your own.

1   Expand the Keyword Set pane in the Keywording panel, if necessary, and then choose Wedding Photography from the Keyword Set menu. You can see that the keywords in the set would indeed be helpful in organizing the shots from a big event. Look at the categories covered by the other Lightroom keyword sets. You can use these as templates for your own keyword sets by editing them to suit your needs and saving your changes as a new preset.

Grouping your keywords in Keyword Sets is one way to keep your keywords organized; another handy technique is to nest related tags in a keywords hierarchy.

▶ **Tip:** Keyword sets are a convenient way to have the keywords you need at hand as you work on different collections in your library. A single keyword tag may be included in any number of keyword sets. If you don't see the Lightroom presets in the Keyword Set menu, open the Lightroom Preferences and click the Presets tab. In the Lightroom Defaults options, click Restore Keyword Set Presets.

2   Ctrl-click / Command-click to select the keywords "France" and "Italy" in the Keyword List panel; then, drag the selected tags onto the keyword "Europe." Click the triangle at the left of the Europe tag to see the France and Italy tags nested inside it.

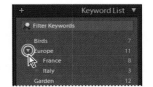

3   In the keyword list, drag the Paris tag from its alphabetical position on the keyword list onto the keyword "France," and then expand the France tag.

4   Right-click / Control-click the keyword "Italy" and choose Create Keyword Tag Inside "Italy" from the context menu.

5   In the Keyword Tag text box, type **Venice**. In the Synonyms text box just below, type **Venezia**. Make sure all the Keyword Tag Options are activated as shown in the illustration below, and then click Create.

Include On Export Includes the keyword tag when your photos are exported.

Export Containing Keywords Includes the parent tag when your photos are exported.

Export Synonyms Includes any synonyms associated with the keyword tag when your photos are exported.

6   Expand the Italy tag; then, right-click / Control-click the keyword "Venice" and choose Create Keyword Tag Inside "Venice" from the menu. Type **Carnival**; then, click Create. Expand the Venice tag to show all the tags in the hierarchy.

7   In the Folders panel, select the Masks subfolder inside the Lesson 5 folder, and then choose Edit > Select All or press Ctrl+A / Command+A. Drag the Venice and Carnival tags from the Keyword List panel onto any of the three selected images in the Grid view.

The check marks in front of the new Venice and Carnival tags in the keyword list, and the image count to the right of each entry, indicate that both keyword tags have been applied to all three of the photos in the selection.

8   In the Folders panel, select the Lesson 2 folder. and then choose Edit > Select All or press Ctrl+A / Command+A.

9   Move the pointer over the Europe tag in the Keyword List panel, and then click the empty check box at the left. Repeat the process to apply the Italy and Venice keywords (but not the Carnival tag) to the selected images.

Searching by keywords

Once you've taken the time to organize your images by adding keywords and other metadata such as ratings, flags, and labels, it will be easy to set up sophisticated and detailed filters to find exactly the photo you're looking for.

For now, we'll look at some techniques for searching the photos in your library by keywords alone.

▶ **Tip:** If you find that you cannot open two panels in one of the side panel groups at the same time, right-click / Control-click the header of any panel in the group and disable the Solo Mode option in the context menu

1   In the left panel group, collapse the Navigator, Collections, and Publish Services panels if necessary, so that you can clearly see the contents of the Catalog and Folders Panels. In the Folders panel, select the Lesson 5 folder, and then choose Edit > Select None or press Ctrl+D / Command+D.

2   Use the Thumbnails slider in the Toolbar to reduce the size of the thumbnails to the minimum, so that you'll be able to see as many images as possible in the Grid view. If the Filter Bar is not already visible above the Grid view, choose View > Show Filter Bar, or press the Backslash key (\).

3   In the right panel group, collapse the Histogram, Quick Develop, and Keywording panels, if necessary, so that you can clearly see the whole of the expanded Keyword List panel.

4   In the Keyword List panel, move your pointer over the entry for the keyword "Europe," and then click the white arrow that appears to the right of the image count.

In the left panel group, All Photographs is now selected in the Catalog panel, indicating that your entire catalog has been searched for photos with the Europe tag.

The Metadata filter has been activated in the Filter bar at the top of the work area, and the Grid view now displays only those images in your library that are tagged with the keyword "Europe."

5   In the Keyword column at the left of the Metadata filter pane, expand the Europe entry; then, expand the nested Italy tag and click Venice.

▶ **Tip:** To transfer lists of keywords between computers or share them with colleagues who are also working in Lightroom, use the Export Keywords and Import Keywords commands, which you'll find in the Metadata menu.

The images in the Grid view are filtered so that only the ten photos with the Venice tag are still visible. Now you'll use a different technique to narrow the search further.

6 Click Text in the Filter Picker in the Filter bar at the top of the work area.

7 In the Text filter bar, choose Any Searchable Field from the first menu and Contains from the second menu, noting the options available in each menu; then type **carnival** in the text box at the right and press Enter.

▶ **Tip:** You can use the lock button at the right end of the Filter bar to keep your current filter settings active when you choose a different image source from the Catalog, Folders, or Collections panels.

Only the three photos of Venetian masks are still displayed in the Grid view. Of course, the true power of the Library filters only comes into play when you set up more complex filters based on a combination of criteria—but this exercise should have given you at least a glimpse of the possibilities.

8 Disable the combined Text and Metadata filter by clicking None in the picker in the center of the Filter bar. In the Folders panel, select the Lesson 5 folder, and then choose Edit > Select None or press Ctrl+D / Command+D.

Using flags and ratings

The Attribute filters in the Filter bar allow you to search and sort your images according to attributes such as flags and ratings.

When you choose Attribute from the Library Filter options in the Filter bar, the Filter bar expands to display controls for sorting your images by flag status, star rating, color label, copy status, or any combination of these attributes.

Flagging images

Assigning flags to sort the good images from the rejects can be a good way to begin organizing a group of photos. An image can be flagged as a pick (⚐), a reject (⚑), or left unflagged (⚐).

1 Choose Attribute from the picker in the Filter bar. The Filter bar expands to show the Attribute filter controls.

2   If the Toolbar is not already visible below the Grid view, press the T key. Click the triangle at the right side of the Toolbar and activate the Flagging tool in the menu to show the Flag As Pick and Set As Rejected buttons in the Toolbar.

▶ **Tip:** In the Grid and Loupe views, you'll find tools for adding ratings, flags, and color labels in the Toolbar. In the Compare and Survey views you can change these attributes using the controls beneath the images. You can also flag, rate, or color label a selected image by using the Set Flag, Set Rating, or Set Color Label commands in the Photo menu.

3   In the Folders panel, select the Architecture subfolder inside the Lesson 5 folder.

4   In the Grid view, select DSCN3538.jpg, a photo of a mausoleum sculpture in the famous Père Lachaise cemetery in Paris. If the Flags option is activated in the Library View Options dialog box, a grey (un-filled) flag icon in the upper left corner of the image cell indicates that this photo is not flagged. If necessary, hold the pointer over the image cell to see the flag, or disable the option Show Clickable Items On Mouse Over Only in the Library View Options dialog box.

5   To change the flag status to Flagged, you can either click the flag badge in the image cell or the Flag As Pick button (⚐) in the Toolbar. Note that the photo is now marked with a white flag icon in the upper left corner of the image cell.

6   Click the white flag button in the Attribute Filter bar. The Grid view displays only the image that you just flagged. The view is now filtered to display only flagged images from the Architecture folder.

► Tip: You can use the Library > Refine Photos command to sort your photos quickly on the basis of their flagging status. Choose Library > Refine Photos, and then click Refine in the Refine Photos dialog box; any unflagged photos are flagged as rejects and the picks are reset to unflagged status.

Lightroom offers a variety of ways to flag a photo. To flag a photo as a pick, choose Photo > Set Flag > Flagged or press the P key on your keyboard. Click the flag icon at the top left corner of the image cell to toggle between Unflagged and Pick status. To flag an image as a reject, choose Photo > Set Flag > Rejected, press the X key, or Alt-click / Option-click the flag icon in the corner of the image cell. To remove a flag from an image, choose Photo > Set Flag > Unflagged or press the U key. To set any flag status for an image, right-click / Control-click the flag icon in the corner of the image cell and choose Flagged, Unflagged, or Rejected from the flagging menu.

7   Click the grey flag button (the flag in the center) in the Attribute Filter bar. The Grid view now displays any photos flagged as Picks and all unflagged photos, so once again we see all of the images in the Architecture folder.

8   In the Filter bar, click None to disable the Attribute filters.

Assigning ratings

A quick and easy way to sort your images as you review and evaluate them is to assign each photo a rating on a scale from one to five stars.

1   In the Grid view, select DSCN3551.jpg: a detail of a wrought iron grille.

2   Press the 3 key on your keyboard. The message "Set Rating to 3" appears briefly and the photo is now marked with three stars in the lower left of its image cell.

► Tip: If you don't see the star rating in the image cell, choose View > View Options and make sure Rating And Label is activated in the image cell display options.

3   If necessary, click the triangle at the right of the Toolbar and make sure that the Rating controls are activated in the menu. The stars in the Toolbar reflect the rating you just applied to the selected image.

It's easy to change the rating for a selected image; simply press another key between 1 and 5 to apply a new rating or press the 0 key to remove the rating altogether. Alternatively, you can click the stars in the Toolbar to change the rating, or click the highest star in the current rating to remove it.

You can also assign ratings in the Metadata panel, by choosing from the Photo > Set Rating menu, or by right-clicking / Control-clicking a thumbnail and choosing from the Set Rating submenu in the context menu.

Working with color labels

Color labeling can be a very versatile tool for organizing your workflow. Unlike flags and ratings, color labels have no predefined meanings; you can attach your own meaning to each color and customize separate label sets for specific tasks.

While setting up a print job you might assign the red label to images you wish to proof, a blue label to those that need retouching, or a green label to mark images as approved. For another project, you might use the different colors to indicate levels of urgency.

Applying Color Labels

You can use the colored buttons in the Toolbar to assign color labels to your images. If you don't see the color label buttons, click the triangle at the right of the Toolbar and choose Color Label from the menu. You can also click the color label icon displayed in a photo's image cell (a small grey rectangle, for an unlabeled image) and choose from the menu. Alternatively, choose Photo > Set Color Label and choose from the menu; you'll notice that four of the five color labels have keyboard shortcuts.

To see—and set—color labels in the Grid view image cells, choose View > View Options or right-click / Control-click any of the thumbnails and choose View Options from the context menu to open the Library View Options dialog box. On the Grid View tab in The Library View Options dialog box, activate Show Grid Extras. In the Compact Cell Extras options, you can choose Label or Rating And Label from either the Bottom Label or Top Label menus. In the Expanded Cell Extras options, activate the Include Color Label checkbox.

Editing Color Labels and using Color Label Sets

You can rename the color labels to suit your own purposes and create separate label sets tailored to different parts of your workflow. The Lightroom default options in the Photo > Set Color Label menu are Red, Yellow, Green, Blue, Purple, and None. You can change the color label set by choosing Metadata > Color Label Set, and then choosing either the Bridge or Lightroom default sets, or the Review Status set.

The Review Status label set gives you an idea of how you might assign your own label names to help you keep organized. The options in the Review Status set are To Delete, Color Correction Needed, Good To Use, Retouching Needed, To Print, and None.

You can use this label set as it is or as a starting point for creating your own sets. To open the Edit Color Label Set dialog box, choose Metadata > Color Label Set > Edit. You can enter your own name for each color, and then choose Save Current Settings As New Preset from the Presets menu.

Searching by color label

In the Filter bar, click Attribute to see the Attribute filter controls. You can limit your search to a single color label by clicking just one button, or activate more than one button at once. To disable an active color label button, simply click it again. You can use the color label search buttons together with other Attribute filters, or to refine a Text or Metadata search.

The Attribute filters, including the Color Label filters, are also available in the bar above the thumbnails in the Filmstrip.

Adding metadata

You can leverage the metadata information attached to the image files to help you organize and manage your photo library. Much of the metadata, such as capture date, exposure time, focal length and other camera settings, is generated by your camera, but you can also add your own metadata to make it easier to search and sort your catalog. In fact, you did just that when you applied keywords, ratings, and color labels to your images. In addition, Lightroom supports the information standards evolved by the International Press Telecommunications Council (IPTC), which includes entries for descriptions, keywords, categories, credits, and origins.

You can use the Metadata panel in the right panel group to inspect or edit the metadata attached to a selected image.

1 In the Folders panel, click the Masks folder; then, Select the image DSC_0252.jpg: the photo featuring a display of Venetian carnival masks.

2 Expand the Metadata panel. If necessary, hide the Filmstrip or collapse the other panels in the right panel group so that you can see as much of the Metadata panel as possible. Choose Default from the Metadata Set menu in the header of the Metadata panel.

Even the default metadata set exposes a great deal of information about the image. Although most of this metadata was generated by the camera, some of it can be very useful in sorting your photos; you could filter images by capture date, search for shots taken with a particular lens, or easily separate photos taken on different cameras. However, the default set displays only a subset of an image's metadata.

3 Choose EXIF And IPTC from the Metadata Set menu in header of the Metadata panel. Scroll down in the Metadata panel to get an idea of the kinds of information that can be applied to an image.

4 For the purposes of this exercise, you can choose Quick Describe from the Metadata Set menu.

In the Quick Describe metadata set, the Metadata panel shows the File-name, Copy Name (for a virtual copy), Folder, Rating, and some EXIF and IPTC metadata. You can use the Metadata panel to add a title and caption to a photo, attach a copyright notice, provide details about the photographer and the location where the photo was shot, and also change the star rating.

5 Click in the Metadata panel to assign the image a rating, and type **Carnival Mask 2** in the Title text box.

6 Control-click / Command-click either of the other two mask photos to add it to the selection. In the Metadata panel you can see that the folder name and the camera model are shared by both files; items not shared by both images now show the entry <mixed>. Changes made to any of the items in the metadata panel, even those with mixed values, will affect both of the selected images. This is a convenient way to edit items such as copyright details for a whole batch of selected images at the same time.

Storage of metadata

File information is stored using the Extensible Metadata Platform (XMP) standard. XMP is built on XML. In the case of camera raw files that have a proprietary file format, XMP isn't written into the original files. To avoid file corruption, XMP metadata is stored in a separate file called a sidecar file. For all other file formats supported by Lightroom (JPEG, TIFF, PSD, and DNG), XMP metadata is written into the files in the location specified for that data.

XMP facilitates the exchange of metadata between Adobe applications and across publishing workflows. For example, you can save metadata from one file as a template, and then import the metadata into other files. Metadata that is stored in other formats, such as EXIF, IPTC (IIM), and TIFF, is synchronized and described with XMP so that it can be more easily viewed and managed. To find out more about Metadata, please refer to Lightroom Help.

—From Lightroom Help

Organizing photos by location

Note: You need to be online to make use of the Map module.

In the Map module, Lightroom enables you to leverage geotagging technology so that you can see exactly where your photos were captured on a Google map, and search and filter the images in your library by location.

Photos that were captured with a camera or phone that records GPS coordinates will appear on the map automatically. You can easily add location metadata to images captured without GPS information by dragging them directly onto the map from the Filmstrip, or by having Lightroom match their capture times to a tracklog exported from a mobile device.

1 In the Library module, click the Import button below the left panel group.

2 If the Import dialog box appears in compact mode, click the Show More Options button at the lower left of the dialog box to see more options.

Tip: If the reverse geocoding feature has not yet been enabled for your catalog, you'll see a dialog box asking you to authorize Lightroom to exchange GPS location information with Google Maps. Click Enable.

3 Under Source at the left of the Import dialog box, navigate to and select the LR5CIB > Lessons > Lesson 5 GPS folder. Make sure that both of the images in the Lesson 5 GPS folder are checked for import. In the import options picker above the thumbnail previews, click Add to add the imported photos to your catalog without moving or copying them. In the Apply During Import panel at the right, type **Lesson 5, GPS** in the Keywords text box, and then click Import.

4 In the Grid view or the Filmstrip, select the image Audreys_House.jpg (Audrey Hepburn's birthplace in Brussels), and then click Map in the module picker.

Working in the Map module

Lightroom has automatically plotted the photo's location by reading the GPS metadata embedded in the image file. The mapped location is marked by a colored pin.

Tip: If you don't see the Map Info overlay and the Map Key, which explains the different color-coded location pins, choose Show Map Info and Show Map Key from the View Menu.

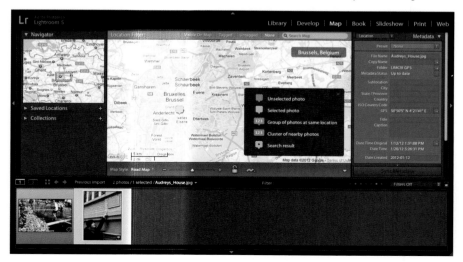

Note: What you see on screen may differ from this illustration, depending on the map style and zoom depth set when you last used the Map module.

The Navigator panel at the left shows a thumbnail overview map, with a white-bordered rectangle indicating the area currently visible in the main map view.

The Toolbar below the map view offers a Map Style menu, a Zoom slider, and buttons for locking marker pins and accessing imported GPS tracklogs. You can add location details and other information in the Metadata panel at the right.

1   Dismiss the Map Key by clicking the Close button (x) in the upper right corner of the overlay, or by disabling the Show Map Key option in the View menu.

2   Experiment with changing the magnification of the map by dragging the Zoom slider in the Toolbar, or by clicking the Zoom In (+) and Zoom Out (-) buttons at either end of the slider. Hold down the Alt / Option key and drag a rectangle in the map to zoom into that area. Drag the map to reposition it in the view, or move the focus by dragging the white-bordered rectangle in the Navigator.

● **Note:** The maximum zoom depth available depends on your choice of map style.

3   In the Map Style menu at the left of the Toolbar, select each of the six styles in turn, then set the map to the look you prefer.

Map styles, clockwise from upper left: Hybrid, Road Map, Satellite, Dark, Light, Terrain.

The Location Filter bar above the map lets you highlight just those photos captured at locations currently visible on the map or filter for tagged or untagged shots.

4   Click each of the four options in the Location Filter bar in turn, noting the effect of the filters on which images are displayed in the Filmstrip.

In the Filmstrip and the Library module's Grid view, images that have been tagged with a GPS location are marked with a location marker badge (⬛).

▶ **Tip:** Click the location marker badge on a thumbnail in the Filmstrip or in the Library module's Grid view to zoom in to the image's map location.

Geotagging images captured without GPS data

Tip: To see whether a selected photo has GPS metadata, choose the Location preset in the Metadata panel; then, look for coordinates in the GPS field.

Even if your camera does not record GPS data, the Map module makes it easy to tag your photos by location.

1 In the header of the Filmstrip, click the white arrow to the right of the name of the currently selected image and choose Folder - Lesson 5 from the Recent Sources list in the menu.

2 In the Filter bar's text search box, type **Venice, Italy**; then, press Enter / Return.

The map is redrawn and the new location is marked with a Search Result marker.

3 Clear the Search Result marker by clicking the X button at the right of the text search box in the Location Filter bar.

4 Select the three photos of carnival masks, and then right-click / Control-click Venice on the map and choose Add GPS Coordinates To Selected Photos.

Tip: If geocoding has been disabled for your catalog, you may see a dialog box asking you to authorize Lightroom to exchange GPS information with Google Maps. Click Enable. You can also disable or activate this feature at any time on the Metadata tab of the Catalog Settings dialog box; choose Catalog Settings from the Edit / Lightroom menu.

5 Choose Edit > Select None. Move the pointer over the marker pin on the map to see a preview of the photos captured at that location. Click the marker pin to select the photos captured at that location. Click the white arrows at the sides of the preview thumbnail to see the other images at this location, and then click away from the preview to close it.

6 In the header of the Filmstrip, click the arrow to the right of the image source information and choose Previous Import from the source menu. Make sure that the image NY_Marathon.jpg is selected.

Adding locations using GPS tracklogs

Although your camera may not record GPS data, many mobile devices such as phones can export a tracklog that records your location over a given period of time. You can import this information, and then have Lightroom tag your photos automatically by matching their capture times to the locations recorded in the tracklog.

Tip: Lightroom can work with tracklogs exported in GPX format. If your device doesn't export in GPX format, you can use GPS Babel to convert its output.

1   Click the GPS Tracklogs button (🔀) in the Toolbar and choose Load Tracklog, or choose Map > Tracklog > Load Tracklog. In the Import Track File dialog box, navigate to your LR5CIB > Lessons > Lesson 5 GPS folder; then, select the file NY_Marathon.gpx and click Open / Choose. Click the small white arrow at the right of the GPS Tracklogs button and choose All Tracks from the menu.

The map is updated to a view of New York, with the recorded GPS track shown as either a blue or yellow line on the map, depending on your choice of map style.

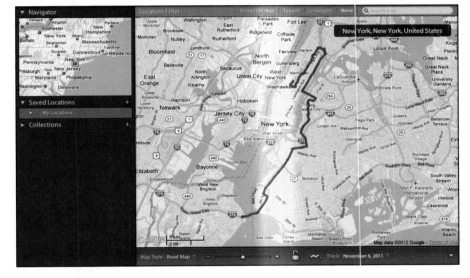

This tracklog was generated by a sports watch that was set to a different time zone than the camera used to capture our lesson photo, so you may need to offset the times recorded. The offset will depend on the time zone setting on your computer.

2   Click the GPS Tracklogs button (🔀) in the Toolbar and choose Set Time Zone Offset, or choose the same command from the Map > Tracklog menu. Use the slider in the Offset Time Zone dialog box, or type a number in the adjacent text box, to shift the starting time for the tracklog to 11:27 AM; then, click OK.

3   Set the map to a style other than Satellite. Select the image NY_Marathon.jpg in the Filmstrip, and then choose Map > Tracklog > Auto-Tag Photos.

Lightroom matches the capture time of the selected image to the corresponding location on the marathon route recorded by the tracklog.

4   Move the pointer over the new marker pin on the map—or double-click the marker—to see a preview of the tagged image.

5   Zoom into the map close enough to read the street names around the new marker pin. As you can see, the photo was taken near the corner of 4th Avenue and Dean Street. Click Library in the module picker at the top of the workspace and double-click the New York marathon thumbnail in the Grid view to enter Loupe view. Zoom into the upper right corner of the image; the street sign confirms that the photo has been correctly placed.

6   Click Map in the module picker to return to the Map module.

Saving map locations

In the Saved Locations panel, you can save a list of your favorite places, making it easy to locate and organize a selection of related images. You could create a saved map location to encompass a cluster of places that you visited during a particular vacation, or to mark a single location that you used for a photo shoot for a client.

1   Zoom out in the map view until you can see all of the GPS track.

2 Expand the Saved Locations panel, if necessary; then, click the Create New Preset button (⊕) at the right of the header.

3 In the New Location dialog box, type **New York Marathon** as the location name. Under Options, set the Radius value to **9.5** miles; then, click Create.

▶ **Tip:** Marking a saved location as Private in the New Location and Edit Location dialog boxes ensures that the GPS information will always be removed when photos from that location are exported or shared, without deleting the location from the images in your catalog. This is useful for protecting your privacy at locations such as your home address. For photos that are not in a saved location, you can choose to omit GPS metadata when you set up an export. For more detail, see Lesson 11.

Your new listing appears in the Saved Locations panel; the image count shows that there is one only tagged image that falls within the specified radius.

On the map, the saved location has a center pin that can be repositioned, and a second pin on the border for increasing or decreasing the radius of the target area.

Selecting or deselecting a location in the Saved Locations panel shows and hides the circular location overlay, and makes the location active for editing. To add photos to a saved location, you can either drag them directly from the Filmstrip onto the location's entry in the Saved Locations panel, or select the images in the Filmstrip and click the check box to the left of the location name.

Click the white arrow button that appears to the right of the location name when you move your pointer over the location in the Saved Locations panel to move to that saved location on the map. To edit a location, right-click / Control-click its entry in the Saved Locations panel and choose Location Options from the menu.

Once your photos are tagged with locations, you can search your library using the filter picker and search box in the Location Filter bar above the map, the Saved Locations panel, and the Library Metadata filters set to GPS Data or GPS Location.

4 Click Library in the module picker to return to the Library module.

Using the Painter tool

Of all the features Lightroom provides to help you organize your growing image library, the Painter tool (🖦) is the most flexible. By simply dragging the Painter tool across your images in the Grid view you can add metadata, assign keywords, labels, ratings, and flags—and even apply developing settings, rotate your photos, or add them to the Quick Collection.

When you pick the Painter tool up from its well in the Toolbar, the Paint menu appears beside the empty tool well. From the Paint menu you can choose which settings or attributes you wish to apply to your images.

The appearance of the Painter tool's spray can icon changes slightly, depending on which option you choose. The illustration below shows the different spray can icons that correspond to the Paint menu options. Reading from left to right, they are: Keywords, Labels, Flag, Rating, Metadata, Settings, Rotation, and Target Collection.

In this exercise you'll use the Painter tool to mark images with a color label.

1   Click the Architecture folder in the Folders panel and make sure that none of the images are selected in the Grid view. If you don't see the Painter tool in the Toolbar, click the triangle at the right side of the Toolbar and choose Painter from the tools menu.

2   Click the Painter tool to pick it up from its well in the Toolbar; then choose Label from the Paint menu, and click the red color label button.

3   The Painter tool is now "loaded." Move the pointer over any of the thumbnails in the Grid view and a red spray can icon appears.

4   Click the thumbnail in the Grid view and the Painter tool applies the red label. Whether you see the color as a tint in the image cell depends on your settings in the Library View Options dialog box. If you don't see the red color label marker (circled in the illustration at the right), choose View > Grid View Style > Show Extras.

5   Move the pointer back over the same thumbnail, and
    then hold down the Alt / Option key and; the cursor
    changes from the Painter tool spray can to an eraser.
    Click the thumbnail with the eraser cursor and the red
    color label is removed.

6   Release the Alt / Option key and click the image once more—but this time drag
    the spray can across all three images. You've applied the red color tag to all the
    images with one stroke. Hold down the Alt / Option key again, and then remove
    the label from all but one of the photos.

7   Click Done at the right side of the Toolbar, or click the Painter tool's empty well,
    to drop the Painter tool and return the Toolbar to its normal state.

Finding and filtering files

Now that you're familiar with the different techniques for categorizing and marking
your photos, it's time to see some results. Next you'll look at how easy it is to search
and sort your images once they've been prepared in this way. You can now filter
your images by rating or label or search for specific keywords, GPS locations and
other metadata. There are numerous ways to find the images you need but one of
the most convenient is to use the Filter bar across the top of the Grid view.

Using the Filter bar to find photos

1   If you don't see the Filter bar above the Grid view, press the backslash key (\) or
    choose View > Show Filter Bar. In the Folders panel, select the Lesson 5 folder.
    If you don't see all eleven photos, choose Library > Show Photos In Subfolders.

The Filter bar contains three filter groups: Text, Attribute, and Metadata filters.
Click any of these options and the Filter bar will expand to display the settings and
controls you'll use to set up a filtered search. You can use these filters separately or
combine them for a more sophisticated search.

Use the Text filter to search any text attached to your images, including filenames,
keywords, captions, and the EXIF and IPTC metadata. The Attribute filter searches
your photos by flag status, star rating, color label, or copy status. The Metadata filter enables you to set up to eight columns of criteria to refine your search. Choose
from the menu at the right end of a column header to add or remove a column.

Library Filter :		Text	Attribute	Metadata	None		No Filter ⇟	
Date		Keyword		Camera		Label		
All (2 Dates)	11	All (2 Keywords)	11	All (2 Cameras)	11	All (1 Label)	11	Add Column
▽ 2012	11	▷ Europe		COOLPIX P7100	8	No Label	11	Remove this Column
▷ April	3	Lesson 5	11	NIKON D5000	3			

2 If the Text or Metadata filters are active, click None to disable them. Click Attribute to activate the Attribute filters. If any of the flag filters is still active from the previous exercise, click the highlighted flag to disable it, or choose Library > Filter By Flag > Reset This Filter.

3 In the Rating controls, click the second star to search for any image with a rating of one star or higher.

The grid view displays only the two images to which you've applied a star rating.

4 There are many options for refining your search. Click Text in the header of the Filter bar to add an additional filter. In the Text filter bar, open the first menu to see the search target options. You can narrow the search to Filename, Copy Name, Title, Caption, Keywords, or searchable IPTC and EXIF metadata, but for this exercise you can choose the search target Any Searchable Field. Click the second menu and choose Contains All.

5 In the search text box, type **Venice**. Your narrowed search returns only one image in the Grid view.

6 In the Rating controls, click the second star to disable the current Rating filter or choose Library > Filter By Rating > Reset This Filter. Click Attribute in the header of the Filter bar to close the Attribute filter controls.

▶ **Tip:** In the search text box, add an exclamation mark (!) before any word to exclude it from the results. Add a plus sign (+) before any word to apply the "Starting With" rule only to that word. Add a plus sign (+) after a word to apply the "Ending With" rule only to that word.

7 In the Text filter bar, clear the search term "Venice" by clicking the x icon at the right of the text box, and then type **Europe**.

The Grid view now displays all eleven of the photos in the Lesson 5 folder.

8 In the Text filter bar, type a space after the word Europe, and then type **!Italy** (note the exclamation mark). The search is narrowed to find those images with searchable text that contains the word Europe, but does not contain the word Italy. The Grid view now displays eight photos. Leave the Text filters set as it is for the next exercise.

Using the Metadata filter

1 Click Metadata in the header of the Filter bar to open the Metadata filter pane. Choose Default Columns from the menu at the far right of the Filter bar header.

2 Click Date in the header of the first column to see the wide range of search criteria from which you can choose for each of up to eight columns. Choose Aspect Ratio from the menu as the criteria for the first column, and then choose Landscape from the Aspect Ratio options in the column. The selection in the Grid view is narrowed to the seven images with a horizontal format.

3 Click Text in the header of the Filter bar to disable the Text filter. This search returns ten photos from the Lesson 5 folder. In the Aspect Ratio column, click Portrait to find the remaining lesson image.

4 Click to close the lock icon at the right of the Filter bar header to lock the current filter so that it remains active when you change the image source for the search.

5 Click the All Photographs listing in the Catalog panel. The Grid view now displays every portrait format image in your catalog.

As you can see, there are endless possibilities for combining filters to find just the image you're looking for.

6 Click None in the Filter bar to disable all filters. Click the Lesson 5 folder in the Folders panel.

Using the filters in the Filmstrip

The Attribute filter controls are also available in the header of the Filmstrip. As in the Filter bar the Filter Presets menu lists filter presets and offers the option to save your filter settings as a custom preset, which will then be added to the menu.

The Default Columns preset opens the four default columns of the Metadata search options: Date, Camera, Lens, and Label. Choose Filters Off to turn off all filters and collapse the Filter bar. Select the Flagged preset to display photos with a Pick flag. Use the Location Columns preset to filter photos by their Country, State/Province, City, and Location metadata. The Rated filter preset displays any photos that match the current star rating criteria. Choose Unrated to see all the photos without a star rating or Used and Unused to see which pictures have been included in projects.

▶ **Tip:** If you don't see any filter presets in the presets menu, open Lightroom Preferences and click Restore Library Filter Presets under Lightroom Defaults on the Presets tab.

1   Choose Flagged from the Filter Presets menu at the top right of the Filmstrip. The Attribute filter bar opens above the Grid view. The Grid view and the Filmstrip show only one photo that you flagged as a pick in a previous exercise.

2   Click the white flag icon in the header of the Filmstrip to disable the current filter, and then click the red color label button. If you don't see the color label buttons in the header of the Filmstrip, click the word Filter to the left of the flag buttons. The Attribute filter settings change in the Filter bar above the Grid view and both the Grid view and the filmstrip display only the image that you labeled with the Painter tool.

▶ **Tip:** To save time and effort setting up searches, save your filter settings as a new preset. Specify criteria for any combination of Text, Attribute, and Metadata filters. Then choose Save Current Settings As New Preset from the Custom Filter menu in the Filter bar or the Filmstrip.

3   To disable all filters and display all the images in the Lesson 5 folder, choose Filters Off from the Filter Presets menu or click the switch at the far right of the Filmstrip's header.

Reconnecting missing files and folders

Remember that when you import a photo into your library, Lightroom adds the image file's name and address to the library catalog file, and displays an entry for the folder in which the photo is stored in the Folders panel.

If you rename or move a photo—or a folder—while you're outside the Lightroom workspace the link to the catalog will be broken and Lightroom may no longer be able to locate the image file.

Lightroom will alert you to the problem by marking the thumbnail of the missing photo—or the entry for the missing folder in the Folders panel—with a question mark icon.

1 In the Grid view, right-click / Control-click one of the photos from the Père Lachaise cemetery and choose Show In Explorer / Show In Finder from the menu.

2 In the Explorer / Finder window, change the name of the selected file to **Cemetery.jpg**. Change the name of the Masks folder inside the Lesson 5 folder to **Carnival**.

3 Back in the Grid view in Lightroom, you'll notice the missing file alert icon in the upper right corner of the image cell (and also just below the Histogram). Click the icon; then click Locate in the dialog box.

4 In the Locate file dialog box, select the renamed file and then click Select.

When you have merely moved, rather than renamed files, you can activate the Find Nearby Missing Photos option in the Locate file dialog box and Lightroom will find any other missing photos in the same folder automatically.

5 Click Confirm to verify that Cemetery.jpg is the correct file despite the changed name. You have now reestablished the link to your renamed file; the missing file icon no longer appears in its image cell.

6 In the Folders panel, the Masks folder is now dimmed and marked with a question mark icon. Right-click / Control-click the Masks folder; you *could* choose Find Missing Folder from the context menu, and then locate the renamed folder as you did for the missing file, but we'll take this opportunity to look at a different method instead.

7 Choose Library > Find All Missing Photos. A new temporary collection named Missing Photographs is created in the Catalog panel. The new collection is automatically selected and the three photos from the Masks folder appear in the Grid view. Select each image in turn; the missing photo icon appears on each image cell.

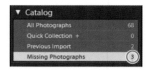

8 Click the missing photo icon on any of the images in the Grid view and follow the same steps you used previously. Navigate to the renamed folder, and then locate the selected file. This time, activate the Find Nearby Missing Photos option in the Locate file dialog box and Lightroom will find the other missing photos in the folder automatically. Click Select.

9 The renamed folder is now listed in the Folders panel. Although the missing Masks folder is still listed in the Folders panel, it now shows an image count of 0. Right-click / Control-click the empty folder and choose Remove from the context menu.

10 Right-click / Control-click the Missing Photographs folder in the Catalog panel and choose Remove This Temporary Collection from the context menu.

This concludes the lesson on organizing your image library. You've learned about structuring your folders, sorting and grouping images into collections, and a variety of methods for tagging and marking your photos to make them easier to find by applying a range of search filters.

However, it's worth discussing a final step that is invaluable in managing your growing library of photos: perform regular catalog backups. The library catalog contains not only your entire image database but also all the preview images and metadata, together with records of your collections and all your settings from the Develop, Slideshow, Web and Print modules. It is as important to make backups of your catalog as it is to keep copies of your image files. You'll learn more about backing-up your library in Lesson 11, "Making Backups and Exporting Photos."

Before you move on to the next lesson, take a moment to refresh some of what you've learned by reading through the review on the next page.

Review questions

1 What is a Smart Collection?

2 Why would you create a Stack?

3 What are keyword tags?

4 What are the three modes in the Filter bar?

5 How can you search for images by location?

Review answers

1 A Smart collection can be configured to search the library for images that meet specified criteria. Smart collections stay up-to-date by automatically adding any newly imported photos that meet the criteria you've specified.

2 Stacks can be used to group similar photos and thereby reduce the number of thumbnails displayed at one time in the Grid view and the Filmstrip. Only the top image in a stack appears in the thumbnail display but the stack can be expanded and contracted by clicking the thumbnail.

3 Keyword tags are text added to the metadata of an image to describe its content or classify it in one way or another. Shared keywords link images by subject, date, or some other association. Keywords help to locate, identify, and sort photos in the catalog. Like other metadata, keyword tags are stored either in the photo file or (in the case of proprietary camera raw files) in XMP sidecar files. Keywords applied in Lightroom can be read by Adobe applications such as Bridge, Photoshop, or Photoshop Elements, and by other applications that support XMP metadata.

4 The Filter bar offers three filter groups: Text, Attribute, and Metadata filters. Using combinations of these filters you can search the image library for metadata text, filter searches by flag, copy status, rating, or label, and specify a broad range of customizable metadata search criteria.

5 Once your photos are tagged with locations, you can search your library from the Map module by using the Location Filter bar above the map and the Saved Locations panel. In the Library you can use the Metadata filters, set to GPS Data or GPS Location.

PHOTOGRAPHY SHOWCASE
MICHAEL CLARK

"I have fallen into quicksand, been hit by falling rocks the size of beach balls, and I've had my rope cut down to only a few strands of the core while hanging from it shooting rock climbing. On some shoots a little agony is just the price of admission."

For the last seventeen years, I have specialized in adventure sports photography. My work as an adventure photographer was born out of my passion for the outdoors. I started out as a climbing photographer and initially shot only rock climbing, ice climbing and mountaineering. As my work evolved I expanded into most all of the other adventure sports and also made huge strides with my portraiture and lifestyle imagery. My clients include a wide range of editorial and commercial clients including Apple, Adobe, Nikon, Red Bull, Patagonia, Outside, Climbing Magazine, Backpacker Magazine and many others.

I have had several close calls over the years while working as an adventure photographer. Because I am a participant in many of the sports I photograph, safety for myself, and the athletes I am working with, is always a major concern. My work is as much about getting into position as it is about getting the image. On some shoots a little agony is just the price of admission. Getting the image is a matter of ignoring those niggling details and getting on with the job. Just as with my career, in the sports I photograph, everything is a risk—albeit a "calculated" risk.

Though my images depict daring adventures, they also reflect a passion for life. I want my images to stop the viewer in their tracks and inspire them to live a passionate life; one where risk is not an impediment to a fulfilled life but just a stop along the way.

www.michaelclarkphoto.com

JON DEVORE - UTAH

TIMY FAIRFIELD - CRYSTAL CAVE, NEW MEXICO

ANDY LYONS - RIO GRANDE, NEW MEXICO

DANNY MACASKILL - SAN DIEGO, CALIFORNIA

DAWN GLANC - OURAY, COLORADO

6 DEVELOPING AND EDITING

Lesson overview

Artificial light sources, unusual shooting conditions, and incorrect camera exposure settings can all lead to faults in an image. In the Develop module Lightroom delivers a suite of powerful developing tools to quickly rectify these problems in your photos.

This lesson introduces you to editing options from easy-to-use presets and retouching tools to an array of specialized settings. Along the way you'll pick up a little digital imaging background knowledge as you become familiar with some basic techniques:

- Applying Develop presets
- Cropping and rotating images
- Working with video
- Using the History and Snapshots panels
- Removing blemishes
- Correcting color problems and adjusting the tonal range
- Sharpening images and removing noise
- Working with black and white and split tone effects
- Adjusting specific areas of an image

 You'll probably need around two hours to complete this lesson.
If you haven't already done so, download the Lesson 6 work files from the Lesson & Update Files tab on your Account page at www.peachpit.com.

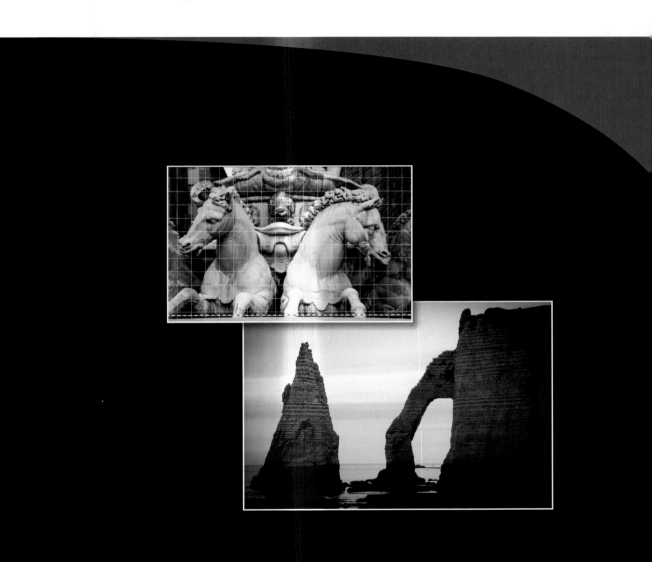

Fine-tune and polish your photographs—and your videos—with precise, easy-to-use tools, secure in the knowledge that the modifications you make in Lightroom won't alter your master file. Take your developing a step beyond just correcting your images; use the Develop module controls creatively to customize your own special effects, and then save them as develop presets.

Getting started

● **Note:** This lesson assumes that you already have a basic working familiarity with the Lightroom workspace. If you find that you need more background informa-tion, refer to Lightroom Help, or review the previous lessons.

Before you start on this lesson, make sure you've set up the LR5CIB folder for your lesson files and created the LR5CIB Catalog file to manage them, as described in "Setting up a work folder" and "Creating a catalog file for working with this book" in the Getting Started chapter at the beginning of this book.

If you haven't already done so, download the Lesson 6 folder from your Account page at www.peachpit.com to the LR5CIB/Lessons folder, as detailed in the section "Accessing the Classroom in a Book files" in the chapter "Getting Started."

1   Start Lightroom.

2   In the Adobe Photoshop Lightroom - Select Catalog dialog box, make sure that the file LR5CIB Catalog.lrcat is selected under Select A Recent Catalog To Open, and then click Open.

![Adobe Photoshop Lightroom – Select Catalog dialog box. Select a recent catalog to open: LR5CIB Catalog.lrcat (/Users/John/Documents/LR5CIB/LR5CIB Catalog) highlighted; Lightroom 5 Catalog.lrcat (/Users/John/Pictures/Lightroom/Lightroom 5 Catalog). Checkboxes: Always load this catalog on startup, Test integrity of this catalog. Note: Lightroom Catalogs cannot be on network volumes or in read-only folders. Buttons: Choose a Different Catalog..., Create a New Catalog..., Quit, Open.]

▶ **Tip:** If you can't see the Module Picker, choose Window > Panels > Show Module Picker, or press the F5 key. If you're working on Mac OS, you may need to press the fn key together with the F5 key, or change the function key behavior in the system preferences.

3   Lightroom will open in the screen mode and workspace module that were active when you last quit. If necessary, switch to the Library module by clicking Library in the Module Picker at the top of the workspace.

![Lightroom menu bar and Module Picker: Lr Adobe Photoshop Lightroom 5 — Library, Develop, Map, Book, Slideshow, Print, Web, with Library circled.]

Importing images into the library

The first step is to import the images for this lesson into the Lightroom library.

1   In the Library module, click the Import button below the left panel group.

2   If the Import dialog box appears in compact mode, click the Show More Options button at the lower left of the dialog box to see all the options in the expanded Import dialog box.

3   Under Source at the left of the expanded Import dialog box, navigate to and select the LR5CIB > Lessons > Lesson 6 folder. Ensure that all six images and the video in the Lesson 6 folder are checked for import.

4   In the import options above the thumbnail previews, select Add so that the imported media will be added to your catalog without being moved or copied. Under File Handling at the right of the expanded Import dialog box, choose Minimal from the Render Previews menu and ensure that the Don't Import Suspected Duplicates option is activated. Under Apply During Import, choose None from both the Develop Settings menu and the Metadata menu and type **Lesson 6** in the Keywords text box. Make sure that your import is set up as shown in the illustration below, and then click Import.

► **Tip:** The first time you enter any of the Lightroom modules, you'll see module tips that will help you get started by identifying the components of the Lightroom workspace and stepping you through the workflow. Dismiss the tips by clicking the Close button. To reactivate the tips for any module, choose [*Module name*] Tips from the Help menu.

The seven media files are imported from the Lesson 6 folder and now appear in both the Grid view of the Library module and in the Filmstrip across the bottom of the Lightroom workspace.

Quick developing in the Library module

▶ **Tip:** You can make a multiple selection in the Grid view or the Filmstrip and apply a develop preset, a new crop ratio, or any of the other Quick Develop adjustments, to all of the selected photos at once.

The Library module's Quick Develop panel offers an array of simple controls that let you apply developing presets, correct tone and color in your images, sharpen them, and even crop them—without ever switching to the Develop module.

1   In the Grid view, double-click the image DSC_6089.NEF (a photograph of the famous cliffs of Etretat, in Normandy) to see it in Loupe view. In the right panel group, expand the Quick Develop panel, if necessary.

Shot in twilight conditions on the shaded side of a rocky bluff, this photo has a blue color cast; the colors are overly cool, resulting in a somewhat flat and gloomy look. You can correct this kind of color imbalance by adjusting an image's *white balance*.

2   In the Quick Develop panel, expand the White Balance pane. Try each of the settings in the White Balance presets menu, noting the effects in the Loupe view. When you're done, choose the Auto white balance preset.

The white balance adjustment has reduced the overall blue cast and increased the depth of color detail in the photo by emphasizing the hues of the fading sunset in the sky and boosting the greens on the cliff-top and at the edge of the beach.

Adjusting the white balance can mean making some very subjective choices. If you wish to stay fairly close to a photo's original look, start with the As Shot preset, and then fine-tune the Temperature and Tint. If you feel that the white balance was set incorrectly at the time of capture—perhaps as a result of artificial lighting—or if you wish to achieve a specific effect, use an appropriate preset as a starting point.

3   Expand the Tone Control pane and click the Auto Tone button.

As the original photo was too dark overall, Auto Tone brightens the entire image considerably—exposing much more detail in the cliffs and the rocky shoreline in the foreground, but effectively losing image detail from the now overly brightened sky.

Next, you can use the controls below the Auto Tone button to fine-tune the tonal balance, recovering detail in the deeper shadows and color in the overexposed sky.

4 If necessary, expand the Tone Control pane by clicking the triangle to the right of the Auto Tone button. Click three times each on the third button beside Contrast (the single, right-facing arrow), the first Highlights button, the third Shadows button, and the right-most buttons for Clarity and Vibrance.

If you lose track of your adjustments, you can reset any control by simply clicking its name. Click the Reset All button to revert the image to its original state.

Increasing the contrast has improved the tonal range of the image as a whole. The highlights adjustment has reduced the exposure in the sky, retrieving burned-out detail without darkening the rest of the photo, while the shadows adjustment has had the inverse effect, revealing detail by increasing exposure in the darker areas of the photo without brightening the sky.

Increasing the Clarity emphasizes *local contrast* between adjacent areas of light and dark. For our photo, this is an ideal way to improve textural definition in the dimly-lit stone of the cliffs. Increasing Vibrance boosts saturation selectively, having most effect on the muted colors in an image, which is also ideally suited to our example.

▶ **Tip:** To see clearly how your adjustments have improved this photo, click Reset All at the bottom of the Quick Develop panel; then, press Ctrl+Z / Command+Z to restore the improvements.

The Quick Develop panel also provides access to over fifty Develop presets, ranging from emulated lens filters and fine-tuned contrast settings to creative effects. Develop presets apply different combinations of developing settings to an image at the same time, enabling you to achieve dramatic results with a single click. You can even save your own settings as custom presets, and then organize them in folders that will be listed as new categories in the Saved Preset menu.

5 Experiment with one or two presets from each category in the Saved Preset menu at the top of the Quick Develop panel. Undo each develop preset before applying the next, so that you can easily return the image to its corrected state.

Color Presets > Yesteryear

B&W Presets > B&W Look 5

B&W Toned Presets > Split Tone 1

Quick and easy video editing

Many digital cameras enable photographers to capture video as well as still images, but for those of us who haven't learned to use video editing software, those videos end up languishing, forgotten and neglected, in dark corners on our hard disks.

Lightroom lets you import your videos, dust them off, catalog and organize them alongside your photos, make simple edits and grab still frames—even share them to Facebook or Flickr—and you can do it all without ever leaving the Library module.

You can import video in many common file formats used by digital still cameras, including AVI, MOV, MPG, MP4, and AVCHD, in exactly the same way that you import photos; in fact, you did just that at the beginning of this lesson.

1   Press the G key or click the Grid view button (▦) in the Toolbar. If you're working with very small thumbnails, use the Thumbnails slider in the Toolbar to make them a little larger.

2   Locate the video file TamilTemple.MPG; then, move the pointer slowly from left to right, and then back again over the thumbnail (or better still, just below it) to scrub forwards and backwards through the video.

The horizontal position of your pointer relative to the width of the thumbnail preview corresponds roughly to the location of the current frame in the video clip.

3   Double-click the thumbnail to see the video in Loupe view; drag the circular current time indicator along the playback control bar to scrub through the video. Click the Play button at the left of the control bar to play the clip.

Trimming video clips

In the Loupe view, you can improve a video by snipping off a slow start or a shaky ending; the video file on your hard disk remains intact, but when you export the clip, or play it in Lightroom, it will be trimmed down to show only the real action.

1   Click the Trim Video button (⚙). The playback control bar expands to display a series of key frames from the video, representing a time-line or film-strip view of the clip. You can lengthen the expanded control bar by dragging either end.

2   Watch the time count at the left end of the control bar as you drag the current
     time indicator to the last frame in the 19th second; then, drag the end marker in
     from the right end of the time-line to meet the current time indicator.

3   Click the Play button at the center of the control bar to view the trimmed clip.

Setting video thumbnails and grabbing still frames

Setting a distinctive poster frame (thumbnail image) for a video clip can make it
easier to locate in the Grid view or the Filmstrip.

1   Make sure that you can see the video clip's thumbnail in the Filmstrip. In the
     Loupe view, move the current time indicator to the frame you want; then, click
     the Frame button (🔲) at the right end of the control bar. Watch the video
     thumbnail in the Filmstrip as you choose Set Poster Frame.

2   Find a frame that you like somewhere in the range between 00:05 and 00:13;
     then, click the Frame button and choose Capture Frame to capture and save the
     current frame as a JPEG image that will be stacked with the clip. You'll use the
     captured frame later in this lesson.

Editing video in the Quick Develop panel

When you're working with video, several of the Quick Develop controls are disabled. Although you can access all of the developing presets in the Saved Preset
menu, only the supported settings within each preset will be applied.

► **Tip:** Presets in the
Lightroom Video Presets
category are tailored
for video; they do not
incorporate any unsup-
ported operations.

1   With the same frame still open in the Loupe view, choose the Video Color Pop
     preset from the Lightroom Video Presets category in the Saved Presets menu.

2   Choose Auto from the White Balance
     menu to make the colors warmer.

3   Click the right-most Contrast button
     and the left-most button for Whites,
     twice each. To see the effect in motion,
     scrub through the clip by dragging the
     current time indicator, or click the Play
     button in the playback control bar.

As imported

Video Color Pop preset, plus
White Balance, Contrast, and Whites

Previews in a nutshell

The issue of previews in Lightroom can be confusing, and much of the information on the subject may seem dauntingly technical, but the concept is really quite simple. *Every* image you see in Lightroom is a preview—from the thumbnails in the Grid view and the Filmstrip to the Develop module Loupe view at its highest zoom ratio. Lightroom extracts some previews from the images themselves, and generates others on the fly; some are used temporarily and then discarded, and others stored.

In the Import, Preferences, and Catalog Settings dialog boxes, you can set up a range of options relating to previews—but basically, you can go ahead and successfully import, organize, and edit your photos without ever changing any of the defaults. The whole process is quite automatic; all of those options are only offered so that, if you choose, you can configure preview handling to improve performance or save disk space. For more information on doing just that, please refer to Lightroom Help.

New in Lightroom, Smart Previews are the exception to this simplified summary; they are created on-demand for your convenience, not generated automatically to Lightroom's operating requirements.

Working with Smart Previews

In previous versions of Lightroom an image that was off-line—perhaps resident on an unconnected hard drive or thousands of miles away on your desktop computer—could still be viewed as a thumbnail or Loupe view preview, but could not be edited; Smart Previews change the rules.

Smart Previews allow you to edit off-line images, and then Lightroom will automatically update the originals when they come back on-line—ideal for working on your laptop when you're away from home. Likewise, your Smart Previews are automatically updated with any adjustments you make when the originals are on-line, so they'll always be up-to-date for the next time you take a trip.

Smart Previews are a new lightweight file type, based on the lossy DNG format—at around 5% of the size of the original raw files, they're also a great way to free up disk space. You can have Lightroom build Smart Previews at import by activating that option in the Import dialog box, invoke the Build Smart Previews command from the Library > Previews menu for a multiple selection, or generate one Smart Preview at a time by clicking the Smart Preview status indicator at the bottom of the Histogram panel when you have an original photo open in the Loupe view.

Viewing an original photo that has no Smart Preview

Viewing an original photo that has a Smart Preview

Viewing a Smart Preview; the original file is off-line

For a multiple selection of images in the Grid view, the Smart Preview status indicator shows a breakdown of the selected files.

Understanding process versions

The latest version of Lightroom uses updated Camera Raw technology to analyze, process, and render images, allowing finer control over color, tone, and detail than was possible in previous versions—so you'll get better results, with fewer artifacts. Taken as a whole, this technology constitutes the current *process version*, PV2012.

Lightroom 1 and 2 used the original process version, PV2003. Lightroom 3 applied the updated PV2010 by default, offering the option to either update images edited in Lightroom 1 or 2, or switch to the old process version to avoid modifying the existing adjustments. Process Version 2012 is applied by default to photos that are edited for the first time in Lightroom 4 or later. For images edited in an earlier version of Lightroom, you can switch to either of the old process versions if you wish.

PV2012 incorporates improved sharpening and noise-reduction routines, as well as new adaptive tone-mapping algorithms that help to protect edge detail and minimize processing artifacts, enabling you to adjust exposure without clipping the whites in your image and to recover more detail from shadows and highlights.

Updating the process version

In this exercise, you'll update the process version for a raw image that was edited in PV2010. Even if you've never used a previous version of Lightroom, this exercise serves as an introduction to the enhanced Develop controls in the latest versions.

1   In the Grid view or the Filmstrip, select the raw image DSC_0151.NEF; then, click Develop in the module picker at the top of the workspace.

In the Develop module, a lightning-bolt marker in the lower right corner of the Histogram panel indicates that the image was not edited with the current process version. Hold the pointer over the marker to see which process version was used.

▶ **Tip:** If you don't see the right panels, press F8 or choose Window > Panels > Show Right Module Panels.

2 Choose Settings > Process. The Process menu also shows that this image was edited using the 2010 process version. For now, leave the setting unchanged.

3 To access update options, click the lightning bolt marker, rather than using the Settings > Update To Current Process (2012) command, which updates the image using the default options, or those that were set for the last update.

4 In the Update Process Version dialog box, activate the option Review Changes Via Before/After; then, click Update.

5 If necessary, expand the Basic panel in the right panel group. Watch the Histogram and the Basic panel settings as you undo and redo the update by pressing Ctrl+Z / Command+Z, and then Shift+Ctrl+Z / Shift+Command+Z.

The histogram shows a significant improvement in the image's tonal spread. In the Basic panel, the old develop settings are mapped to a new set of slider controls.

Tip: Updating to Process Version 2012 may result in significant changes in the appearance of your photos; it's a good idea to update images one at a time until you're familiar with the new processes. Use one of the Before & After views while you tweak the PV2012 settings, to help you match the look of the photo before it was updated.

In PV2012, the Exposure setting combines elements of both the Exposure and Brightness settings from earlier process versions. The new Exposure control works more like camera exposure; shifting the midtones without clipping the highlights.

The Highlights and Shadows sliders replace Recovery and Fill Light, enabling you to bring out even more detail from the darkest and brightest parts of your photos. The improved processes in PV2012 target their respective tonal ranges more effectively, without affecting the rest of the image; your Highlights and Shadows adjustments won't overlap, so there's less chance of color shifts and other artifacts.

The Whites and Blacks controls correct clipping at the ends of the histogram; for PV2012, blacks are calculated automatically. The new Clarity process produces a different look, with less likelihood of halo effects; the upgraded setting is reduced.

About white balance

In order to correctly display the full range of color information recorded in an image file, it's critical to balance the distribution of color in the photo—that is, to correct the photo's *white balance*.

This is achieved by shifting the image's *white point*: the neutral point around which the colors in the image are distributed on the two axes of temperature (blue to red, visualized in the illustration at the right as a curved axis) and tint (green to magenta).

An image's white point reflects the lighting conditions in which the photo was captured. Different types of artificial lighting have different white points; they produce light that is dominated by one color or deficient in another. Weather conditions also have an effect on the white balance.

The higher the red component in the lighting, the warmer the colors in the photo will appear; the higher the blue component, the cooler the image, so movement along this axis defines the photo's color *temperature*, while the term *tint* refers to shifts in the direction of green or magenta.

The sensors in a digital camera record the amount of red, green, and blue light that is reflected from an object. Under pure white lighting, an object that is a color-neutral gray, black, or white reflects all color components of the light source equally.

If the light source is not pure white but has a predominant green component for example (typical of fluorescent lighting), a higher amount of green will be reflected. Unless the composition of the light source is known—and the *white balance* or *white point* is corrected accordingly—even objects that should appear color-neutral will have a green color cast.

When shooting in auto white balance mode, your camera attempts to estimate the composition of the light source from the color information measured by the sensors. Although modern cameras are doing better at automatically analyzing lighting and setting the white balance to meet conditions, the technology is not infallible; it's preferable—if your camera supports it—to use your camera to measure the white point of the light source before shooting. This is usually done by photographing a white or neutral, light gray object in the same lighting conditions as the intended subject.

Together with the color information collected by the camera sensors, Raw images also contain "As Shot" white balance information; a record of the white point determined automatically by the camera at the moment of capture. Lightroom can use this information to correctly interpret the recorded color data for a given light source. The recorded white point information is used as a calibration point in reference to which the colors in the image will be shifted to correct the white balance.

(continues on next page)

About white balance (continued)

You can use the White Balance Selector tool, located in the top left corner of the Basic panel, to correct the white balance in your photo. Click to sample an area in your photo that you know should appear on screen as a light neutral gray; Lightroom will use the sampled information to determine the point around which the image can be calibrated and set the image's white balance accordingly.

As you move the White Balance Selector tool across the image you will see a magnified view of the pixels under the eyedropper cursor and RGB values for the central target pixel. To avoid too radical a color shift, try to click a pixel where the red, green, and blue values are as close as possible. Do not use white or a very light color (such as a spectral highlight) as the neutral target; in a very bright pixel, one or more of the color components might already have been clipped.

Color temperature is defined with reference to a concept known as *black-body radiation* theory. When heated, a black-body will first start glowing red, then orange, yellow, white, and finally blue-white. A color's temperature is the temperature—in kelvin (K)—to which a black-body must be heated to emit that particular color. Zero K corresponds to −273.15 °C or −459.67 °F and an increment of one unit kelvin is equivalent to an increment of one degree Celsius.

What we generally refer to as a warm color (with a higher red component) actually has a lower color temperature (in kelvin) than what we would call a cool color (with a higher blue component). The color temperature of a visually warm scene lit by candlelight is about 1,500 K. In bright daylight you would measure around 5,500 K and light from an overcast sky results in a color temperature in the photo of about 6,000 to 7,000 K.

The Temperature slider adjusts the color temperature (in kelvin) of the designated white point, from low at the left side of the range to high on the right side. Moving the Temp slider to the left reduces the color temperature of the white point. In consequence, the colors in the image are interpreted as having a higher color temperature relative to the adjusted white point and are shifted towards blue. The colors displayed in the track of the Temp slider control indicate the effect a change in that direction will have on the image. Moving the slider to the left will increase the blue in the image, moving the slider to the right will make the image look more yellow and red.

The Tint slider works in the same way. For example, to remove a green cast in an image you would move the Tint slider to the right, away from the green displayed inside the slider control. This increases the green component in the white point so the colors in the image are interpreted as less green relative to the adjusted white point.

Adjusting the Temp and Tint sliders corresponds to shifting the white point within the color gamut.

The Develop module

Although the Library module's Quick Develop panel offers access to many basic image editing options, you'll work in the Develop module to make more detailed adjustments and modifications to your photos. The Develop module is a comprehensive editing environment, presenting all the tools you'll need to correct and enhance your images in a single workspace. The controls are simple enough for a beginner to use, and yet have the depth and power required by the advanced user.

The Develop module offers two viewing modes: the Loupe view, where you can focus on a single image, and the Before/After view, which has several layout options that make it easy to compare the original and edited versions of a photo.
The Toolbar across the bottom of the work area presents buttons for switching between the views and a slightly different suite of controls for each viewing mode.

The tools and controls in the Develop module's right panel group are arranged from top to bottom in the order in which they would ordinarily be used: a layout that guides you intuitively through the editing workflow.

The left panel group contains the Navigator panel, which can be collapsed but not hidden, and any combination of the Presets, Snapshots, History, and Collections panels, which can be shown or hidden to suit the way you prefer to work.

At the top of the left panel group, the Navigator panel helps you find your way around a zoomed image, and lets you preview the effects of developing presets before you apply them. You can also use the Navigator to review past stages in an image's developing history. At the right of the Navigator's header is a zoom picker for setting the magnification level in the working views.

The Navigator can be collapsed, but not hidden.

While the History panel keeps track of every modification made to the image, including Quick Edit adjustments made in the Library module, you can use the Snapshots panel to record important stages in a photo's development, so you can return to a key state quickly and easily, without searching through the history list.

At the top of the right panel group is the Histogram panel. Immediately below the Histogram is an array of tools for cropping, removing image flaws, applying local adjustments through graduated or radial masks, and painting develop settings directly onto an image selectively. Clicking any of these tools expands a tool options pane with controls and settings for that tool.

Below these editing tools is the Basic panel: your starting point for color correction and tonal adjustments. In many cases this may be the only panel you need to achieve the result you want. The remaining panels offer specialized tools for various image enhancement tasks.

For example, you can use the Tone Curve panel to fine-tune the distribution of the tonal range and increase mid-tone contrast. Use the controls in the Detail panel to sharpen an image and reduce noise.

It's not intended that you use every tool on every photo. In many circumstance you may make only a few slight adjustments to an image; however, when you wish to polish a special photo—or if you need to work with shots captured at less than ideal camera settings—the Develop module gives you all the control you need.

In the next exercise you'll use the first of the tools in the strip below the Histogram.

Cropping and rotating images

The Crop Overlay tool makes it simple to improve your composition, crop away unwanted edge detail, and even straighten your image.

1   You should still be in the Develop module (press the D key or choose View > Go To Develop) with the raw image DSC_0151.NEF selected.

2   Hide the Filmstrip and the left panel group to enlarge the work area; you'll find keyboard shortcuts for showing and hiding any or all of the workspace panels listed beside the commands in the Window > Panels menu. If you're not already in the Loupe view, press the D key, or click the Loupe view button ( ) in the Toolbar. If you don't see the Toolbar, press the T key.

3   Click the Crop Overlay tool (▦)button just below the Histogram panel, or press R. A crop overlay rectangle appears on the image in the Loupe view and a control pane for the Crop Overlay tool opens above the Basic panel.

4   From the Aspect menu, choose Original. If the lock button shows an open lock icon, click to close the lock; this will constrain the aspect ratio.

The Crop & Straighten pane also contains the Straighten tool, which lets you mark a horizontal or vertical element in a tilted photo as a reference around which the image will be straightened automatically. As there is no reliable straight-line reference in our lesson photo, we'll rotate it manually instead.

5   In the Loupe view, drag outside the crop rectangle to rotate the image. Release the mouse button when the blue-gray stone fountain-rim across the bottom of the photo is aligned with the grid.

Whether you use the Straighten tool or rotate the photo manually, Lightroom will automatically trim the angled edges of the rotated photo when you commit the crop by clicking the Crop Overlay tool or double-clicking the image in the Loupe view. Lightroom will find the largest crop possible with the specified aspect ratio. Changing or unlocking the aspect ratio can minimize the amount of the photo that will be trimmed away.

6 Drag the lower right handle of the crop overlay rectangle upwards and to the left. As you drag, the image moves so that the cropped portion is always centered in the Loupe view. Release the mouse button when the lower edge of the crop rectangle is clear of the curved fountain rim, as shown below.

7 Click inside the crop overlay rectangle and drag the image. You'll notice that you can't drag the photo downwards or to the right because the image will move only until its edge touches the border of the cropping rectangle. Position the photo so that the horses' noses have the same amount of clearance on each side.

8 To exit cropping mode, press the R key or click the Crop Overlay tool button again. The cropped and straightened image is displayed in the Loupe view.

▶ **Tip:** Thanks to non-destructive editing, you can return at any time and adjust your crop—or the angle of the photo—by simply reactivating the Crop Overlay tool. The crop becomes "live"—the trimmed portions of the image become visible once more and you can rotate the photo or resize and reposition the cropping rectangle as you wish.

Removing unwanted objects

The impact of a photo can easily be spoiled by an unwanted object in the frame. In the modern world, it's often difficult to photograph even a remote landscape without capturing a fence, power lines, satellite dishes, or litter, if not a tourist or two—mundane clutter that can reduce the drama of an otherwise perfect shot.

In this exercise, we'll stay with our marble horses as we take a look at the latest enhancement to the Spot Removal tool—free-form *brush spots*, which make it easy to paint an extraneous element out of a photo with just a few strokes.

1   Click the white triangle at the left edge of the workspace window to show the left panel group.

2   In the header of the Navigator panel, click the small white triangles to the right of the zoom picker and choose 1:2 from the zoom level menu. Drag the white view area overlay to the top right corner of the Navigator preview; keep dragging until you see a little of the empty grey image canvas at the top and right edges of the Loupe view.

3   Click to activate the Spot Removal tool—the second tool in the strip below the Histogram panel. In the tool options pane right below the tool strip, click Clone to set the Spot Removal tool to cloning mode. Set the brush size to 75 and the opacity to 100.

▶ **Tip:** As a general rule, Clone mode is the best option for areas with repeated patterns, such as brickwork, floor boards or foliage.

4   Position the circular Spot Removal tool cursor over the green pipe in the background; then, starting with the central cross-hairs just inside the upper edge of the photo, drag downwards to paint over the pipe. Make sure that the bottom of your stroke covers the pipe, while avoiding the sculpture in the foreground. Watch as you release the mouse button; Lightroom analyzes the detail around your brush stroke and automatically finds a sample area to clone.

The target and sample areas are both marked with adjustment pins. You can move either area by dragging its pin. To delete the Spot Removal adjustment, hold the Alt / Option key and click the target area's pin. Press the H key to hide and show the brush spot overlays.

The sample area chosen by the Spot Removal tool will vary depending on the placement, shape, and direction of your target stroke. As you can see in the illustration at the left, below, our brush spot produced a less than ideal result; the cloned sample is noticeably darker than the area around the target. If you're not satisfied with the automatic result, you can move either area by dragging its adjustment pin. In the next step, we'll look at two other techniques to achieve a seamless patch.

5   Press H, or move the pointer away from the preview image to hide the brush spot overlays while you examine the result of the preceding step. Press H again, if necessary, to show the overlays.

● **Note:** Brush spots can be moved or made more or less opaque, but they can not be scaled or reshaped.

6   Right-click / Control-click either of the brush spot marker pins and choose Select New Source from the context menu. Examine the result; then, undo the new source and click Heal in the tool options pane to change the brush mode for the active spot adjustment. Examine the result in the Loupe view; in Heal mode, the Spot Removal tool will still copy well-defined detail from the source, but will attempt to match the color and tone of the sample to the target zone.

Automatic clone source selection

Select New Source (context menu)

Original source in Heal mode

▶ **Tip:** When an object more complex than the pipe in our example proves hard to remove, try using more strokes, or vary the direction, brush size and mode.

7   Apply the solution you prefer; then, press Q or click the Spot Removal tool in the tool strip to deactivate the tool and hide the adjustment overlays.

8   Reactivate the Spot Removal tool and move the pointer over the Loupe view; the target marker pin for your spot overlay becomes visible once more. Move the pointer over the pin to see the outlines of the brush spot; then, click the pin to select and activate the adjustment. Leave the Spot Removal tool active.

You can reactivate a Spot Removal adjustment at any time and tweak it by moving the target or source, changing the mode, or adjusting the opacity as needed.

Retouching spots

The Spot Removal tool can also be used to create *circle spot* adjustments, which are ideal for fixing image flaws such as the unsightly spots or blurs often caused by water droplets or dust on the camera lens, especially in photos captured outdoors or in harsh lighting conditions. In this exercise however, you'll use circle spots to improve a portrait photo by retouching blemishes on the subject's skin.

1   If necessary, press F6 or use the Window > Panels menu to show the Filmstrip. Click to select the image DSC_0069.NEF; then, hide the Filmstrip. Press T if you don't see the Toolbar across the bottom of the Loupe view. In the header of the Navigator panel, make sure that the zoom level is still set to 1:2; then, hide the left panel group.

2   Hold down the space bar on your keyboard and drag the photo in the work area to center the Loupe view on the young girl's face.

3   The Spot Removal tool should still be active from the previous exercise, with the size and opacity set to 75 and 100 respectively. Set the tool to Heal mode.

In Clone mode, the Spot Removal tool replaces the target area with an exact copy of the source—ideal for dealing with regular patterns or textures. Use the Heal mode for areas with smooth color transitions such as skin or sky, and for fine, random textures like sand or lawn. In Heal mode, the Spot Removal tool matches color and tone to blend the sample into the target area, rather than replacing it.

4   Center the cross-hairs just below and to the right of the darkest part of the red blemish on the girl's cheek; then click—but don't drag. Lightroom automatically locates a sample source. Keep the pointer over the image. On your screen you should see something similar to the illustration at the right, below; the bolder circle marks the sample area, linked by an arrow to the target area—the lighter white circle with the central cross-hairs.

▶ **Tip:** Depending on exactly where you clicked, the automatic source area you see on screen may differ from the illustration.

● **Note:** Unlike *brush spots* created by dragging in the image with the Spot Removal tool, one-click *circle spots* do not have marker pins. Clicking inside either the target or source circle will select it for adjustment with the size and opacity sliders.

5   The automatically selected sample may sometimes include unwanted detail or create repetition in the target area. To try a different source, press the forward slash (/) key or right-click / Control-click either of the circles and choose Select New Source. If the source circle doesn't move far, repeat the command.

▶ **Tip:** To cancel and remove an active spot correction, simply press Backspace / Delete.

6 Click inside the target circle to select it. Move the pointer over the edge of the circle and drag outwards from the target circle's center to enlarge both circles together. Release the mouse button to see the target area's outline; then, tweak the circle until it's the same size as that in the illustration at the left, below. Drag the source circle to touch the target area as shown below at the right.

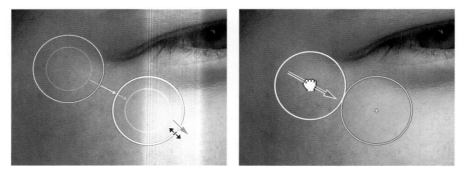

7 To blend the source sample more subtly with the target, use the slider in the tool options pane to reduce the opacity for the selected spot to 60%. Press H to hide the circle overlays while you assess the blend; then, show the overlays again and drag either of the circles as needed to improve the results. Press Q to deselect the current adjustment; then press Q again to reactivate the Spot Removal tool.

Although this young lady's skin really needs no further retouching, we have one more circle spot technique to try; this time, rather than let Lightroom select the sample automatically, you'll specify the target and source in one stroke.

8 Position the cross-hairs over the tiny spot on the girl's chin. Press the left bracket key ([ ) repeatedly to reduce the brush size until the Size value in the tool options pane is approximately 50. Hold the Ctrl / Command key and drag from the target to find a source that blends well; then, release the mouse button.

9 Examine the options in the Tool Overlay menu in the Toolbar below the Loupe view. The default setting, Auto, shows the Spot Removal tool overlays only while the pointer remains over the photo. Change the setting to Always.

10 The white Spot Removal tool overlays can be difficult to see against light-colored or "busy" areas in a photo, especially when not they are not selected. In the Toolbar, activate the Visualize Spots check box; then, use the slider to reduce the image detail enough to see the white overlays clearly. A selected spot adjust-ment shows both source and target overlays; inactive spots show a source area only when you move the pointer over them.

11 Disable Visualize Spots, reset the Tool Overlay to Auto, and then click Done to deactivate the Spot Removal tool. Click the Before & After view button (Y|Y) in the Toolbar to admire your handiwork; then, return to the Loupe view.

Correcting color balance and tonal range

In the Develop module, the basic tone and color corrections your photos are likely to need are generally best made in the following order:

- Inspect the Histogram as an aid to understanding the photo's deficiencies. As you work on the image, the Histogram provides feedback on the effects of your adjustments.

- In the Basic panel, set the white point to correct the color balance.

- Maximize the image's tonal range using the Basic panel's tone controls.

- Tweak the contrast selectively using the Tone Curve panel.

- Adjust specific colors in the HSL / Color / B & W panel.

- Apply sharpening and noise reduction in the Detail panel.

- Correct lens effects such as distortion, color fringes, and vignetting in the Lens Corrections and Camera Calibration panels.

- Add special effects such as duo-tone treatments, simulated film grain, and decorative vignetting, using the Split Toning and Effects panels.

As you can see in the illustration at the right, this order is reflected in the layout of the panels in the right group; although you may often make only a handful of adjustments to any one image, you can work your way down the right panel group, using it as an image processing check-list.

1 If you're not in the Develop module, press the D key. Show the Filmstrip, if necessary, and select the image DSC_5945.NEF, an inadequate exposure of a difficult subject: a brightly sunlit courtyard enclosed by a shaded arcade.

2 Hide the Module picker (F5), the left panel group (F7), and the Filmstrip (F6). Make sure that both the Histogram panel and the Basic panel are expanded; then, drag the left edge of the right panel group to make it as wide as possible. Wider adjustment sliders give you finer control.

The controls in the Basic panel are also arranged from top to bottom in the order that's likely to produce the best results; if you're new to image correction, you can let the layout guide you through the workflow.

▶ **Tip:** If the colors you see on-screen differ significantly from those illustrated, consider calibrating your display. See Windows / Mac OS help for instructions. Slighter differences may be a result of the CMYK printing process.

3 Starting at the top of the Basic panel, try a few of the White Balance (WB) presets; then set the white balance to the Flash preset for this photo.

4 Moving down the Basic panel to the Tone controls, click Auto Tone. Undo and redo the Auto Tone adjustment, noting the effect it has on the Histogram and the tone settings in the Basic panel, as well the changes in the image itself.

▶ **Tip:** Auto Tone may be all you need for some photos, but for others it may produce unacceptable results. You can use it as a base for manual adjustment, or read the settings as a diagnosis of the photo's problems; then, undo and devise your own treatments.

The adjustment to the photo's tonal distribution has revealed color and detail that was almost invisible in the more deeply shadowed areas such as the wooden ceiling and increased definition in mid-toned areas like the stone floor in the courtyard. Overall the image has far more color and depth, though the sunlit portion of the courtyard and the wall above it now appear over-exposed.

Though the result is less than optimal, Auto Tone has improved the photo's tonal range markedly. The Histogram curve is still far from ideal, but the dominant peak of information clumped in the Blacks and Shadows ranges has become much broader and shifted to the right to fill out the mid-tones a little.

Undoing, redoing, and remembering changes

Lightroom offers several options for undoing and redoing changes and recalling key stages in the develop process. The Edit > Undo command (Ctrl+Z / Command+Z) lets you undo the last command executed; pressing Ctrl+Y / Command+Shift+Z will redo the last command undone. To jump backward and forward in the editing history by more than one step at a time, you'll use the History panel instead.

The History panel

1   Press F7 or click the triangle at the left edge of the workspace to show the left panel group. If necessary, collapse any other panels that are open (except the Navigator) to see the History panel.

2   Expand the History panel; you'll see a list of every operation that has already been performed; with the most recent command at the top.

3   Watch the Navigator panel as you move the pointer slowly up the list of commands in the History panel. The Navigator preview shows how the image looked at each stage of its developing history.

4   Click the top entry—Auto Tone—to return the image to its most recent edited state.

● **Note:** If you return an image to a previous state by clicking an entry in the History panel, and then make any new adjustment, all of the entries above your current position will be replaced by the new command.

Creating snapshots

The History list can quickly become long and unwieldy, so it's a good idea to save key steps in an image's developing history as Snapshots for quick and easy recovery. In this case, you'll use a snapshot as a reference to guide you as you work.

1   In the History panel, right-click / Control-click the Auto Tone entry and choose Create Snapshot from the context menu.

2   In the New Snapshot dialog box, type **Flash / Auto Tone** to name the snapshot; then, click Create. Your new snapshot appears in the Snapshots panel.

Getting more from the Before & After view

By default, the un-edited photo as imported is displayed as the Before image in the Before & After view. However, this is not always helpful; it may be more meaningful to compare the results of your latest adjustments to a more recent state.

You can designate any stage in the developing history—or any saved snapshot—as the Before image. Change the Before image when you're happy with your work thus far, then work beside it so that you can see exactly what gains you're making.

1 Click the Before & After view button in the Toolbar, repeatedly if necessary, until the two states of the photo are displayed one above the other.

▶ **Tip:** If you don't see the Toolbar below the work area, press T.

Cycles between before and after views
Before & After : □ Soft Proofing

2 Right-click / Control-click your saved snapshot in the Snapshots panel and choose Copy Snapshot Settings To Before. Both sides of the view should now be showing the photo as it appears with the Auto Tone adjustment.

3 In the Basic panel, double-click the name of each of the six adjustment controls in the Tone pane to zero the current settings.

Each of these six actions is listed as a new entry in the History panel. The Auto Tone adjustment hasn't really been undone—it merely became history, superseded by more recent events. Once you've zeroed all six controls, the After view is identical to the history state just before you applied the Auto Tone adjustment.

▶ **Tip:** In the Loupe view, you can quickly toggle between the most recent state of an image and the designated Before state by pressing the Backslash key (\) on your keyboard.

Now you can go back to your exploration of the Basic panel, with the Flash / Auto Tone snapshot serving as a benchmark to which you can compare your efforts.

Working with the Tone controls

As with the panels in the right panel group, you'll start at the top.

The first step is to use the Exposure control to set the overall image brightness by correcting the midtones range; then, you can retrieve detail from the lightest and darkest areas with the Highlights and Shadows controls and correct clipping at the ends of the curve by tweaking the Whites and Blacks settings.

1   Hide the left panel group to make more room for your working view.

2   In the Basic panel, drag the Exposure slider all the way to the left, and then back up through its range. Watch the effect on the curve in the Histogram as well as in the After image. When you're done, set the Exposure value to **1.75**.

● **Note:** In terms of camera f-stops, increasing the exposure by 1 is equivalent to opening the aperture one stop.

3   Experiment with the Contrast slider, and then set the contrast to **+25** (%).

4   Watch the Histogram, as well as the After image, as you drag the Highlights slider slowly, all the way to the left. Notice the dramatic effect on the lighter parts of the image, while very little changes elsewhere, even in the adjacent mid-tones. The peak in the Whites zone of the Histogram curve disappears, and the right end of the curve moves towards the center. Set the Highlights to -75.

▶ **Tip:** To modify any of the settings, you can either drag the slider, scrub horizontally over the numerical value, or click the setting's name to activate it, and then use the Plus (+) and Minus (-) keys.

5   Drag the Shadows slider slowly, all the way to the right. Watch how little effect this has on the mid-tones and highlights in the image, relative to the gain in the darkest areas. When you're done, leave the Shadows set to **+75**.

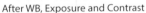

After WB, Exposure and Contrast   Highlights -75   Shadows +75

These Highlights and Shadows settings are somewhat extreme; at these levels you'll notice a glowing halo effect where light and dark areas meet, giving the scene an unreal look—and there is also the risk of introducing noticeable noise. As a general rule, set values between -50 and +50 for image correction and use higher settings sparingly to rescue problem photos or to achieve creative effects.

6   Leave both the Whites and the Blacks at the zero setting—for this image, just short of levels that would result in clipping at the ends of the Histogram curve. In the Presence pane, set the Clarity to **25** to enhance image definition.

● **Note:** Clarity effects local contrast between small adjacent areas of light and dark.

The photo now has a little less detail in the brightest areas than the auto-toned Before image, but a great deal more detail through the mid-tones and shadows. Though the image is much improved, the problem now is that any attempt to further improve the brightly lit courtyard area using the Tone controls in the Basic panel will adversely affect the more predominant shadowed areas.

In Lesson 1, you used the new Radial Filter tool to create custom vignette effects; for this image, you can use it to create a feathered elliptical mask through which you can adjust the overexposed courtyard without affecting the rest of the photo. You'll start by setting the adjustments that will be applied through the Radial Filter.

7   Click the Loupe view button (▣) in the Toolbar; then, click the Radial Filter tool, the fifth of the tools in the strip just below the Histogram, to activate it. Lower the Exposure setting for the local adjustment to **-0.5** and reduce the Highlights to **-25**. Set both the Clarity and Saturation values to **25**.

8   By default, your adjustments would be applied to the area outside the elliptical mask; activate the Invert Mask option to target the area inside the ellipse instead. Make sure that the Feather control is set to the default value of **50**.

▶ **Tip:** The Radial Filter is being applied over global adjustments, so the cumulative values add up to some fairly extreme settings. As a result, the effect you see on-screen may not look like the illustration at the right if your display is calibrated differently from ours. Try adjusting the filter's settings; if the problem is a color-cast, for example, tweak the Temperature and Tint.

9   Starting in the fork of the branches of the closest potted tree, drag with the Radial Filter tool to create an ellipse as shown in the illustration below; mostly avoiding the sunlit wall above the arches on the far side of the courtyard.

10 Press Shift+M to deactivate the Radial Filter tool. The Histogram shows that this image now has no true whites; hold down the Alt / Option key and drag the Whites slider to the right until you see the first white spots begin to appear on the black background of the clipping preview (we set a Whites value of **50**).

11 Return to the Before & After view and show the left panel group (F7). In the History panel, right-click / Control-click the Import entry and choose Copy History Step Settings To Before; then, hide the left panels again.

Creating your own developing presets

When you've spent time setting up an effect that you'd like to use again, you can save all your current settings as a developing preset that will be listed in both the Develop module's Presets panel and the Library module's Quick Develop panel.

You might set up a preset to achieve a unified look for every image in a photo book or web gallery, to add a romantic glow to wedding shots, or to correct the color in your underwater photos. Whatever the purpose, develop presets streamline your workflow by enabling you to apply multiple develop settings with a single click.

In this exercise, you'll create a custom preset tailored to a very specific purpose. Earlier in this lesson you trimmed a video clip in the Library module, where your editing options were limited to those offered in the Quick Develop panel. You can't bring video into the Develop module, but by working on a captured frame, and then saving your settings as a custom preset, you can effectively bring the power and subtlety of Develop module editing back to your video in the Library module.

1   Staying in the Develop module, click the Loupe view button ( ) in the Toolbar. Show the Filmstrip, if it's hidden, and then select the still image that you captured from the TamilTemple video earlier in the lesson.

The colors in our still frame are cold and de-saturated, and the tone is flat and dull; the video was shot in fading light just a few seconds before the arrival of a tropical storm. You'll use the White Balance (WB) controls to make the color warmer, and then add depth and definition by boosting the Contrast, Vibrance, and Saturation.

2   Starting at the top of the Basic panel, set the Temperature to **+15** and the Tint to **+30**; then, set a Contrast value of **55**. Reduce the Whites setting to **-100**, increase the Blacks to **+100**, and set both Vibrance and Saturation to **20**.

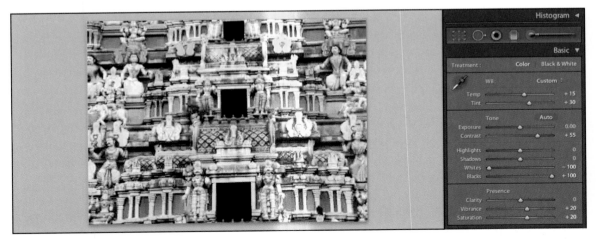

3   Choose Develop > New Preset. Name your custom preset **IceCreamCake** and accept the User Presets folder as the destination to which it will be saved.

Note: Because this preset is intended for use with our lesson video, we avoided modification to the Highlights, Shadows, and Clarity settings, as those adjustments are amongst several not supported for video. If you choose a Develop preset that includes un-supported operations, you'll se an alert listing the adjustments that *can* be applied to video. For any given clip, some Lightroom presets not specifically intended for use with video may produce very little effect. Some other presets, including the Lightroom Effect Presets category, will not work at all for video.

4   Inspect the Settings pane in the lower half of the New Develop Preset dialog box for an overview of just how many separate developing adjustments you can build into a single preset. The illustration below shows the default options; make sure you have the same set activated, and then click Create.

If you apply your custom preset to the lesson video now, you'll overwrite the video preset and manual adjustments you applied earlier. In the next exercise, you'll create a *virtual copy* of the video file, so that you can compare the two edited versions.

Working with virtual copies

Note: In fact, *every* photo or video in your catalog is a virtual copy of the master file.

When you wish to explore different treatments for a photo or video, without losing the work you've already done, you can create *virtual* copies of your image or clip, and edit each one independently, just as if they were separate master files.

If a particular photo is included in more than one collection, any changes you make to that image while you're working in one collection will be visible in all the others. If you wish to modify an image for a specific collection without affecting the way the photo appears elsewhere in your catalog, you should use a virtual copy.

You might include a full-frame, full-color version of your photo in a collection that you've assembled for a slideshow—and a tightly cropped, sepia-toned virtual copy in another collection intended for a print layout. You can apply a unifying special effect to an entire collection of virtual copies for a photo book without affecting the way the same images appear in any of your other projects and presentations.

Another important advantage of working with virtual copies is that you save a great deal of disk space by keeping only one master file for each photo. A virtual copy is actually just an additional catalog entry for that master file. This new entry will be updated to record every change you make to the virtual copy, while your developing settings for other virtual copies—and the master file itself—remain unchanged.

1 If you're still in the Develop module, switch to the Grid view in the Library. In the Grid view or the Filmstrip, right-click / control click the video file TamilTemple.MPG and choose Create Virtual Copy from the context menu.

2 If necessary, press F6 to show the Filmstrip. You can see that there are now two copies of the video side by side in the Filmstrip.

In both the Grid view and the Filmstrip, virtual copies are identified by a page peel (or dog-ear) icon in the lower left corner of the thumbnail, though this is difficult to see on video thumbnails, as it appears behind the duration indicator.

By default, Lightroom will automatically stack the virtual copy with the original video. In this case, the original video was already stacked with the still frame you captured, so Lightroom has added the virtual copy to the existing stack. The original video at the top of the stack is marked with a stack badge.

> **Tip:** If you don't see the virtual copy dog-ear markers in the Grid view or the Filmstrip, choose View Options from any thumbnail's context menu, and then activate thumbnail badges.

3 Move the pointer over either of the stacked videos to see a file count indicating the position of that copy in the stack.

> **Tip:** To unstack photos or videos, select one of the thumbnails in the stack in the Grid view; then, right-click / Control-click the stack icon on the selected thumbnail and choose Unstack from the menu.

You can use the Kind filter—one of the Attribute filters in the Filter bar—to filter your library by file kind, isolating master images, virtual copies, or video files.

4 If you don't see the Filter bar above the Grid view, press Backslash (\) . Click Attribute in the filter picker; then click the third of the Kind filters—the button with a film-strip icon—at the right of the Filter bar. The Grid view displays the original video. Click to disable the video filter; then, click the next Kind filter to the left—the button with a turned-up corner—to isolate the virtual copy.

5 Click None in the filter picker; then, press Backslash (\) to hide the Filter bar.

6 Double-click the virtual copy, TamilTemple.MPG / Copy 1, in the Grid view or the Filmstrip, to open the clip in the Loupe view. Expand the Quick Develop panel, if necessary, and click the Reset All button at the bottom of the panel to clear all of the current settings and set the copy to the video's un-edited state.

7 Click the Saved Preset menu (currently set to Default Settings) and choose your custom IceCreamCake preset from the User Presets category. Scrub or play through the clip to see the effect.

Your custom preset has improved the video significantly, correcting the cold, blue-green color cast, boosting the flat tonal range to add contrast and definition, and replacing the dull, de-saturated hues with the cheerful colors of the candy counter.

8 Choose Edit > Select None. In the Filmstrip, select the original video; then, hold down the Ctrl / Command key and click the virtual copy. Press the C key to switch to Compare view where you can see the two treatments side by side.

Beyond the Basic panel

Once you've adjusted the white balance and the tonal distribution in the Basic panel, you can move on to the rest of the panels in the right panel group.

1   In the Filmstrip, select the image DSC_6051.NEF, another shot of the cliffs of Normandy; then, press D on your keyboard to switch to the Develop module.

2   You can make more space in the Loupe view for this portrait-format photo by hiding the top panel (F5) and the Filmstrip (F6). Press T to hide the Toolbar. Make sure that both side panel groups are visible.

3   Inspect the settings in the Basic panel; you can see that the developing settings for this Raw image have already been adjusted to maximize and balance the overall tonal range. Expand the Histogram and Tone Curve panels. For a clearer view, collapse the Basic panel and any other panels that are currently expanded.

Adjusting contrast using the tone curve

Working with the Tone Curve enables you to adjust contrast in different parts of the tonal range selectively. Tone curve corrections should not be applied until after the imaged has been processed as necessary with the controls in the Basic panel.

The tone curve maps the distribution of tonal values in the input image along the x-axis to a new distribution of tonal values in the output image along the y-axis. The dark end of the range is at the lower left and the light at the upper right.

A linear tone curve at a 45° incline from the lower left corner to the upper right corner has no effect on the image; each tone value in the input image is mapped to the identical tone value in the output image. Raising the tone curve above this line maps tone values to a lighter value; lowering it darkens the tonal values.

A tone curve section that is flatter than 45° compresses a range of tone values from the input image (x axis) to a narrower range in the output image (y axis). Some tone values which were distinguishable in the input image become indistinguishable in the output image, resulting in a loss of image detail.

A tone curve section that is steeper than 45° expands tone values; the differences between tone values becomes more noticeable and therefore the image contrast is increased.

In Lightroom, the tone curve is constrained so that the curve is always ascending. This means that if you increase the incline of one section of the curve you'll end up with a decreased incline somewhere else; you'll have to make a compromise. When using the tone curve, the trick is to increase the contrast in the range where you have the most tonal information; recognizable by a peak in the histogram. At the same time, try to place the flatter parts of the tone curve in ranges where there is less information in the image (troughs in the histogram) or where a lack of contrast is not as disturbing or noticeable.

A typical tone curve intended to increase mid-range contrast starts flat in the lower left corner (less contrast in the shadows), is steep in the center (more contrast in the mid-tones), and ends flat in the upper right corner (less contrast in the highlights).

For the photo at hand we'll customize the tone curve to selectively increase the contrast in the brightly-lit portion of the cliff face, which dominates the image. For this substantial enhancement it will be worthwhile sacrificing a little tonal depth in the shadowed area at the lower right and in the sky.

1   In the header of the Navigator, set the Loupe view zoom level to FIT.

● **Note:** The choice of point curve preset also constrains the amount of play in the adjustment controls.

2   From the Point Curve menu at the bottom of the Tone Curve panel, choose Linear, Medium Contrast, and Strong Contrast in turn and notice the effect each setting has on the image. You can use a tone curve preset as a starting point for your adjustments; for this image, set a Medium Contrast curve.

Note the silhouette of the histogram plotted in the background in the tone curve display. This gives you an indication of the tonal ranges where an increase in contrast might be most effective.

▶ **Tip:** By default, the four tonal ranges are of equal width. You can change their width by dragging the controls below the tone curve to reposition the dividing lines between adjacent tonal ranges.

3   Position the pointer over the tone curve. As you move along the curve, you'll notice the name of the range currently under your pointer displayed at the bottom of the tone curve grid, while the corresponding slider is highlighted in the Region controls below.

Whether you use the sliders, enter numeric values, or drag directly in the tone curve grid, the tone curve controls raise or lower the curve by moving the center points of these four ranges: Shadows, Darks, Lights, and Highlights. The overall shape of the tone curve changes to accommodate your adjustments, becoming flatter in one place and steeper in another.

The extent to which you can adjust each section of the tone curve is indicated by the lighter gray area that appears when you position the pointer over that section.

4   To see which areas in the image correspond to the different tonal ranges, click the Target button (◉) in the top left corner of the Tone Curve panel and move the pointer over the image in the Loupe view. As you move the pointer over the shadowed area in the lower part of the image you can see that these tones account for much of the first peak in the histogram around the 25% mark. Most of the tonal values in the blue sky are represented in the second peak in the histogram silhouette near the 50% input level. The tones in the well-lit parts of the church wall are mostly spread between input levels of 60% to 90%. The third peak in the histogram corresponds to a mid-beige tone in the striated limestone.

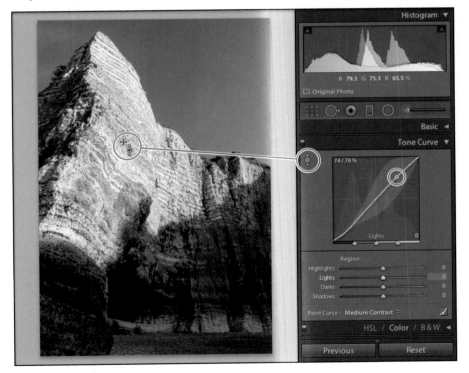

Lowering the Lights value in the curve should increase the contrast in the sunlit cliff face by steepening the curve for input values above 60%. The compromise will be a flattening of the curve for lower input values, which will reduce contrast in the shadowed areas and the sky where a loss of detail is less noticeable.

5   Watch the tone curve as you move the target cursor over the rock face. When you see the Lights adjustment control selected on the Tone Curve, click and drag downwards in the image. Release the mouse button when the Lights value is reduced to –55. Remember: you can only adjust the tone curve by dragging directly in the image when you are using the Tone Curve Target mode.

6   Click the Target button again to turn off target mode.

7   To compare your image with and without the tone curve adjustment, switch the tone curve controls off and on by clicking the On/Off switch at the left side of the Tone Curve panel's header. Review the effect in the image at 100% zoom level. Note how much your adjustment has enhanced the detail in the sunlit stone.

The image was also darkened as a whole because the tone curve was pushed below the diagonal. This works quite well for the photo at hand. In another case, you could lessen the effect, if you wished, by raising the Shadows value in the Tone Curve or by readjusting the levels using the controls in the Basic panel.

8   When you're done, set the zoom level to FIT and make sure the tone curve adjustment is turned on.

Overall, the photo's tonal balance now looks quite acceptable. To improve the image further, you'll need to increase definition in the darker areas selectively.

Making local corrections

All the adjustments applied to this photo thus far (including those we made when preparing the lesson image) have been applied across the entire image. For example, the tone curve affects tones throughout a photo; you can't use it to lighten or darken one area more than another. The local correction tools—the Graduated Filter, the Radial Filter, and the Adjustment Brush tool—enable you to do just that.

Using the Graduated Filter tool

With the Graduated Filter tool you can create a gradient mask through which you can apply an adjustment so that the effect is strongest in one area and fades off across the rest of the image.

1   You should still have the image DSC_6051.NEF active in the Loupe view. Click the Graduated Filter tool below the Histogram panel, or press M. Controls for the tool appear below the tool buttons.

2   Make sure New is selected as the Mask setting; then, choose Exposure from the Effect menu above the Temperature and Tint sliders. Use the slider or type a new value in the text box at the right to set the Exposure setting to **1.00**.

3   With the Graduated Filter tool, drag upwards and to the left, starting near the lower right corner of the image; then, release the mouse button.

You've just created a gradient mask, through which your adjustment has been applied; the exposure increases gradually towards the lower right corner of the photo. In the Graduated Filter controls, the Mask setting has changed from New to Edit. Next you'll fine-tune both the adjustment and the mask itself.

4   Set the Temperature to 25, the Tint to -5, and the Contrast to 25. Increase the Shadows setting to 50 and set both the Clarity and the Saturation to 25.

5   Adjust the gradient mask as shown in the illustration below. Drag the pin to center it on the edge of the shadow that runs diagonally across the cliff face. To set the angle, move the pointer over the center line and drag with the curved double-arrow cursor to rotate the mask around its pin; then, drag either of the outer lines to make the band of the gradient narrower or broader.

▶ **Tip:** You can use more than one graduated filter on a single image, each with its own position, direction, size, and adjustment settings.

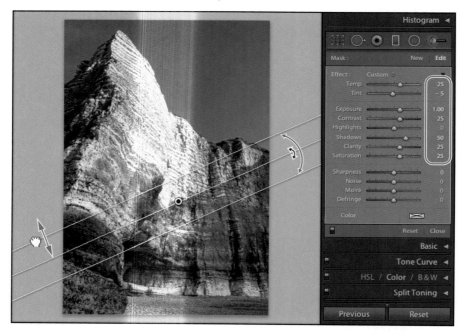

The broader the band, the "softer" the gradient—the narrower the band, the more abruptly the adjustment is faded into the image. While you're dragging the outer lines, you can keep the center line fixed at its current position by holding down the Alt / Option key. The outer lines represent the boundaries beyond which the adjustment is applied—at 100% of the specified value on one side, and at 0% on the other. Press the H key to hide or show the adjustment pin.

6   To evaluate the image with and without the graduated filter adjustment, click the On/Off switch icon in the lower left corner of the Graduated Filter controls pane. When you're done, make sure the graduated filter adjustment is activated.

7   Click the Graduated Filter button again to disable the Graduated Filter tool.

Using the Adjustment Brush tool

You can use the Adjustment Brush tool to edit different areas selectively by painting adjustments directly onto the image. In this exercise, you'll use this technique to liven up the sky, which was darkened and dulled by the tone curve adjustment.

1   Click the Adjustment Brush tool (circled at right) below the Histogram panel, or press K. Controls for the Adjustment Brush tool appear below the tool strip. Make sure that Mask is set to New in the Adjustment Brush tool controls pane.

▶ Tip: You can apply multiple brush adjustments to a single image, each with its own effect. Try overlapping and layering adjustments.

2   Set the Exposure value for the brush adjustment to **0.75** and the Contrast to **100**.

3   Below the Effect pane, click brush A. Set the brush size to **20** and activate the Auto Mask option. With Auto Mask activated, the brush will detect the edges of the area you're painting, and automatically mask the parts of the image outside those edges.

● Note: You can set up two brushes to apply the adjustment and one that will erase it—each with a different size, softness, flow, and density.

4   Starting with the cursor cross-hairs a little above the top of the cliff face and just inside the right edge of the photo, drag to the left. As you drag, allow the inner circle (the full-effect area) to overlap the cliff-top, but make sure that the cross-hairs always remain over the sky area. Release the mouse button when you reach the left edge of the photo. Hold the pointer above the new brush adjustment's marker pin for a second or two to show a translucent overlay that makes it easy to see the area affected by your brush-on adjustment.

You'll probably find that the Adjustment Brush fails to detect the edge between sky and stone at the upper left of the photo, as shown here. You could easily erase the spill-over by holding down the Alt / Option key and painting over the area, but for our sample image, the extra exposure in this shaded corner of the rock face is not at all unwelcome.

5   Make sure that the brush adjustment is still selected and active; then, paint over the rest of the sky area, making sure to overlap your strokes for even coverage. When you've admired your handiwork, click the switch in the lower left corner of the Adjustment Brush controls panel to switch the effect off; in the next exercise, you'll explore a different technique for correcting the color and intensity of the sky. Press K or click the Adjustment Brush tool to disable it.

Making discrete color adjustments

You can use the controls in the HSL / Color / B & W panel to adjust discrete shades of color in your image, changing the hue, saturation, or luminance values for specific color ranges independently.

When converting an image to black and white, you can fine-tune the way that each color in the image will contribute to the grayscale mix. Use the Split Toning panel to apply creative duotone effects to a black and white image.

Understanding hue, saturation, and luminance

The color of each pixel in your image can be expressed either as a set of RGB values or as a combination of hue, saturation, and luminance values. Hue, saturation, and luminance values can be calculated from RGB values, and vice versa.

Once you understand hue, saturation, and luminance, defining color in these terms seems far more natural than using RGB values, especially when it comes to describing changes made to color.

For example; in RGB values, R: 42, G: 45, B: 63 describes a light blue, while a darker blue has the values R: 35, G: 38, B: 56. This is certainly not a very intuitive model for understanding color adjustments. In terms of hue, saturation and luminance, however, darkening the blues in your image can be expressed as simply reducing the luminance value for the blue color component.

When you describe a color by name—red, yellow, green, blue—you're referring to its *hue*. The full range of hues can be displayed as a color wheel. Changing the hue is equivalent to moving around the wheel in one direction or the other.

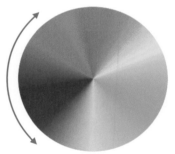

Saturation is the boldness or intensity of a hue, ranging from neutral and grayed to vivid and un-muted. Saturation can be visualized on a color wheel with fully saturated colors around the edge of the circle and less saturated colors closer to the center. As the saturation of a color is increased it moves from a neutral gray in the center of the wheel to a pure, vivid hue on the rim.

Luminance is the measure of brightness of a color, ranging from the minimum value for black to the maximum value for white. On the color wheel model, luminance can be represented by adding a third dimension, with a completely underexposed—or black—wheel below the color wheel and a completely overexposed—or white—wheel above it.

The terms tint, shade, and tone can all be expressed with reference to hue, saturation, and luminance.

A *tint* is a pure hue mixed with white; a hue with increased luminance and a reduced saturation. In our three-dimensional color wheel model the tints of a hue are found along the line from the pure hue on the rim of the wheel in the middle to the center point of the white wheel at the top.

A *shade* is a pure hue mixed with black; a hue with decreased luminance and saturation, located along a line from the pure hue on the rim of the wheel in the middle to the center point of the black wheel at the bottom.

A *tone* is a pure hue mixed with a neutral gray, located along a line from the pure hue on the rim of the wheel in the middle to the respective gray on the central axis.

Adjusting colors selectively

Understanding color in an image in terms of hue, saturation and luminance can help you both in identifying the changes you need to make to achieve the effect you want and in choosing the most effective way to make those changes.

In this exercise you'll darken the blue of the sky in the photo of the stone church. You can do this by reducing the luminance of the blue color range while leaving the hue and saturation unchanged.

1   You should still be in the Develop module, with the image of the limestone cliffs, DSC_6051.NEF, open in the Loupe view.

2   In the Navigator panel, set the zoom level to FIT.

3   In the right panel group, scroll or collapse other panels, if necessary, and then expand the HSL / Color / B & W panel. If it's not already selected, click HSL (Hue, Saturation, Luminance) in the panel header, and then click the Luminance tab.

4　Click the Target tool button () in the upper left corner of the Luminance pane.

5　In the Loupe view, click in the sky area and drag upwards to increase the luminance of the color range under the pointer. Release the mouse button when the Luminance value for Blue reaches **+50**. Depending on where you click, you may see a small shift in the Aqua or Purple values.

6　While the target mode is still active, click the Saturation tab at the top of the HSL controls and repeat the process to set the Saturation value for Blue to **+50**. Click the Target button again to disable target mode.

● **Note:** Hue, saturation, and luminance adjustments are not restricted to a single, discrete color but are applied across a range of colors to either side of the target hue.

7　To compare the image with and without the saturation and luminance adjustments, switch the HSL adjustment off and on by clicking the switch at the left of the HSL / Color / B & W panel header. Note that the adjustment has not affected the gradient from lighter blue near at the right to darker blue at the top of the photo. When you're done, make sure the HSL adjustment is turned on.

8　Collapse the Basic and tone Curve panels, if they're open, and press K to reactivate the Adjustment Brush. Compare your HSL adjustment to the brush adjustment by switching them on and off in turn.

9　Try switching both adjustments on at the same time; the effects are cumulative. Click the brush adjustment's pin to make it "live" for editing; then, drag or "scrub" over the pin to reduce the effect, noting the change in the control sliders as well as the image. Stop when the Contrast value has dropped to **75**. Press K to deactivate the Adjustment Brush, leaving the effect switched on.

Sky untreated　　　Exposure & Contrast brush　　Saturation & Luminance　　Combined effects, tweaked

10　Examine the Hue and All tabs in the HSL pane. To check out the options in the Color pane, click Color on the header of the HSL / Color / B & W panel.

Converting an image to black and white

Lightroom converts a photo to black and white by analyzing the image and mapping each color value to a different tone of gray according to a default routine.

You can create very different grayscale looks for the same photo by adjusting the relative predominance of each color in the mix.

1   In the Filmstrip, select the Raw image of the marble horses: DSC_0151.NEF.

2   Click B & W in the header of the HSL / Color / B & W panel. You can see the result of the default black and white mix in the Loupe view and in the settings of the control sliders in the B & W pane. You can tweak the slider for each color manually or, if you wish, you can adjust the black and white mix visually by dragging in different areas of the image with the adjustment target tool.

3   Click the Target button (⊙) at the upper left of the B & W tab. In the Loupe view, click one of the darker tones on the left shoulder of the "white" horse on the right; then, drag downwards to set both Orange and Yellow to approximately -100. Click the right shoulder of the dark horse that is partially visible at the right of the photo and drag upwards until the Blue value reaches +100.

4   Move the target cursor over the brighter part of the first horse's right shoulder. Look for a point that highlights the Yellow slider; then, drag upwards to increase the Yellow value to -50 (you may also see a small change in the Orange setting).

5   Click the Black And White Mix Target button (⊙) again to turn target mode off.

6   To compare the image before and after your adjustments to the grayscale mix, switch the Black And White Mix adjustments off and on by clicking the On/Off switch icon at the left side of the HSL / Color / B & W panel header. When you're done, make sure the Black And White Mix control is turned on.

Split toning

A split toning effect replaces the dark tones (shadows) in a black and white image with shades of one color and the lighter tones (highlights) with tints of another. The effect can be quite subtle and restrained or very striking and unusual depending on your choice of colors and your intention.

1 In the right panel group, expand the Split Toning panel. If possible, keep the HSL / Color / B & W panel open so you can see the settings for the grayscale mix at the same time.

2 Right-click / Control-click the image in the Loupe view and choose Settings > Lightroom BW Toned Presets > Split Tone 2 from the menu. Note the changes in the Black & White Mix pane as well as the Split Toning panel. This split tone effect uses a light olive tone for the highlights and a slightly darker, de-saturated French blue for the shadows.

3 In the right panel group, expand the Basic and Tone Curve panels in turn, using Undo and Redo to see how the Split Tone 2 preset changes the settings. Collapse each panel when you're done with it.

This preset has built-in settings for the black and white mix, tone controls, and tone curve that override the look you created earlier. To counter this, you can copy just the color settings from the Split Toning panel, without the preset tone adjustments.

4 Right-click / Control-click the image and choose Settings > Copy Settings from the context menu. In the Copy Settings dialog box, first click the Check None button, and then activate only the Split Toning option. Click Copy.

5   Choose Edit > Undo Split Tone 2 to return to the black and white image with all your customized settings. Right-click / Control-click the image in the Loupe view and choose Settings > Paste Settings from the context menu.

By checking the panels in the right panel group, you can confirm that this time, only the settings in the Split Toning panel have changed; there are no alterations to the tone settings that make up the high-contrast look that you set up earlier.

Split Tone 2 preset applied   Preset's Split Toning settings only applied

Synchronizing settings

You can copy, or *synchronize*, settings from one photo to a multiple selection of images by using the Synchronize Settings command.

1   In the Filmstrip, Ctrl-click / Command-click to select the photo of the horses together with three or four of the other raw images, avoiding the two video files and the associated JPEG image. Click the split tone image to make sure that it's the active (the most selected) image.

2   Click the Sync button below the right panel group. In the Synchronize Settings dialog box, click the Check None button, and then activate the Basic Tone, Treatment (Black & White) and Split Toning options. Click Synchronize.

All the selected images have been converted to black and white and have had the duo-tone effect that you copied from the Split Tone 2 preset applied.

▶ **Tip:** The Synchronize Settings command in the Develop module copies absolute values from one image to the others. To apply relative changes to a selection of images—such as increasing exposure by 1/3 step independent of the current exposure settings in each of the destination images— you can use the Quick Development panel in the Library module.

3   Undo the Synchronize operation to restore the images in your selection to the settings you applied in previous exercises.

Removing camera-generated image artifacts

Before moving to the Detail panel to look at image noise and sharpening, you need to visit the Lens Corrections panel to deal with two unwelcome image artifacts.

1 Show the Filmstrip if it's hidden and select the photo of the courtyard cafe. Use the zoom picker and preview in the Navigator panel to set a 2:1 or 3:1 zoom level and center the view on the closest table in the arcade at the left.

Our lesson photo exhibits *chromatic aberration*, an image artifact usually most noticeable near the edges of a photo shot with a wide-angle lens, resulting in color fringes (blue/green and magenta/purple) where the lens has been unable to correctly align the different wavelengths of incoming light on the sensor.

Note: Though you may not notice it until you magnify an image, chromatic aberration can cause even a well focused photo to look blurred, similar to off-register printing in a cheap magazine.

Tip: For information on using camera and lens profiles optimize corrections, please refer to Lightroom Help.

2 In the right panel group, expand the Lens Corrections panel. If it's not already active, click the Basic tab at the top of the panel. Note that profile-based corrections have already been enabled; lens correction operations work better if Lightroom can access the camera and lens profiles in the image's metadata. Watch the zoomed image as you activate the Remove Chromatic Aberration option. The operation was largely successful, but a trace of magenta is still discernible at the left edges of lighter toned objects such as the table-cloths.

3 Drag the rectangle in the Navigator preview to center the view on the patch of sky under the nearest arch.

Note: If Lightroom can't detect the hues usually produced by chromatic aberration, you'll be asked to pick a different color.

4 In the Lens Corrections panel, click the Color tab, and then pick up the Defringe eyedropper. Move the eyedropper over the image; a pixel-level preview gives you a clear view of the colors under the pointer. Click to sample a magenta/purple pixel under the apex of the arch.

5 Press the Esc key to drop the Defringe eyedropper. In the Lens Corrections panel, move the purple Amount slider to the right until the fringe disappears; a setting of 4 or 5 should suffice for this image. If there was any movement in the green Amount slider, reset that value to zero. Zoom out to the FIT view.

The lesson photo also shows *lens vignetting*, an effect that varies with different lens types, focal lengths, and filters and results in reduced brightness or saturation of color towards the edges of the image. In this image with its shaded edges, the lens vignette is not immediately apparent—but you'll definitely notice its removal.

6   Click the Manual tab in the Lens Corrections panel. Drag the Lens Vignetting Amount slider all the way to the right; then back down to a value of **75**.

Correcting lens distortion

While you're still on the Manual tab, we'll look at the Transform controls that let you manually correct distortion caused by the camera lens. Our lesson photo was shot with a (very) wide-angled lens; it exhibits classic *fish-eye* or *barrel distortion*, but even "standard" lenses produce some degree of distortion.

Once again, it's important to enable profile-based correction so that both automatic and manual adjustments are tailored to the idiosyncrasies of your lens.

1   Note that the controls in the Transform pane have pre-applied settings; toggle the switch in the Lens Corrections panel's header to turn their effects off and on. In preparing the lesson image, we applied these settings manually to remove most of the fish-eye effect. Make sure to return the switch to the on position.

● **Note:** Switching Lens Corrections off will also hide your lens vignetting correction.

2   Drag each of the Transform sliders back and forth to see its effect on the photo, making sure that you restore the original setting before moving on to the next.

Correcting perspective effects automatically

Even though a photo may not exhibit distortion as obvious as a fish-eye effect, objects in the image can be affected by perspective in ways that can diminish the impact of the image by distracting attention from the subject.

The new Upright feature can correct perspective effects automatically by analyzing image content in the light of information from the lens profile, looking for elements affected in various ways by perspective.

Every photo will perform differently with the Upright feature. For some photos, one or more of the Upright modes may produce no result at all if Lightroom can't find a viable correction; try all four modes for any image you wish to correct.

1   In the Filmstrip, select the image DSC_0055.NEF. Set the zoom level to FIT.

2   Click the Basic tab at the top of the Lens Corrections panel, and then make sure that the Enable Profile Corrections option is still activated.

For the best result, you should always enable the lens profile before applying Upright corrections; for some photos, Upright might work well without reference to a lens profile, but in many cases the results can be unpredictable.

Original image

Upright: Full mode, lens profile enabled   Upright: Full mode, no lens profile

3   In the Upright pane, click Level, Vertical, Auto and Full in turn.

Level corrections (left) are weighted in favor of horizontal elements in the image; you can use the Level button to straighten a tilted image automatically, even when the horizon is hidden and all the so-called horizontal details in the image are angled by perspective, as is the case with our lesson photo. Upright analyzes converging horizontals, calculates the hidden horizon, and straightens the image accordingly.

Vertical corrections are weighted towards vertical detail, but also level the image. The Vertical mode corrects *keystone distortion*, the perspective effect that causes vertical lines to converge when your camera is tilted upwards.

The Auto mode usually produces the most "realistic" results; intelligently blending level, vertical and perspective corrections in a way that makes the most of your image without forcing or favoring any particular aspect.

The Upright feature's Full mode (illustrated on the facing page) combines the full effects of the Level, Vertical, and Auto perspective corrections; with the right photo, it can produce a striking result.

Enable the Constrain Crop option to have Upright crop away areas left empty after a perspective correction. If the upright correction gives your photo a stretched or compressed look, adjust it with the Aspect slider in the manual Transform controls. If you enable or disable profile corrections, or change the lens profile, after you've applied an Upright correction, you'll need to click Reanalyze in the Upright pane; Lightroom will re-configure the existing correction accordingly.

● **Note:** An Upright correction will reset cropping and override any manual distortion transforms unless you hold Alt / Option when you apply the feature.

Sharpening detail and reducing noise

The Detail panel hosts controls for sharpening image detail and reducing noise. Sharpening helps make edges more pronounced and gives the image a crisper look. Lightroom applies a slight amount of sharpening to your Raw images by default, so you should apply additional sharpening with caution.

1 In the Filmstrip, select the photo of the sculpted horses. Set the zoom level to 1:1 (100%); sharpening and noise reduction edits are always best executed at 100%; the pixel-for-pixel view gives you the clearest appreciation of the results. Scroll down in the right panel group and expand the Detail panel.

2 To compare the image with and without the default 25% sharpening, switch the Detail controls off and on by clicking the switch at the left of the panel header. Review the effect in several areas of the image at 100% magnification. When you're done, make sure that the Detail settings are switched on.

Though the default sharpening has done a good job of emphasizing the edges in this image, you can still make it crisper. Before you apply extra sharpening, however, it's best to set up a mask that will restrict your adjustment to areas with edge detail: this will enable you to sharpen detail without accentuating image noise.

3 Position the photo in the Loupe view so that you can see the face of the horse on the right. Hold down the Alt / Option key and drag the Masking slider to the right. Release the pointer when most of the finer lines in the cheek, fore-head, and nose have disappeared, leaving the main edges clearly outlined in white (we set a value of **90**). The black areas will be protected from sharpening.

Tip: If you can't see the effect clearly, set a higher zoom ratio.

4 To sharpen the image, drag the Amount slider to the right. With the mask in place, you can afford to increase the value significantly. We raised the Amount to **100**, the Radius to **3**, and the Detail to **50**. Compare the image with and without sharpening once again by clicking the switch at the left side of the panel's header. Make sure to return the switch to the on position.

5 To assess the effect of the sharpening mask, drag the Masking slider back to its default setting of zero. Undo and Redo to see the effect of the sharpening with and without the mask. When you're done, return the Masking setting to **90**.

Most of the noise apparent in this image is *luminance noise*—variations in the brightness of pixels which should be equally bright. In general, Luminance noise is less of a problem than color noise, or *chrominance noise*—blue, red and purple spots in areas that should be a uniform hue. In the Noise Reduction pane, you can see that a little Color noise reduction has been applied to this image by default.

6 In the Filmstrip, select the photo of the courtyard cafe. Set the zoom level to 2:1 and focus the view on the top of the nearest pillar.

7 To assess the effect of the default reduction in color noise, drag the Color slider all the way to the left. Undo and Redo to see the image with and without the noise reduction. When you're done, set the Color noise reduction value to **35**.

Tip: You should use Noise Reduction with caution; both forms can blur image detail. You can use the Detail sliders for the Noise Reduction controls to help maintain the sharpness of the image, despite this effect.

8 Position the photo so that you can see the windows and second-floor balustrade visible under the arch at the right of the pillar. Drag the Luminance slider all the way to the right. The luminance noise has now disappeared; however, there is marked blurring of the detail in the background. You'll need to find a compromise between reducing noise and maintaining the sharpness. Drag the Luminance slider back to 0, and then slowly to the right until you notice that the noise is improved with only slight blurring image details. We set a value of **55**.

9 Use the Detail and Contrast controls below the Luminance slider to reduce the blurring effect. Try Detail and Contrast values of **75** and **50** respectively.

Adding effects

● **Note:** The illustration at the right shows a fairly extreme application of Post-Crop Vignetting that suggests the look of a film transparency. You can control the softness and shape of the vignette, and specify how you want it to interact with colors and highlights.

In the Lens Corrections panel, you removed accidental lens vignetting; in the Effects panel you can deliberately put it back! A post-crop vignette can be used creatively to frame a photo (as illustrated here), to draw the viewer's attention to the center of an image, or even to simulate an accidental vignette for an atmospheric or "antique" effect.

The Effects panel also offers a configurable Grain effect that simulates the distinctive look of a film photograph.

Congratulations, you've completed the lesson. Take a moment to refresh what you've learned by reading through the review on the facing page.

Review questions

1 How do you undo changes or return quickly to a previous develop state?

2 What is white balance?

3 What does a tone curve represent and what is it used for?

4 What are the two kinds of noise you might encounter in a digital image and what can you do about them?

5 Which tools are used to perform local corrections?

6 What are the four Upright modes and what do they do?

Review answers

1 You can undo one modification at a time using the Undo command. You can jump back multiple steps at once in the History panel. You can create snapshots of important develop states so that you can return to them quickly.

2 An image's white balance reflects the composition of the red, green, and blue components in the light source when the picture was taken. It is used as a calibration benchmark to correctly render the color information recorded by the camera's sensors.

3 A tone curve adjusts the distribution of the tonal ranges in an image. The curve shows the way tonal information from the original image will be mapped to the adjusted image. It can be used to increase or decrease the contrast in specific tonal ranges.

4 Digital images may contain two kinds of noise: luminance noise, which is a result of variation in the brightness of pixels which should be of the same luminance, and color (chrominance) noise: bright blue, red and purple spots in an area that should be a uniform hue. Each kind of noise can be reduced using the appropriate noise reduction slider in the Detail panel.

5 You can restrict adjustments to selected areas of your image with the Graduated Filter tool and the Adjustment Brush tool.

6 The four Upright perspective correction modes are Auto, Level, Vertical, and Full. Level mode straightens tilted images, Vertical mode corrects converging verticals, Auto mode blends Level, Vertical, and aspect corrections intelligently to produce a natural-looking correction, and Full mode combines the full effects of the other three.

PHOTOGRAPHY SHOWCASE
JOHN BATDORFF

"I think the best images are created to stand on their own, superseding the photographer's eye."

My natural curiosity comes from years of working in our family's small town newspaper. Over the years I have found myself traveling more in an effort to better understand the world around me. It's during these moments of observation that I try to reconcile what I see with who I am. It is this process that continues to drive my creativity.

Over the years I've become naturally drawn to black and white images. For me, when an image is stripped of it's color it become vulnerable and the composition becomes the cornerstone for the message. It's that sort of honesty that I look for in my images and in myself. I think the best images are created to stand on their own, superseding the photographer's eye. While my style is ever evolving, without dispute my journalism foundation runs deep and continues to bolster my curious nature.

John Batdorff is an award-winning landscape and travel photographer and a nationally recognized authority on black and white photography. When John's not teaching workshops or writing books he can be found wandering the streets looking for his next image.

www.johnbatdorff.com

SMOKE, 2011

THE SWEEPER, 2010

UNGUARDED, 2011

EYES OF JAIPUR, 2010

HIS MAJESTY, 2011

7 CREATING A PHOTO BOOK

Lesson overview

Whether it's produced for a client or as a professional portfolio, designed as a gift or as a way to preserve precious memories, a photo book makes a stylish way to share and showcase your images. The Book module makes it easy to design beautiful, sophisticated book layouts, and then publish them without leaving Lightroom.

In this lesson, you'll learn the skills you need to create your own professional-looking photo book:

- Grouping the images for your photo book as a collection
- Modifying page layouts
- Specifying page numbering options
- Setting a page background
- Placing and arranging images in a layout
- Adding text to a book design
- Working with text cells and photo cells
- Using the Text Adjustment Tool
- Saving a photo book
- Exporting your creation

 You'll probably need between one and two hours to complete this lesson. If you haven't already done so, download the Lesson 7 work files from the Lesson & Update Files tab on your Account page at www.peachpit.com.

Whether it's produced for a client or as a professional portfolio, designed as a gift or as a way to preserve precious memories, a photo book makes a stylish way to share and showcase your images. The Book module makes it easy to design beautiful, sophisticated book layouts, and then publish them without leaving Lightroom.

The Book module delivers everything you need to create polished book designs that can be uploaded directly from Lightroom for printing through the on-demand book vendor Blurb, or exported to PDF and printed on your own printer.

Template based page layout, an intuitive editing environment, and state-of-the-art text tools make it easy to present your photographs in their best light.

in the detail

in the
detail

The Book module delivers everything you need to create polished book designs that can be uploaded directly from Lightroom for printing through the on-demand book vendor Blurb, or exported to PDF and printed on your own printer. Template-based page layout, an intuitive editing environment, and state-of-the-art text tools make it easy to present your photographs in their best light.

Getting started

● **Note:** This lesson assumes that you already have a basic working familiarity with the Lightroom workspace. If you find that you need more background information, refer to Lightroom Help, or review the previous lessons.

Before you start on this lesson, make sure you've set up the LR5CIB folder for your lesson files and created the LR5CIB Catalog file to manage them, as described in "Setting up a work folder" and "Creating a catalog file for working with this book" in the Getting Started chapter at the beginning of this book.

If you haven't already done so, download the Lesson 7 folder from your Account page at www.peachpit.com to the LR5CIB/Lessons folder, as detailed in the section "Accessing the Classroom in a Book files" in the chapter "Getting Started."

1　Start Lightroom.

2　In the Adobe Photoshop Lightroom - Select Catalog dialog box, make sure the file LR5CIB Catalog.lrcat is selected under Select A Recent Catalog To Open, and then click Open.

Adobe Photoshop Lightroom - Select Catalog

Select a recent catalog to open

LR5CIB Catalog.lrcat	C:\Users\John\Pictures\LR5CIB Catalog
Lightroom 5 Catalog.lrcat	C:\Users\John\Pictures\Lightroom

☐ Always load this catalog on startup　　　　☐ Test integrity of this catalog

Note: Lightroom Catalogs cannot be on network volumes or in read-only folders.

[Choose a Different Catalog...] [Create a New Catalog...]　　　[Open] [Quit]

▶ **Tip:** The first time you enter any of the Lightroom modules, you'll see module tips that will help you get started by identifying the components of the Lightroom workspace and stepping you through the workflow. Dismiss the tips by clicking the Close button. To reactivate the tips for any module, choose [*Module name*] Tips from the Help menu.

3　Lightroom will open in the screen mode and workspace module that were active when you last quit. If necessary, switch to the Library module by clicking Library in the Module Picker at the top of the workspace.

LR5CIB Catalog - Adobe Photoshop Lightroom - Library

File　Edit　Library　Photo　Metadata　View　Window　Help

Lr Adobe Photoshop **Lightroom 5**　　　(Library)　Develop | Map | Book | Slideshow | Print | Web

---

Importing images into the library

The first step is to import the images for this lesson into the Lightroom library.

1　In the Library module, click the Import button below the left panel group.

2   If the Import dialog box appears in compact mode, click the Show More Options button at the lower left of the dialog box to see all the options in the expanded Import dialog box.

3   In the Source panel at the left of the expanded Import dialog box, navigate to and select the LR5CIB > Lessons > Lesson 7 folder. Ensure that all nineteen images are checked for import.

4   In the import options above the thumbnail previews, select Add so that the imported photos will be added to your catalog without being moved or copied. Under File Handling at the right of the expanded Import dialog box, choose Minimal from the Render Previews menu and ensure that the Don't Import Suspected Duplicates option is activated. Under Apply During Import, choose None from both the Develop Settings menu and the Metadata menu and type **Lesson 7, Architecture** in the Keywords text box. Make sure that the Import dialog box is set up as shown in the illustration below, and then click Import.

The nineteen images are imported from the Lesson 7 folder and now appear in the Grid view of the Library module and also in the Filmstrip across the bottom of the Lightroom workspace.

Assembling photos for a book

The first step in creating a book is to assemble the photos you wish to include.

Having just been imported, the images for this lesson are already isolated from the rest of your catalog. In the Catalog panel, the Previous Import folder is selected as the active image source.

The Previous Import folder is merely a temporary grouping and, as an image source, it is not flexible—you can't rearrange the images inside it, or exclude a photo from your project without removing it from the catalog entirely.

You should always use either a collection or a single folder without subfolders as the source for the images in your book; both will let you reorder photos in the Grid view or the Filmstrip. For this exercise, you'll create a collection—a virtual grouping from which you can also exclude an image without deleting it from your catalog.

1   Make sure that either the Previous Import folder in the Catalog panel, or the Lesson 7 folder in the Folders panel, is selected as the image source; then, press Ctrl+A / Command+A or choose Edit > Select All.

2   Click the New Collection button (➕) in the header of the Collections panel and choose Create Collection from the menu. In the Create Collection dialog box, type **Details** as the name for the collection. Make sure that the option Include Selected Photos is activated and the options Inside A Collection Set, Make New Virtual Copies, and Set As Target Collection are disabled; then, click Create.

Your new collection appears in the Collections panel, where it is automatically selected as the active image source. The image count indicates that the Details collection contains 19 photos.

3   Choose Edit > Select None; then, click Book in the Module Picker to switch to the Book module.

Library | **Develop** | Map | **Book** | Slideshow | Print | Web

Working in the Book module

Whether you want to commemorate a family milestone, frame your memories from a special trip, or put together a photographic package for a client, a photo book is an attractive and sophisticated way to showcase your work. The Book module, new in Lightroom 5, delivers everything you need to create stylish book designs that can be uploaded directly from Lightroom for printing through the on-demand book vendor Blurb, or exported to PDF and printed on your own printer.

Setting up a photo book

In the work area, you may or may not see photos already placed in page layouts, depending on whether you've already experimented with the Book module's tools and controls. You can start this project by clearing the layout and setting up the workspace so that we're all on the same page.

1   Click the Clear Book button in the header bar across the top of the work area. If you don't see the header bar, choose View > Show Header Bar.

2   In the Book Settings panel at the top of the right panel group, choose Blurb from the Book menu and make sure that the Size, Cover, Paper Type, and Logo Page are set to Standard Landscape, Hardcover Image Wrap, Premium Lustre, and On, respectively. The estimated price of printing the book at the current settings is displayed at the bottom of the Book Settings panel.

3   If it's not already selected, click the Multi-Page View button at the far left of the Toolbar at the bottom of the work area. In the View menu, disable Show Info Overlay.

4   Choose Book > Book Preferences. Examine the options; you can choose whether photos are zoomed to fit their image cells or cropped to fit them, toggle the Autofill feature for new books, and set your preferences for text behaviors. Leave the settings at the defaults and close the Book Preferences dialog box.

The Autofill feature is activated by default; if you just entered the Book module for the first time, you would have seen the images from the Details collection already placed in the default book layout. An automatically generated layout can be a great starting point for a new book design, especially if you're beginning without a clear idea of exactly what you want.

5   Expand the Auto Layout panel, if necessary. From the Auto Layout Preset menu, choose Left Blank, Right One Photo, Caption; then, click the Auto Layout button. Scroll down in the work area, if necessary, to see all the page thumbnails. Click the Clear Layout button and repeat the procedure for the auto-layout preset One Photo Per Page.

Note: If you're publishing to Blurb.com, auto-layout is limited to books of 240 pages. There is no auto-layout page limit for books published to PDF.

6   Examine the result in the work area; scroll down, if necessary, to see all the page thumbnails arranged as two-page spreads in the Multi-Page view. Hide the module picker and the left panel group by pressing F5, and then F7, or by clicking the triangles at the top and left edges of the Lightroom workspace. Drag the Thumbnails slider in the Toolbar to reduce or enlarge the thumbnails.

Note: Blurb offers a discounted price for photo books that incorporate the Blurb logo on the last page.

Lightroom generates a book with a cover, a separate page for each of the nineteen lesson photos—placed in the order in which they appear in the Filmstrip—and a twentieth page reserved for the Blurb logo. You can't place a photo on the Blurb logo page, but you can disable it in the Book Settings panel, if you wish.

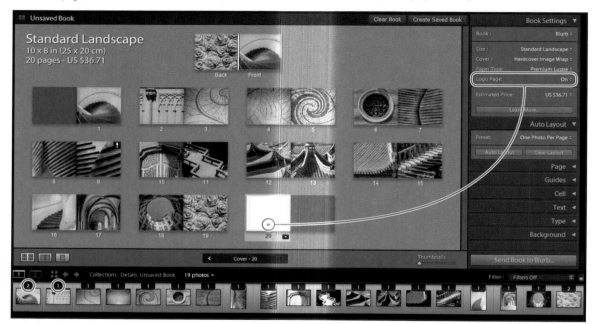

Tip: If you want to rearrange the order of images in the Filmstrip before you click Auto Layout, you'll first need to save your book.

The first image in the Filmstrip is placed on the front cover; the last photo in the series becomes the back cover image. The number above each photo in the Filmstrip indicates how many times it has been used in the book; the first and last images have each been used twice—on the cover and also on pages 1 and 19.

Changing page layouts

Using an auto-layout preset can help you get started on your book; you can then focus on individual spreads and pages to introduce subtlety and variety to the design. For this project, however, you'll build your book layout from scratch.

1   In the Auto Layout panel, click the Clear Layout button.

2   Right-click / Control-click the header of the Page panel and choose Solo Mode from the context menu. If you see the overlay detailing the book's layout, size, page count, and estimated price from Blurb, choose View > Show Info Overlay.

3 In the Multi-Page view, double-click the front cover: the right side of the spread.

The cover layout fills the work area, with the front cover's photo cell selected, as indicated by the yellow border. The Page panel shows a diagrammatic preview of the default cover template: two image cells (identifiable by central cross-hairs) and a narrow text cell positioned along the book's spine.

4 Click the Change Page Layout button ( ) to the right of the layout preview thumbnail in the Page panel, or in the lower right corner of the cover spread displayed in the work area.

5 Scroll down in the page template picker to see all of the available cover layout templates. Grey areas with central cross-hairs indicate image cells; rectangles filled with horizontal lines represent text cells. Click to select the third template in the list. The single cross-hairs at the center of the spread shows that this template has a single image cell that extends across both covers, and three text cells: one on the back cover, one on the spine, and one on the front cover.

6 Expand the Guides panel. Make sure that the Show Guides option is activated; then, watch the layout in the work area as you toggle each of the four guides in turn. Move the pointer over the layout to see the borders of the text cells.

The Page Bleed guide's wide gray border shows the area to be cut off after printing. A thin gray line borders the Text Safe Area, where your text will be well clear of accidental trimming. The Filler Text guide shows filler text (here, the word "Title") to mark the position of text cells. Filler text disappears when you click a text cell.

7 Disable Photo Cells, leaving the other three guides options activated; then, click the Multi-Page View button ( ) in the Toolbar.

The first page in a photo book is always on the right side of the first spread; the grayed-out left side represents the inside of the front cover, which is not printed. Likewise, the last page in a photo book to be published to Blurb must always occupy the left side of the final spread. At this stage, your book consists of a cover and a single, double-sided page, the back of which is the Blurb logo page.

8 Right-click / Control-click page 1 and choose Add Page from the context menu. A second spread appears in the Multi-Page view. Right-click / Control-click page 2 and choose Add Page to copy the same page layout to page 3.

9 Click to select page 2, and then click the Change Page Layout button ( ) below the lower right corner of the page.

For inside pages, unlike the cover, the page template picker groups layout templates in categories according to style, project type, or by the number of photos per page.

▶ **Tip:** To add a page layout to the Favorites category in the template picker, click the circle that appears in the top right corner of the template's thumbnail when you move the pointer over it.

10 Click "2 Photos" to see all the templates with two image cells. Select the fourth template: a layout without text cells that fills the page with two portrait-format images, side by side. In the Guides panel, activate Photo Cells so that you can see the changed page layout.

Adding page numbers to a photo book

● **Note:** The context menu of a page number cell also lists commands that enable you to hide the page number on a selected page, or set the page numbering to start from a page other than page 1.

1 Double-click page 1 to shift to single page view; then, check the box at the top of the Page panel to activate page numbers. From the adjacent positioning menu, choose Bottom Corner. Right-click / Control-click page 1 and make sure that the option Apply Page Number Style Globally is activated in the context menu.

2 Click the new page number cell in the page preview; then, expand the Type panel and inspect the default font, style, size, and opacity settings. With the option Apply Page Number Style Globally activated, any changes to these type style settings would be made throughout the book; for now, leave them unchanged.

Placing photos in a book layout

You can add photos to a page layout in any of the three Book Editor views.

1 Click the Multi-Page view button at the left of the Toolbar; then, drag the seventh thumbnail in the Filmstrip, the image DSC_1534.jpg, onto the cover spread.

2 Drag the image DSC_6230.jpg from the Filmstrip to page 1 in the Multi-Page view. Place the photos DSC_0180.jpg and DSC_5865.jpg in the left and right image cells on page 2, respectively, and the sixth image DSC_0149.jpg on page 3.

● **Note:** An exclamation mark badge in the upper right corner of an image cell indicates that the image may not be of a high enough resolution to print well at the current size. You can either reduce the size of the image in your layout, or ignore the alert if you are prepared to accept a lower print resolution.

Changing the images in a photo book

You can remove a photo from a page layout by right-clicking / Control-clicking the image in the Book Editor and choosing Remove Photo from the context menu. If you simply want to replace a photo, you needn't remove it first.

1 Drag the photo DSC_0131.jpg—the second image in the Filmstrip—onto the right-hand image on page 2. DSC_0131.jpg replaces the original image.

2 In the Multi-Page view, drag the image on page 1—DSC_6230.jpg—onto the photo on page 3; the photos on pages 1 and 3 swap places.

▶ **Tip:** You should see the image thumbnail move as you drag, not the page itself. If you move the page instead, drag it back into place and try again, making sure to drag from well inside the photo cell.

▶ **Tip:** You can easily rearrange the order of the pages in your photo book—or even shuffle entire spreads—in the same way; simply drag them to new positions in the Multi-Page view.

Working with photo cells

The photo cells in a page layout template are fixed in place; you can't delete them, resize them, or move them on the page. Instead, you can use the *cell padding*—the adjustable space around a photo within its cell—to position the images in your page layout exactly as you want them.

1 Double-click page 3. The Book Editor switches from Multi-Page view to Single Page view; in the Toolbar, the Single Page View button is highlighted.

2 Click the photo to select it, and then experiment with the Zoom slider. When you enlarge the image too much (for this photo, above 43%), an exclamation-point badge appears in the upper right corner to alert you that the photo may not print well. Right-click / Control-click the photo and choose Zoom Photo To Fill Cell; the image is scaled so that its shortest edge fills the cell (at a zoom value of 29%, for this photo). Drag the photo to position it vertically within the cell. Drag the slider all the way to the left; the minimum setting reduces the image so that its longest edge fits within the image cell. Click well within the borders of the photo and drag it to the right side of the cell.

▶ **Tip:** If you don't see the Amount slider, click the triangle above the padding values.

3 Leave the photo at the 0% zoom setting. Expand the Cell panel and increase the padding by dragging the Padding Amount slider or typing a new value of **150** pt.

4 Click the black triangle above the Padding value to expand the padding controls. By default, the four controls are linked; the adjustment you made in the previous step changed all four values. Disable the Link All option (the checkbox darkens); then, set both the Right and Top padding to **0** pt and the Bottom value to **300** pt.

5 Set the Left and Right padding to **250** pt, and the Top and Bottom padding to **205** pt. Click the photo in the Single Page view to select it; then, use the slider to set the zoom level to 22% and drag the image to position it within its cell padding as shown in the illustration at the right.

By starting with the right template, and then setting the photo cell padding, you can position an image anywhere on the page, cropped however you wish.

6 In the Cell panel, activate Link All, and then drag any of the sliders to set all of the padding settings to zero. Right-click / Control-click the photo in the Single Image view and choose Zoom Photo To Fill Cell from the context menu. Drag the image vertically inside its cell to find a pleasing crop.

7 Click the Spread View button in the Toolbar to see pages 2 and 3 as a spread.

8 Select the image on the left of page 2. Set the linked padding controls to **50** pt, then unlink them and reduce the Right padding to **15** pt. Repeat the process for the photo on the right side of page 2, but this time, reduce the Left padding to 15, rather than the Right.

9 Double-click the yellow frame below page 2 to see it enlarged in the Single Image view. Zoom the photo on the left to 70%; then, drag the image inside its cell padding to position it as shown in the illustration at the right. Zoom the photo on the right to 45%; then, reposition it as shown in the illustration. For a clearer view, click the gray space outside the page to deselect it.

10 In the Toolbar below the Single Image view, click the left navigation arrow to jump to page 1. The circular grille is slightly off-center; zoom the photo to 20% and drag in the photo cell to center the image on the page.

11 Click away from the page to deselect it, and then click the Multi-Page View button (⊞) in the Toolbar for an overview of the changes you've made.

Setting a page background

By default, all the pages in a new book share a plain white background. You can change the background color, set up a partially transparent backdrop image, or choose from a library of graphic motifs, applying your background design to the entire book, or just a selected page.

You can start by adding two more spreads to your book layout.

1   Right-click / Control-click page 4 and choose Add Page from the context menu. To apply the default layout to page 5, Right-click / Control-click page 5 and choose Add Page. Right-click / Control-click page 6 and choose Add Blank Page.

2   Click to select page 6 in the Multi-Page view, and then click the Spread View button (▭) in the Toolbar.

3   Expand the Background panel. Disable the option Apply Background Globally; then, drag the last photo in the Filmstrip, DSC_9777.jpg, to the preview pane in the Background panel. Drag the slider to set the opacity of the image to 50%.

> **Tip:** You can also apply a background image to a selected page (or pages) by dragging a photo directly onto the page background area from the Filmstrip, making sure not to drop the image into a photo cell.

4   Activate the Background Color option, and then click the adjacent color swatch to open the color picker. Drag the saturation slider at the right of the color picker about two thirds of the way up its range; then, drag the eyedropper cursor in the picker to find a muted tone; we chose a color with R, G, and B values of 70, 55, and 90, respectively. Click away from the color picker to close it.

5   In the Background panel, activate the Apply Background Globally option, and then click the Multi-Page View button (⊞) in the Toolbar.

Your background is applied to every page (except the Blurb logo page, where only the color is applied); it can be seen on page 7 and behind the images on page 2. On other pages, the background design is hidden behind photo cells.

6　Disable the Background Color option; then, right-click / Control-click the image in the background preview pane and choose Remove Image. Disable Apply Background Globally.

7　Select page 2 in the Multi-Page view, and then reactivate the Background Color option. Click the color swatch to open the color picker, and then click the black swatch at the top of the picker. Click away from the color picker to dismiss it.

8　Refresh the skills you've learned in this lesson by replicating the pages in the illustration below. You'll need to adjust photo cell padding on pages 5, 6, and 7.

Adding text to a photo book

There are several ways to add text to your pages in the Book module, each useful in different situations:

- Text cells that are built into page layout templates are fixed in position; they can't be deleted, moved, or resized, but you can use the adjustable cell padding to position text anywhere on a page.

- A *photo caption* is a text cell that is linked to a single image in the layout; a photo caption can be positioned above or below an image, or overlaid on the photo, and can be moved vertically on the page.

- A *page caption* is a text cell that is linked to the page as a whole, rather than any particular image. Page captions span the full width of the page; you can move them vertically, and then adjust the cell padding to position text horizontally, enabling you to place custom text anywhere in your layout.

On a single page, you can add a page caption, and a separate photo caption for each image—even if the page is based on a layout template that has no fixed text cells. Fixed text cells and photo captions can be configured for custom text, or set to display captions or titles extracted automatically from your photos' metadata.

The Book module incorporates state-of-the-art text tools that give you total control over every aspect of the text styling. Type attributes can be adjusted using sliders or numerical input, or tweaked visually with the Text Adjustment Tool.

Working with text cells

Text cells incorporated in a page layout template are fixed in place; you can't delete them, resize them, or move them on the page. Instead, you can use the adjustable cell padding—the space surrounding the text within its cell—to position text in your page layout exactly as you want it.

► **Tip:** To select a page or a spread, rather than the text and image cells in the layout, click near the edge of the thumbnail, or just below it.

1 Click the Multi-Page View button () to see your entire book layout; then, double-click below the cover spread to zoom in on the layout. Click in the center of the front cover to select the fixed text cell.

2 Expand the Type panel. Make sure that the Text Style Preset is set to Custom, to accommodate manually entered text, rather than metadata from the image.

3 Choose a font and type style from the menus below the preset setting. We chose American Typewriter, Regular. Click the Character color swatch to open the color picker; click the white swatch at the left of the row at the top of the picker; then, click away from the color picker to dismiss it. Set the type size to 70 pt, and leave the opacity set to 100%. Click the Align Center button at the lower left of the Type panel.

4 Type the words **in the**; then, press Enter / Return and type **detail**. Swipe to select the word detail, and then type in the Size text box to increase the size of the selected text to **140** pt.

5 Keeping the text selected, click the black triangle to the right of the Character color swatch to see the type attribute controls. Reduce the Leading—the spacing between the selected text and the line above it—to **100** pt.

► **Tip:** Once you've changed the Leading value, the Auto Leading button becomes available below the text adjustment controls, making it easy for you to quickly reinstate the default setting. The Auto Kerning button works the same way.

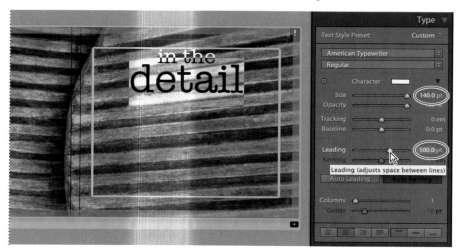

6   Click inside the text cell, but away from the text, to keep the cell selected while deselecting the text; then, expand the Cell panel. Disable the Link All option, and then increase the Top padding to **320** pt.

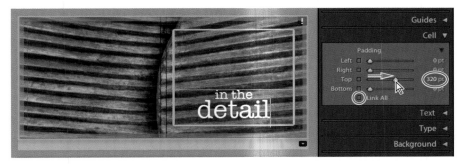

Fine-tuning type

In The Type panel, Lightroom incorporates a suite of sophisticated yet easy-to-use type tools that allow you detailed control over the text styling. You can use the adjustment sliders and numerical input to set type attributes in the Type panel, or tweak your text visually in any view using the intuitive Text Adjustment Tool.

1   Expand the Type panel and examine the four controls below the Size and Opacity sliders: Be sure to undo any changes you make at this stage.

- **Tracking** adjusts the letter spacing throughout a text selection. You can use tracking to change the overall appearance and readability of your text, making it look either more open or more dense.

- **Baseline** adjusts the vertical position of selected text relative to the baseline—the imaginary line on which the text sits.

- **Leading** adjusts the space between selected text and the line above it.

- **Kerning** adjusts the letter spacing between specific pairs of letters. Some pairings produce optical effects that cause letter spacing to appear uneven; place the text insertion cursor between two letters to adjust the kerning.

2   Swipe across all of the text in the front cover text cell to select it, and then click to activate the Text Adjustment Tool, to the left of the Character color setting in the Type panel.

3 Drag horizontally across the selection to adjust the text size. The adjustment is applied relatively; the different sizes of text are changed by relative amounts. Choose Edit > Undo or press Ctrl+Z / Command+Z to undo the change.

4 Drag vertically over the selection to adjust the leading; then, choose Edit > Undo or press Ctrl+Z / Command+Z to reverse the change.

5 Hold down the Alt / Option key—to temporarily disable the Text Adjustment Tool—and drag to select the words **in the**, leaving the word **detail** deselected; then, release the Alt / Option key and hold down the Ctrl / Command key as you drag horizontally over the selected text to increase the tracking slightly. Watch the Tracking control in the Type panel as you drag to set a value of **5** em.

6 Hold down the Alt / Option key and drag to select the word **the**, leaving the rest of the text deselected. Release the Alt / Option key, and then hold down the Ctrl / Command key and drag vertically over the selected text to shift it in relation to its baseline. Undo the change and click away from the text to deselect it.

7 If necessary, press F7, or choose Window > Panels > Show Left Module Panels. In the zoom ratio picker in the header of the Preview panel, click 1:1. Drag the white rectangle in the preview to focus on the front cover text. Make sure that the Text Adjustment Tool is still active; then, click once to position the text insertion cursor to the left of the word **in**. Drag to the right over the insertion point. Watch the Type panel as you drag to set a Kerning value of **135** em.

At this large point size, the first three letters of the word **detail** appear to be more loosely spaced than the last four.

8 Click once to place the insertion point between the letters **e** and **t**, and then drag to the left over the insertion point to set the Kerning value to **-30**. Set the Kerning value to **-40** for the **d-e** pair.

9 Click the Text Adjustment Tool in the Type panel to disable it; then, click the Multi-Page View button (⊞) in the Toolbar to see your entire book layout. Double-click page 1 to zoom to the Single Page view.

Working with captions

Unlike the fixed text cells built into layout templates, page and photo caption cells can be moved vertically; horizontal placement of captions is achieved by adjusting padding. Each page can include one page caption text cell and one photo caption cell for each photo on the page, even if the page template has no built-in text cell.

1   Right-click / Control-click the header of the Type panel and disable Solo Mode; then, leaving the Type panel open, expand the Text panel.

2   Move the pointer over page 1. The template for this page has no fixed text cell; hence, nothing is highlighted. Click the photo; then click the Add Photo Text button. In the Text panel, the Photo Text controls become active. Press Ctrl+Z / Command+Z to undo the photo caption. Now click the yellow footer below the photo; the Add Photo Text button changes to read Add Page Text. Click the Add Page Text button; the Page Text controls are activated in the Text panel.

3   To anchor the page caption to the top of the page, click the Top button in the Page Text controls; then, drag the Offset slider to set a value of **110** pt.

4   With the page caption active in the Single Page view, set up the Type panel as you did for steps 2 and 3 of the exercise "Working with text cells" on page 238, other than the size and leading. Set the size to **40** pt and click Auto Leading. Type whatever you like in the page caption, using the Enter/Return key to break the lines so that the text is shaped to fit the image, as in the illustration below.

> ▶ **Tip:** If you prefer, you can add a photo or page text caption by activating the respective option in the Text panel, rather than using the floating buttons.

> ● **Note:** Unlike fixed template text cells and photo captions, page captions can't be set to display information drawn from a photo's metadata; they can only be used for custom text.

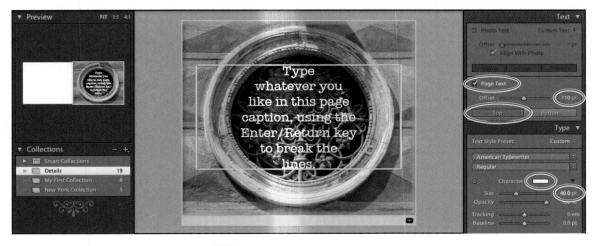

5   Click the Multi-Page View button (▦) in the Toolbar.

Creating a custom text preset

To save your text settings as a custom text preset, so that you can apply the same style elsewhere in your book, or re-use it in a different project, choose Save Current Settings As New Preset from the Text Style Preset menu in the Type panel.

Saving and re-using custom book page layouts

Once you've used cell padding and caption text to modify a page layout, you can save your design as a custom template that will be listed in the Page Layout menus.

1   Expand the Page panel; then, watch the layout thumbnail as you right-click / Control-click the page 1 preview and choose Save As Custom Page.

The original single-photo layout is overlaid by a text cell with the proportions and position of our page caption.

2   Click the Change Page Layout button (▼) below the lower right corner of the page preview, or to the right of the Page panel's layout thumbnail; the saved layout is listed in the Custom Pages category.

Another way to re-use the work you've put into a layout is to copy and paste it directly onto another page in your book, where you can use it as is, or make further modifications to the design. You'll find the Copy Layout and Paste Layout commands in the same context menu you used in step 1.

Creating a saved book

Since you entered the Book module, you've been working with an *unsaved book*, as is indicated in the bar across the top of the Book Editor work area.

Unsaved Book   Clear Book   Create Saved Book

Until you save your book layout, the Book module works like a scratch pad. You can move to another module, or even close Lightroom, and find your settings unchanged when you return, but if you need to clear the layout to begin another project, all your work will be lost.

Converting your project to a Saved Book not only preserves your work, but also links your book layout to the particular set of images for which it was designed.

Your photo book is saved as a special kind of collection—an *output collection*—with its own listing in the Collections panel. Clicking this listing will instantly retrieve the images you were working with, and reinstate all of your settings, no matter how many times the book layout scratch pad has been cleared.

1   Click the Create Saved Book button in the bar at the top of the preview pane, or click the New Collection button (⊕) in the header of the Collections panel and choose Create Book.

2   In the Create Book dialog box, type **Details Book** as the name for your saved layout. In the Placement options, activate Inside and choose the collection Details from the menu; then, click Create.

Your saved book appears in the Collections panel, marked with a Saved Book icon () and nested inside the source collection. The image count shows that the output collection includes only ten of the photos in the source collection. The bar above the work area shows the name of the book.

▶ **Tip:** Adding more images to your saved photo book is easy: simply drag photos to the book's listing in the Collections panel. To jump directly from the Library to your layout in the Book module, move the pointer over your saved book in the Collections panel and click the white arrow that appears to the right of the image count.

Depending on the way you like to work, you can save your book layout at any point in the process; you could create a Saved Book as soon as you enter the Book module with a selection of images, or wait until your design is finalized.

Once you've saved your book project, any further changes you make to the design are auto-saved as you work.

Copying a saved book

Your saved photo book design represents a lot of effort; if you want to go ahead and try something different, or add pages and photos without a clear idea of what you'd like to achieve, you can duplicate your output collection and make changes to the copy without the risk of losing your work thus far.

1   Right-click / Control-click your saved book in the Collections panel and choose Duplicate Book from the context menu.

If you're happy with your extended design, you can delete the original saved book, and then rename the duplicate.

2   Right-click / Control-click the original saved book in the Collections panel and choose Delete from the context menu; then, confirm the deletion.

3   Right-click / Control-click the duplicated book in the Collections panel and choose Rename from the context menu. In the Rename Book dialog box, delete the word Copy from the end of the book's name, and then click Rename.

Exporting a photo book

You can upload your book to Blurb.com, or export it to PDF and print it at home.

1   To publish your photo book to Blurb.com, click the Send Book To Blurb button below the right panel group.

2   In the Purchase Book dialog box, either sign in to Blurb.com with your email address and password, or click "Not A Member?" in the lower left corner and register to get started.

3   Enter a book title, subtitle, and author name. You'll see an alert at this stage warning that your book must contain at least twenty pages; the Upload button is disabled. Click Cancel, or sign out of Blurb.com first, and then cancel.

Books published to Blurb must have between 20 and 240 pages, not including the front and back covers. Blurb.com prints at 300 dpi; if a photo's resolution is less than 300 dpi, an exclamation point badge (!) appears in the upper-right corner of the image cell in the work area. Click the exclamation point to find out what print resolution can be achieved for that photo. Blurb.com recommends a minimum of 200 dpi for optimum quality.

For help with printing, pricing, ordering, and other Blurb.com issues, visit the-Blurb.com Customer Support page.

4   To export your photo book as a PDF file, first choose PDF from the Book menu at the top of the Book Settings panel. Examine the controls that appear in the lower half of the Book Settings panel. You can leave the JPEG Quality, Color Profile, File Resolution, Sharpening, and Media Type settings unchanged for now. Click the Export Book To PDF button below the right panel group.

5   In the Save dialog box, type InTheDetail as the name for the exported book. Navigate to your LR5CIB > Lessons > Lesson 7 folder, and then click Save.

6   To export your Blurb photo book as a PDF file for proofing purposes, leave the Book selection set to Blurb and click the Export Book To PDF button below the left panel group.

Well done! You've successfully completed another Lightroom lesson. In this lesson you learned how to put together an attractive photo book to showcase your images.

In the process, you've explored the Book module and used the control panels to customize page templates, refine the layout, set a backdrop, and add text.

In the next chapter you'll find out how to present your work in a dynamic slide-show, but before you move on, take a few moments to reinforce what you've learned by reading through the review questions and answers on the next page.

Review questions

1 How do you modify a photo book page layout?

2 What options are available for page numbering?

3 What is cell padding and how is it used?

4 What text attributes are affected by the Tracking, Baseline, Leading, and Kerning controls in the Type panel?

5 How can you use the Text Adjustment Tool to fine-tune text?

Review answers

1 Click the Change Page Layout button ( ) to the right of the layout preview thumbnail in the Page panel, or in the lower right corner of a selected page or spread displayed in the work area. Choose a layout category, and then click a layout thumbnail to apply that template. Use cell padding to tweak the layout.

2 Page numbering can be activated in the Page panel, where you can also set the global position for the numbers. Use the Type panel to set text style attributes. Right-click / Control-click a page number to apply the style globally, hide the number on a given page, or have the page numbering start on a page other than page 1.

3 Cell padding is the adjustable space around an image or text within its cell; it can be used to position text or a photo anywhere on the page. In combination with the Zoom slider, photo cell padding can be used to crop an image any way you wish.

4 Tracking adjusts the letter spacing throughout a text selection. You can use tracking to change the overall appearance and readability of your text, making it look either more open or more dense. The Baseline setting shifts selected text vertically in relation to the baseline. The Leading control affects the space between selected text and the line above it. Kerning adjusts the letter spacing between specific pairs of letters.

5 Drag horizontally across selected text to adjust the text size. Drag vertically over the selection to increase or decrease the leading (line spacing). Hold down the Ctrl / Command key as you drag horizontally over selected text to adjust the tracking. Hold down the Ctrl / Command key and drag vertically over a text selection to shift it in relation to its baseline. Hold down the Alt / Option key to temporarily disable the Text Adjustment Tool when you wish to change the text selection. Click between a pair of letters to place the text insertion cursor, and then drag horizontally across the text insertion point to adjust kerning.

PHOTOGRAPHY SHOWCASE
CARSTEN SCHAEL

"Photography is the challenge to grab the eye
and then have the mind follow."

The inspiration for my personal work is all around me in every day Hong Kong life. The city is a mixing bowl of extremes in which I wander around and constantly sample the results of its energetic hustle.

"FAI DI! FAI DI! (Hurry! Hurry!) is the colloquial Cantonese phrase that describes the rush which is part of local life, always maximizing time and space. My images explore the omnipresent visual density, then tweaking the captured RAW data allows me to create the tonal compression, which further dramatizes the scenes.

Color and texture are part of my signature style in personal and commercial work. Therefore food photography plays to my visual sensibilities. The dish, as a result of the chef's creativity and precision, produces this most interesting still life subject; its fleeting beauty has to be captured within seconds, or at most minutes.

In all my photography I like to start with a plan that addresses all the relevant components of a shoot (concept, technique, execution) and therefore being well prepared, something which I teach my students at the Polytechnic University, will help to take more chances once the shooting begins. Then again, if chance provides unforeseen opportunities, leaving all the preparation behind can be equally important.

The unexpected is often the muse for more creative work.

www.carstenschael.com

FAI DI! FAI DI! (HURRY! HURRY!), #04

TIGER PRAWN

OYSTER SHOOTERS

FAI DI! FAI DI! (HURRY! HURRY!), #02

FAI DI! FAI DI! (HURRY! HURRY!), #07

8 CREATING A SLIDESHOW

Lesson overview

Once you've spent time bringing out the best in your images, showing them off in a slideshow is one of the easiest and most effective ways to share your photos with friends and family or to present them to a client. Choose a template as a starting point; then customize the layout, color scheme, and timing. Add backdrops, borders, text overlays—even music and video—to create a dynamic presentation that will complement your work and captivate your audience.

In this lesson, you'll create your own slideshow by following these easy steps:

- Grouping the images for your slideshow as a collection
- Choosing a slideshow template
- Adjusting the slide layout and setting a backdrop image
- Adding a text overlay
- Adding music and adjusting the playback settings
- Saving your slideshow and your customized template
- Exporting your presentation
- Viewing an impromptu slideshow

 You'll probably need between one and two hours to complete this lesson. If you haven't already done so, download the Lesson 8 work files from the Lesson & Update Files tab on your Account page at www.peachpit.com.

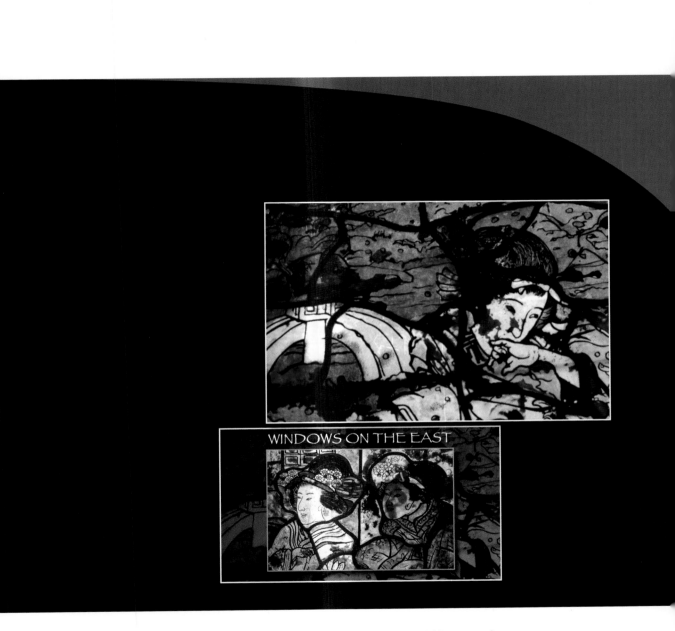

In the Slideshow module you can quickly put together
an impressive on-screen presentation complete with
stylish graphic effects, transitions, text, music, and
even video. Lightroom makes it easier than ever to
share your images with family and friends, clients, or
the world at large by giving you the option of exporting your slideshow to PDF or video.

Getting started

Note: This lesson assumes that you already have a basic working familiarity with the Lightroom workspace. If you find that you need more background information, refer to Lightroom Help, or review the previous lessons.

Before you start on this lesson, make sure you've set up the LR5CIB folder for your lesson files and created the LR5CIB Catalog file to manage them, as described in "Setting up a work folder" and "Creating a catalog file for working with this book" in the Getting Started chapter at the beginning of this book.

If you haven't already done so, download the Lesson 8 folder from your Account page at www.peachpit.com to the LR5CIB/Lessons folder, as detailed in the section "Accessing the Classroom in a Book files" in the chapter "Getting Started."

1   Start Lightroom.

2   In the Adobe Photoshop Lightroom - Select Catalog dialog box, make sure that the file LR5CIB Catalog.lrcat is selected under Select A Recent Catalog To Open, and then click Open.

Tip: If you can't see the Module Picker, choose Window > Panels > Show Module Picker, or press the F5 key. If you're working on Mac OS, you may need to press the fn key together with the F5 key, or change the function key behavior in the system preferences.

3   Lightroom will open in the screen mode and workspace module that were active when you last quit. If necessary, switch to the Library module by clicking Library in the Module Picker at the top of the workspace.

Lightroom   File   Edit   Library   Photo   Metadata   View   Window   Help

LR5CIB Catalog.lrcat – Adobe Photoshop Lightroom – Library

Lr Adobe Photoshop Lightroom 5   **Library** Develop | Map | Book | Slideshow | Print | Web

Importing images into the library

The first step is to import the images for this lesson into the Lightroom library.

1   In the Library module, click the Import button below the left panel group.

2 If the Import dialog box appears in compact mode, click the Show More Options button at the lower left of the dialog box to see all the options in the expanded Import dialog box.

3 At the top of the Source panel, just below the Select A Source menu, activate the Include Subfolders option; then, navigate to and select the LR5CIB > Lessons > Lesson 8 folder. Ensure that all twelve images are checked for import.

4 In the import options above the thumbnail previews, select Add so that the imported photos will be added to your catalog without being moved or copied. Under File Handling at the right of the expanded Import dialog box, choose Minimal from the Render Previews menu and ensure that the Don't Import Suspected Duplicates option is activated. Under Apply During Import, choose None from both the Develop Settings menu and the Metadata menu and type **Lesson 8, Japan, Art** in the Keywords text box. Make sure that your import is set up as shown in the illustration below, and then click Import.

The twelve images are imported from the Japan 1 and Japan 2 subfolders inside the Lesson 8 folder and now appear in the Grid view of the Library module and also in the Filmstrip across the bottom of the Lightroom workspace.

Assembling photos for a slideshow

▶ **Tip:** In the latest version of Lightroom, you can include video as well as still images in your slideshow.

The first step in creating a slideshow is to assemble the images you wish to include. Having just been imported, the images for this lesson are already isolated from the rest of your catalog. In the Catalog panel, the Previous Import folder is selected as the active image source.

Although you could move to the Slideshow module now, the result would be less than ideal. The Previous Import folder is merely a temporary grouping and, as an image source, it is not flexible—you can't rearrange the images inside it, or exclude a photo from your slideshow without removing it from the catalog entirely.

1 In the Folders panel, click to select the Lesson 8 folder. If you don't see the twelve lesson images in the Grid view and the Filmstrip, activate the option Show Photos In Subfolders in the Library menu.

2 In the Grid view or the Filmstrip, drag any of the lesson images to a new position in the group. An alert message appears to let you know that you can't reorder the images in a folder that contains subfolders; click OK to dismiss it.

If the selected image source for your slideshow was a folder without subfolders, you *would* be able to rearrange photos in the Grid view or the Filmstrip to create a custom order for your slideshow, but you would still not be able to exclude an image without removing it from the catalog.

▶ **Tip:** You can reorder photos in a collection by simply dragging the thumbnails in the Grid view or the Filmstrip. Your custom display order will be saved with the collection.

The solution is to create a collection to group the photos for your project, where you can rearrange the image order—just as you can with a single folder—and also remove an image from the virtual grouping, without deleting it from your catalog. A collection has a permanent listing in the Collections panel, making it easy to retrieve the set of images you've assembled at any time, even if they're stored across multiple folders, as is often the case for the results of a complex search.

3 Check that the Lesson 8 folder is still selected in the Folders panel; then, press Ctrl+A / Command+A or choose Edit > Select All. Click the New Collection button (➕) in the header of the Collections panel and choose Create Collection from the menu. In the Create Collection dialog box, type **Japan** as the name for the new collection, and make sure that the option Inside A Collection Set is disabled under Location. Activate the Include Selected Photos option and disable Make New Virtual Copies and Set As Target Collection; then, click Create.

Your new collection appears in the Collections panel, where it is automatically selected as the active image source. The image count indicates that the Japan collection contains twelve photos.

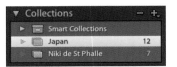

4 Choose Edit > Select None; then, press Ctrl+Alt+5 / Option+Command+5, or click Slideshow in the Module Picker to switch to the Slideshow module.

Working in the Slideshow module

At center stage in the Slideshow module is the Slide Editor view where you'll work on your slide layouts and preview your slideshow in operation.

In the left panel group, the Preview panel displays a thumbnail preview of whichever layout template is currently selected (or under the pointer) in the Template Browser panel, while the Collections panel provides easy access to your photos.

Tip: The first time you enter any of the Lightroom modules, you'll see tips that help you identify the components of the workspace and understand the workflow order. You can dismiss the tips by clicking the Close button. To reactivate the tips for any module, choose [*Module name*] Tips from the Help menu.

The Toolbar below the Slide Editor view offers controls for navigating through the images in your collection, previewing the slideshow, and adding text to your slides.

The settings and controls in the right panel group enable you to customize the selected template by tweaking the layout, adding borders, shadows, and overlays, changing the backdrop, adding title screens, and adjusting the playback settings.

Note: Your preview may look slightly different from the illustration, depending on the size and proportions of your computer display.

Choosing a slideshow template

Each of the preset Lightroom slideshow templates incorporates a different combination of layout settings, such as image size, borders, backgrounds, shadows, and text overlays that can be customized to create your own slide designs.

▶ **Tip:** The Plus sign (+) after the name of the Default template is not part of the name but denotes that this is the template that will be used when you launch the Impromptu Slideshow from another module. To designate a different template for this purpose, right-click / Control-click its name in the Template Browser and choose Use For Impromptu Slideshow.

1 In the Template Browser panel, expand the Lightroom Templates folder, if necessary; then, move the pointer slowly up and down the list of Lightroom templates. The Preview panel shows you how the selected image looks in each template layout. Select a different image in the Filmstrip, and then preview the templates again.

2 When you're done previewing the options in the Template Browser, click to select the Widescreen template.

3 In the Toolbar, right below the slide preview, choose All Filmstrip Photos from the Use menu. In the Filmstrip, select the first image, SlideShow-01.jpg.

4 Click the Preview button at the bottom of the right panel group to preview your presentation in the Slide Editor view. When you're done, press the Esc key on your keyboard, or click in the Slide Editor view to stop the preview.

Template options for slideshows

As a convenient starting-point for creating your own slide layouts, you can choose from these customizable Lightroom templates:

Caption And Rating This template centers the images on a grey background and displays the star rating and caption metadata for each photo.

Crop To Fill Your photos fill the screen and may be cropped to fit the screen's aspect ratio, so this is probably not a good option for images in portrait format.

Default This template centers your photographs on a black background and incorporates your custom identity plate.

EXIF Metadata The slides are centered on a black background and include star-ratings, EXIF (Exchangeable Image Format) information, and your identity plate.

Widescreen Your images are centered and sized to fit the screen without being cropped: any empty space outside the image is filled with black.

Customizing your slideshow template

For the purposes of this lesson, you won't be adding an identity plate or metadata information to your slides, so the Widescreen template will serve as a good basis. You'll customize the template by tweaking the layout, creating a background, and overlaying text, and then liven up the show by adding a soundtrack.

Adjusting the slide layout

Once you've chosen a slide template, you can use the controls in the right panel group to customize it. For this project you'll start by modifying the layout, and then change the background to set up the overall look of the design before you make decisions about the style and color of borders and overlaid text. The Layout panel enables you to change the size and position of the photo in the slide layout by setting the margins that define the image cell.

1 If the Layout panel in the right panel group is currently collapsed, expand it by clicking the triangle beside its name. Make sure that the Show Guides and Link All options are activated.

> **Tip:** Video clips in a slideshow are placed in your slide layout in the same way as still images, complete with borders and shadows.

2 Move the pointer over the lower edge of the image in the Slide Editor view. When the pointer changes to a double-arrow cursor, drag the edge of the image upwards. As you drag, grey layout guide lines appear against the black background around the scaled-down image. All four guides move at the same time because the Link All option is activated in the Layout panel. As you drag upwards, watch the linked sliders and numerical values change in the Layout panel and release the mouse button when the values reach 75 px (pixels).

> **Tip:** You could also drag the sliders in the Layout panel, or click the pixel values and type new numbers, to adjust the size of the image in the slide layout. With the settings linked, you only need to drag one slider or enter one value. Remember that the proportions of your slides may differ from what you see in the illustrations in this lesson, depending on the aspect ratio of your computer display.

Now you can increase the width of the slide's top margin to create a space where you can add text later in the lesson.

3 In the Layout panel, disable the Link All option, and then either drag the Top slider to the right, type over the adjacent pixel value, or drag the top guide in the Slide Editor, to set a value of 150 px (pixels). Disable the Show Guides option, and then collapse the Layout panel.

Setting up the slide background

● **Note:** When all three of the backdrop options are disabled, the slide background is black.

▶ **Tip:** You can also drag an image from the Filmstrip directly onto the slide background in the Slide Editor view.

In the Backdrop panel you can set a flat background color for your slides, apply a graduated color wash, or place a background image—you can even mix all three elements to create an atmospheric frame for your photos.

1 In the Filmstrip, select any image other than the third photo in the series.

2 If necessary, expand the Backdrop panel in the right panel group. Activate the Background Image option, and then drag the third image, SlideShow-03.jpg, from the Filmstrip into the Background Image pane. Drag the Opacity slider to the left to reduce the value to 70%, or click the Opacity value and type **70**.

With the Background Color option disabled, the default black background shows through the partially transparent image, effectively darkening it. However, the background is still competing too much with the featured photos. You can use the Color Wash feature to create an angled lighting effect that will darken the backdrop a little more. Color Wash applies a graduated wash that fades from whatever color is set in the Color Wash swatch to the background color or image.

3 Activate the Color Wash option. Click the Color Wash swatch, and then click the black swatch in the row at the upper right of the Color Picker.

4 Click the Close button at the upper left of the Color Picker, and then use the Opacity slider to set the color wash opacity to **75%**. Set the Angle of the wash to **135°**. When you're done, collapse the Backdrop panel.

With the background photo set to partial transparency, your backdrop design is now a composite of all three optional elements: a graduated color wash, an image, and the default background color.

▶ **Tip:** A sophisticated backdrop design that includes a related background image can be a stylish and effective way to create an overall theme or atmosphere for your slideshow.

Adjusting stroke borders and shadows

Now that you've established the overall layout and feel for your slides, you can "lift" the images to make them stand out more against the background by adding a thin stroke border and a drop shadow. We'll choose a border color that will provide a contrast to the predominately blue backdrop.

1 In the right panel group, expand the Options panel. Activate the Stroke Border option, and then click the color swatch beside it to open the Color Picker.

2 To set a dull gold color for the stroke border, click to select the R, G, and B percentages at the lower right of the Color Picker in turn and type values of **65**, **50**, and **20** respectively. Click outside the Color Picker to close it.

3 Use the Width slider to set a width of 4 pixels or type **4** in the text box.

4 Activate the Cast Shadow option in the Options panel and experiment with the controls. You can adjust the opacity of the shadow, the distance the shadow is offset from the image, the angle at which it is cast, and the Radius setting, which affects the softness of the shadow's edge. When you're done, set the controls as in the illustration at the right, and then collapse the Options panel.

Adding a text overlay

● **Note:** For this exercise, you won't incorporate an identity plate or watermark in your slideshow. For more information on identity plates, refer to Lesson 2, Lesson 10, or the Lightroom Help topic "Add your identity plate to a slideshow."

In the Overlays panel you can add text, an identity plate, or a watermark to your slides and have Lightroom display the rating stars you've assigned to your images or the captions that you've added to their metadata. In this exercise, you'll add a simple headline that will be overlaid on the background for every slide.

1 Expand the Overlays panel and activate the Text Overlays option.

2 If the Toolbar is not visible just below the Slide Editor view, press the T key. In the Toolbar, click the Add Text To Slide button (ABC).

3 Type **WINDOWS ON THE EAST** in the Custom Text box.

4 Press Enter / Return. The text appears in the lower left corner of the slide, surrounded by a bounding box. The Text Overlays settings are updated to show the default font details (Myriad Web Pro is selected in the illustration below).

5 Click the double triangle beside the font name and choose a different font. We chose Papyrus, but Optima or even Lithos Pro would suit our design. From the Face menu, we chose Regular.

6 Drag the text upwards and allow it to attach itself to the anchor at the center of the upper edge of the slide. Drag the handle at the bottom of the text bounding box downwards to scale the text to the width of the photo; then, use the up and down arrow keys to center the text vertically in the space above the image.

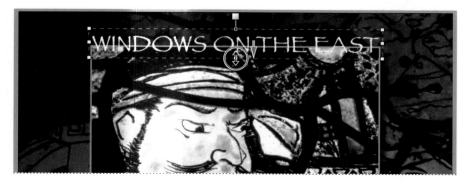

As you drag text on a slide layout, Lightroom tethers the bounding box either to the nearest of various reference points around the edge of the slide, or to a point on the border of the image itself.

7 To see this in operation, drag the text around the slide, both inside and outside of the image, and watch the white tether-line jump from point to point. When you're done, return the text to its original position.

Throughout a slideshow, the tethered text will maintain the same position either relative to the slide as a whole or to the border of each image, whatever its shape.

You can use this feature to ensure that photo-specific caption text, for instance, will always appear just below the left corner of each image no matter what its size or orientation, while a title that applies to the presentation as a whole—as does the text in our example—will remain in a constant position on the screen. In the latter case, the text is tethered to one of the anchors around the edge of the slide; in the former, the text would be tethered to an anchor on the border of the feature image.

The color and opacity controls in the Text Overlays operate just as they do for the Color Wash and Stroke Border. For this exercise, we'll use the default white at 100% opacity. On Mac OS, you can also set up a drop shadow for your text.

8 Collapse the Overlays panel and deselect the text box in the Slideshow Editor.

9 Select the first slide in the Filmstrip and click the Preview button at the bottom of the right panel group to preview your slideshow in the Slideshow Editor view. When you're done, press Esc to stop playback.

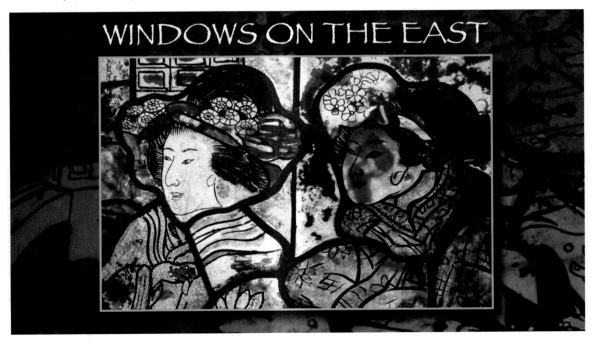

Using the Text Template Editor

In the Slideshow module, you can use the Text Template Editor to access and edit the information stored as metadata in your photos—and to specify which elements of that information you would like to display as text overlays on each slide.

You can add titles or display captions, capture dates, image sizes, or any of numerous other options, and then save your choices as a text template preset. Stream-line and automate your workflow by creating presets with different sets of information to suit different types of presentation.

In the Slideshow module, click the Add Text To Slide button (ABC) in the Toolbar. Type anything at all in the Custom Text box and press Enter / Return. The text appears as an overlay in the Slide Editor. Make sure the text overlay is selected; then click the double triangle beside the Custom Text box in the Toolbar and choose Edit from the menu.

The Text Template Editor appears. In the Example text box, you will see a Custom Text *token*.

A token is a placeholder for whatever custom text you wish to specify. If you did not specify any other content for the token in the Text Template Editor the token would represent whatever custom text you already entered in the Toolbar.

Double-click the token to select the text and type anything you wish. Click Done and the new custom text replaces the original in the Slide Editor view.

Open the Text Template Editor again by clicking the double triangle beside the Custom Text box in the Toolbar and choosing Edit from the menu. This time you will replace the custom text with another token chosen from the options in the Text Template Editor. Select the custom text in the Example box and delete it. In the Image Name options, click the top Insert button. A Filename token appears in the Example box. Click Done and the file name appears in the Slide Editor view.

Drag the file name overlay to the upper left corner of the slide and click outside the bounding box to deselect it. Click the Add Text To Slide button (ABC) in the Toolbar; then click the double triangle beside the Custom Text box and choose Edit from the menu. The text "untitled" appears on the slide as a new text overlay. In the Text Template Editor, delete the new Custom Text token in the Example box and choose Image # (01) from the upper menu in the Numbering options. Click the Insert button at the right of the menu to add the new numbering token; then, click Done and the image number (in two-digit format) replaces the text "untitled" on the slide in the Slide Editor view.

(continues on next page)

Using the Text Template Editor (continued)

In this way you can create as many text overlays as you wish and each text overlay can contain more than one token. Change the font, color and other options for your overlays using the Text Overlays controls in the Overlays panel. Scale the text by dragging the handles of the bounding box.

Explore the options in the Text Template Editor:

Preset menu Apply, save, delete, or rename presets, which are saved sets of information tokens customized for different presentation purposes.

Image Name Specify a text string containing the filename, folder name, or a custom name.

Numbering Number the slideshow images and display image capture dates in various formats.

EXIF Data Choose from Exchangeable Image Format data including image dimensions, exposure, flash settings and numerous other options.

IPTC Data Choose from International Press Telecommunications Council data including copyright and creator details and numerous other options.

Custom Add a custom text string.

For more details on using the Text Template Editor please refer to Lightroom Help.

Creating a Saved Slideshow

Since you entered the Slideshow module, you've been working with an *unsaved slideshow*, as is indicated in the bar across the top of the Slideshow Editor view.

Unsaved Slideshow	Create Saved Slideshow

Until you save your slideshow, the Slideshow module works like a scratch pad. You can move to another module, or even close Lightroom, and find your settings unchanged when you return, but if you click a new slideshow template—or even the one you started with—in the Template Browser, the "scratch pad" will be cleared and all your work will be lost.

Converting your project to a Saved Slideshow not only preserves your layout and playback settings, but also links your design to the particular set of images for which it was designed. Your slideshow is saved as a special kind of collection—an *output collection*—with its own listing in the Collections panel. Clicking this listing will instantly retrieve the images you were working with, and reinstate all of your settings, no matter how many times the slideshow scratch pad has been cleared.

▶ **Tip:** Once you've saved your slideshow, any changes you make to the layout or playback settings are auto-saved as you work.

1 Click the Create Saved Slideshow button in the bar at the top of the Slideshow Editor view, or click the New Collection button (⊕) in the header of the Collections panel and choose Create Slideshow.

▶ **Tip:** The Make New Virtual Copies option is useful if you wish to apply a particular treatment, such as a developing preset, to all the pictures in your slideshow, without affecting the photos in the source collection.

2 In the Create Slideshow dialog box, type Japan Slideshow as the name for your saved presentation. In the Placement options, activate Inside and choose the collection Japan from the associated menu; then, click Create.

▶ **Tip:** Adding more photos to your saved slideshow is easy: simply drag images to the slideshow's listing in the Collections panel. Click the white arrow that appears to the right of the image count when you move the pointer over your saved slideshow in the Collections panel to jump from the Library to your presentation in the Slideshow module.

Your saved slideshow appears in the Collections panel, marked with a Saved Slideshow icon (▣), and nested inside the original source collection, Japan. The image count shows that the new output collection, like the source, contains twelve photos.

The title bar above the Slide Editor now displays the name of your saved slideshow, and no longer presents the Create Saved Slideshow button.

Depending on the way you like to work, you can save your slideshow at any point in the process; you could create a Saved Slideshow as soon as you enter the Slideshow module with a selection of images or wait until your presentation is polished.

For the purposes of this lesson, saving the project at this stage enables you delete and rearrange slides to refine your presentation, without affecting the source collection—any image you exclude from the slideshow now will be removed from the Japan Slideshow output collection, but will remain a part of your Japan collection.

This could be useful if you also intended to use the photos in the Japan collection to produce a print layout and a web gallery, for instance—your original collection will remain intact, while the output collection for each project might contain a different subset of images, arranged in a different order.

Refining your slideshow

It's a good idea to finalize the photo set for your slideshow at this point, before you go on to specify playback settings—if you remove an image later, you might need to readjust the time allocated for each slide and transition, especially if your slideshow is timed to match the duration of a sound file.

1 In the Filmstrip, right-click / Control-click the image SlideShow-03.jpg—the photo you used as a background image—and choose Remove From Collection.

Note that although the photo disappears from the Filmstrip, and will not feature on any slide in the presentation it is not removed from the slide background in the Slide Editor view. The background image has become part of the slide layout, rather than merely one of the selection photos to be displayed. Even if you "re-fill" your slideshow with a different set of photos entirely, the background image will remain in place. Your saved slideshow includes a link to the photo that is independent of the output collection or its parent collection.

In the Collections panel, the nested Japan Slideshow output collection now shows an image count of eleven photos, while its parent collection still contains the original count of twelve.

2   In the Filmstrip, drag the photo SlideShow-07 to a new position between the images SlideShow-05 and SlideShow-06, releasing the mouse button when the black insertion bar appears.

Adjusting the playback settings

Now that you've finalized the photo set for the slideshow, you can go ahead and fine-tune your presentation by specifying the playback settings.

In the Playback panel you can add a soundtrack to your presentation, set the duration for slides and transitions, or set the slideshow to display your images in random order. Adding a soundtrack can make your slideshow much more dynamic and compelling, so let's start with that.

Adding music to your slideshow

You'll find a sound file named Shogun.m4a in your Lesson 8 folder. This piece of music will underline the Japanese theme of the slideshow. However, feel free to choose any other file from your music library that you'd like to audition.

1   Expand the Playback panel in the right panel group, and then activate the Audio option.

2   Click the Select Music button; then, navigate to your LR5CIB > Lessons > Lesson 8 folder, select the file Shogun.m4a, and click Open / Choose.

> **Tip:** If you have a second display attached to your computer, you'll see the Playback Screen pane in the Playback panel. You can choose which screen will be used when your slide-show is played at full screen and whether to blank the other screens during playback.

Tip: The Audio pane in the Playback panel incorporates an Audio Balance slider that enables you to mix your soundtrack music with the audio from video clips in your slideshow.

The name of the sound file and its duration are now displayed in the Audio pane of the Playback panel.

3   Click the Preview button at the bottom of the right panel group to preview the slideshow in the Slideshow Editor view. The new soundtrack adds atmosphere to the slideshow. When you're done, press Esc to stop playback.

The next step is to fine-tune the timing of the slideshow by setting the duration of slides and fades to match the length of the music file.

4   In the Audio pane, click the Fit To Music button, keeping an eye on the default Slides and Fades values in the Slide Duration settings towards the bottom of the Playback panel as you do so.

Lightroom adjusts the Slides and Fades values to fit the duration of the music file.

5   Drag the Fades slider to the right to increase the duration of the fade transitions to 4 seconds, and then click the Fit To Music button once more, keeping an eye on the Slides value in the Slide Duration settings as you do so.

Lightroom automatically re-calculates the duration for which each slide will be shown so that the slideshow still fits the music file despite the lengthened fades.

6   At the bottom of the Playback panel, disable Random Order and Repeat.

7   Select the first photo in the Filmstrip, and then click the Play button at the bottom of the right panel group to see the slideshow in full-screen mode. Press the spacebar to pause and resume playback, and then press the Esc key to end the slideshow.

Saving a customized slideshow template

Having spent so much time customizing your slideshow template, you should now save it so that it becomes available as a new choice in the Template Browser menu.

This is different from saving your slideshow, as you did earlier.

A saved slideshow is actually an output collection—an arranged grouping of images, saved together with a slide layout, text overlays, and playback settings. In contrast, a saved custom template records only your slide layout and playback settings—it is an empty container that is not linked to any particular set of images.

Saving your customized slideshow template will save you a lot of time later should you wish to put together a related presentation, or simply use the template as a starting point for creating a new design.

Modifying and organizing user templates

The Template Browser offers numerous options for organizing your templates and template folders:

Renaming a template or template folder
You cannot rename the Lightroom Templates folder, any of the Lightroom templates, or the default User Templates folder. To rename any of the templates or template folders that you have created, right-click / Control-click the template or folder in the Template Browser and choose Rename from the context menu.

Moving a template
If you wish to move a template into another folder in the Template Browser, simply drag the template to that folder. If you wish to move a template into a new folder, right-click / Control-click the template and choose New Folder from the context menu. The selected template will be moved into the new folder as it is created. If you try to move one of the Lightroom templates, the template will be copied to the new folder but will still remain in the Lightroom Templates folder.

Updating a custom template's settings
If you wish to modify one of your own custom templates select it in the Template Browser and make your changes using any of the controls in the right panel group. To save your changes, right-click / Control-click the template in the Template Browser and choose Update with Current Settings.

Creating a copy of a template
You may wish to create a copy of a template so that you can safely make modifications without affecting the original. If you wish to create a copy of the currently selected template in an existing template folder, click the Create New Preset button (+) in the Template Browser panel header. In the New Template dialog box, type a name for the copy, choose the destination folder from the Folder menu, and click Create. If you wish to create a copy of the currently selected template in a new folder, click the Create New Preset button (+) in the Template Browser panel header. In the New Template dialog box, type a name for the copy and choose New Folder from the Folder menu. In the New Folder dialog box, type a name for the new folder and click Create. The new folder appears in the Template Browser. Click Create in the New Template dialog box to dismiss it. The copied template will be created in the new folder.

Exporting a custom template
To export your custom slideshow template so that you can use it in Lightroom on another computer, right-click / Control-click the template name in the Template Browser menu and choose Export from the context menu.

Importing a custom template
To import a custom template that has been created in Lightroom on another computer, right-click / Control-click the User Templates header or any of the templates in the User Templates menu and choose Import from the context menu. In the Import Template dialog box, locate the template file and click Import.

(continues on next page)

Modifying and organizing user templates (continued)

Deleting a template

To delete a custom template, right-click / Control-click the template name in the Template Browser and choose Delete from the context menu. You can also select the template and click the Delete Selected Preset button in the header of the Template Browser. You cannot delete the templates in the Lightroom Templates folder.

Creating a new templates folder

To create a new empty folder in the Templates Browser, right-click / Control-click the header of any other folder and choose New Folder from the context menu. You can drag templates into the new folder.

Deleting a templates folder

To delete a template folder, you'll first need to delete all the templates within that folder—or drag them to another folder. Right-click / Control-click the empty folder, and choose Delete Folder from the context menu.

By default, your customized template will be listed with the User Templates in the Template Browser panel.

1   With your slideshow still open, click the Create New Preset button (⊕) in the header of the Template Browser panel, or choose Slideshow > New Template.

► **Tip:** When saving a customized template it's a good idea to give it a descriptive name. This will make it easier to find as you add more choices to the Template Browser menu.

2   In the New Template dialog box, type **Centered Title** as the new template name. Leaving the default User Templates folder selected as the destination folder in the Folder menu, click Create.

Your new customized template is now listed under User Templates in the Template Browser panel.

Exporting a slideshow

To send your slideshow to a friend or client, play it on another computer, or share it on the Web, you can export it as a PDF file or as a high-quality video file.

1   In the Slideshow module, click the Export PDF button at the bottom of the left panel group.

2 Review the options available in the Export Slideshow To PDF dialog box, noting the settings for size and quality, and then click Cancel.

● **Note:** PDF slide-show transitions work when viewed using the free Adobe Reader® or Adobe Acrobat®. However, slideshows exported to PDF will not include music, random-ized playback order, or your customized slide duration settings.

3 Repeat the process for the Export Video button. Review the Export Slideshow To Video dialog box, noting the range of options available in the Video Preset menu. Select each export option in turn to see a brief description below the Video Preset menu.

Lightroom exports slideshows in the mp4 movie format so that you can share your slideshow movies on popular video sharing sites or optimize them for playback on mobile media. Preset size and quality settings range from 320 x 240, optimized for personal media players and email, to 1080p, optimized for high quality HD video.

4 In the Export Slideshow To Video dialog box, type a name for your exported video and specify a destination folder. Choose an option from the Video Preset menu, and then click Export.

A progress bar in the upper left corner of the workspace shows the status of the export process.

Playing an impromptu slideshow

Even outside the Slideshow module you can play an impromptu slideshow. In the Library module, for instance, this makes a convenient way to see a full-screen preview of the photos you've just imported.

The Impromptu Slideshow can be launched from any of the Lightroom modules. The slide layout, timing, and transitions for the Impromptu Slideshow will depend on the template currently set in the Slideshow module for use with the Impromptu Slideshow.

▶ **Tip:** To change the slideshow template used for the impromptu slideshow, right-click / Control-click a template in the Slideshow module Template Browser and choose Use For Impromptu Slideshow.

1 Switch to the Library module.

2 Use the Sort menu in the Grid view Toolbar to set the sorting order to either Capture Time or File Name. Choose View > Sort > Ascending, or click the Sort Direction button ([A/Z]) beside the Sort menu, if necessary, to set an ascending sort direction (the Sort Direction button should show an "A" above a "Z").

3 Press Ctrl+A / Command+A or choose Edit > Select All to select all of the images that you've just imported.

4 Choose Window > Impromptu Slideshow or press Ctrl+Enter / Command+Return to start the impromptu slideshow.

5 Use the spacebar to pause and resume playback. The slideshow will repeat, cycling through the selected images until you either press the Esc key on your keyboard or click the screen to stop playback.

▶ **Tip:** In the Library and Develop modules, you can also use the Impromptu Slideshow button in the Toolbar. If you don't see the Impromptu Slideshow button in the Toolbar, choose Slideshow from the content menu at the right end of the Toolbar.

Well done! You have successfully completed another Lightroom lesson. In this lesson you learned how to create your own stylish slideshow presentation.

In the process, you've explored the Slideshow module and used the control panels to customize a slideshow template—refining the layout and playback settings and adding a backdrop, text, borders, and a soundtrack.

In the next chapter you'll find out how to present your work in printed format, but before you move on, take a few moments to reinforce what you've learned by reading through the review questions and answers on the next page.

Review questions

1 How can you change which template is used for the Impromptu Slideshow?

2 Which Lightroom slideshow template would you pick if you wished to display metadata for your images?

3 What options do you have when customizing a slideshow template?

4 What are the four Cast Shadow controls and what are their effects?

5 What is the difference between saving your customized slideshow template and saving the slideshow you've created?

Review answers

1 In the Slideshow module, right-click / Control-click the name of a slideshow template in the Template Browser and choose Use For Impromptu Slideshow.

2 The EXIF Metadata template, which centers photos on a black background and displays star ratings and EXIF information for the images, as well as an identity plate.

3 In the right panel group you can modify the slide layout, add borders and text overlays, create shadow effects for images or text, change the background color or add a backdrop image, adjust the durations of slides and fades, and add a soundtrack.

4 The four Cast Shadow controls have the following effects:

• Opacity: Controls the opacity of the shadow ranging from 0% (invisible) to 100% (fully opaque).

• Offset: Affects the distance that the shadow is offset from the slide. As the offset is increased, more shadow becomes visible.

• Radius: Controls how sharp (lower settings) or soft (higher settings) the edges of the shadow appear.

• Angle: Sets the direction of the light source, which affects the angle at which the shadow is cast.

5 A saved custom template records only your layout and playback settings—it is like an empty container that is not linked to any particular set of images, whereas a saved slideshow is actually an output collection—an arranged grouping of images, saved together with a slide layout, text overlays, and playback settings.

PHOTOGRAPHY SHOWCASE
NICOLE YOUNG

"I believe we are all photographers;
we all have a story to tell and memories to create,
so why not do it beautifully."

I can recall sitting in photography class when I was a teenager and having that "light-bulb" moment when I understood photography; aperture and shutter speed were no longer a mystery, and I could create a beautiful photograph just with some film and a chemical-filled darkroom. Years later, I can remember dusting off my camera and eventually learning to "see" light. An entirely new world had just been revealed to me, and it was that moment that I became a photographer.

These days I spend my time creating food, landscape and stock photographs. When I have free time I travel the world with my camera, and when I'm behind my computer I'm either blogging, writing books or creating digital content for other artists. Sharing my thought on photography is very important to me; my goal is to inspire others to become artists, learn their craft and hone their skills.

As a photographer and educator, Lightroom plays a very huge role in my daily process of organizing, creating and sharing photographs. At its basic level, Lightroom is a raw processor: you use it to enhance your photographs. However the more my business grows and the more projects I become involved with, Lightroom has very quickly become the most crucial piece of the puzzle when it comes to file management and organization. We all have so little time, and as a photographer I want to spend the majority of it behind my camera, and not behind my computer. Lightroom gives me the tools I need to do just that.

http://nicolesy.com

GHOSTLY SAILS

SEATTLE SUPERMOON

PINK SKY PURPLE FIELDS

BLUE ADVENTURE

THE GOLDEN GATE BRIDGE

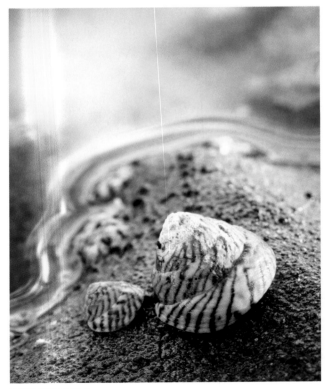

TINY SEASHELL

9 PRINTING IMAGES

Lesson overview

The Lightroom Print module offers all the tools you'll need to quickly prepare any selection of images from your library for printing. You can print a single photo, repeat one image at different sizes on the same sheet, or create an attractive layout for multiple images. Add borders, text, and graphics, and then adjust print resolution, sharpening, paper type, and color management with just a few clicks.

In this lesson, you'll explore the Print module as you become familiar with the steps in the printing workflow:

- Choosing a print template

- Customizing the layout and output settings

- Creating a Custom Package print layout

- Adding an identity plate, borders and a background color

- Captioning photos with information from their metadata

- Saving a custom print template

- Specifying print settings and printer driver options

- Choosing appropriate color management options

- Saving a print job as an output collection

 You'll probably need between one and two hours to complete this lesson. If you haven't already done so, download the Lesson 9 work files from the Lesson & Update Files tab on your Account page at www.peachpit.com.

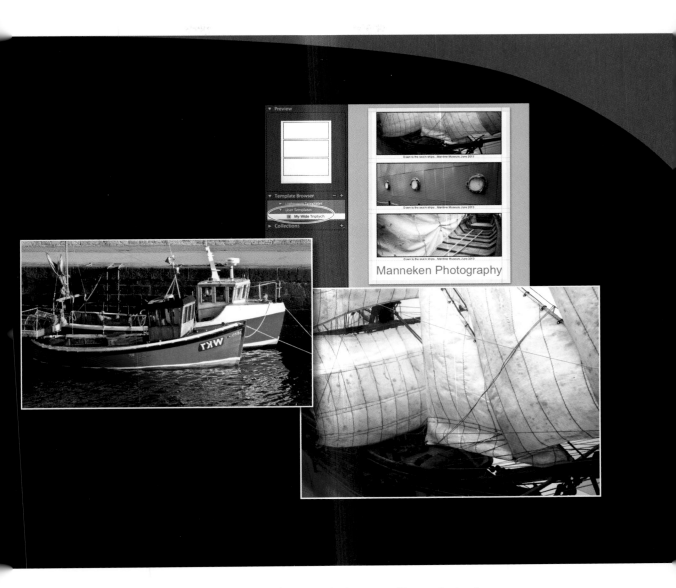

Lightroom makes it easy to achieve professional results, with device-specific soft proofing to help you produce prints that match the color and depth you see on screen, and customizable layout templates for anything from a contact sheet to a fine art mat.

Getting started

Note: This lesson assumes that you already have a basic working familiarity with the Lightroom workspace. If you find that you need more background information, refer to Lightroom Help, or review the previous lessons.

Before you start on this lesson, make sure you've set up the LR5CIB folder for your lesson files and created the LR5CIB Catalog file to manage them, as described in "Setting up a work folder" and "Creating a catalog file for working with this book" in the Getting Started chapter at the beginning of this book.

If you haven't already done so, download the Lesson 9 folder from your Account page at www.peachpit.com to the LR5CIB/Lessons folder, as detailed in the section "Accessing the Classroom in a Book files" in the chapter "Getting Started."

1   Start Lightroom.

2   In the Adobe Photoshop Lightroom - Select Catalog dialog box, make sure the file LR5CIB Catalog.lrcat is selected under Select A Recent Catalog To Open, and then click Open.

▶ **Tip:** If you can't see the Module Picker, choose Window > Panels > Show Module Picker, or press the F5 key. If you're working on Mac OS, you may need to press the fn key together with the F5 key, or change the function key behavior in the system preferences.

3   Lightroom will open in the screen mode and workspace module that were active when you last quit. If necessary, switch to the Library module by clicking Library in the Module Picker at the top of the workspace.

Importing images into the library

The first step is to import the images for this lesson into the Lightroom library.

1   In the Library module, click the Import button below the left panel group.

2 If the Import dialog box appears in compact mode, click the Show More Options button at the lower left to expand it.

3 Under Source at the left of the Import dialog box, navigate to and select the Lesson 9 folder (inside the LR5CIB > Lessons folder). Make sure that all six images in the Lesson 9 folder are checked for import.

4 In the import options picker above the thumbnail previews, select Add so that the imported photos will be added to your catalog without being moved or copied. Under File Handling at the right of the Import dialog box, choose Minimal from the Render Previews menu and ensure that the Don't Import Suspected Duplicates option is activated. Under Apply During Import, choose None from both the Develop Settings menu and the Metadata menu, and type **Lesson 9, Boats** in the Keywords text box. Make sure that your import is set up as shown in the illustration below, and then click Import.

The six images from the Lesson 9 folder appear in both the Library module Grid view and the Filmstrip across the bottom of the Lightroom workspace.

5 You won't be able to rearrange the images for your print job as long as Previous Import is selected as the image source in the Catalog panel. In the Folders panel, click the Lesson 9 folder to change the image source. In the Toolbar, set the Sort order to File Name; then, click Print in the Module Picker at the top of the workspace to switch to the Print Module.

Library | Develop | Map | Book | Slideshow | Print | Web

▶ **Tip:** The first time you enter any of the Lightroom modules, you'll see module tips that will help you get started by identifying the components of the Lightroom workspace and stepping you through the workflow. Dismiss the tips by clicking the Close button. To reactivate the tips for any module, choose [*Module name*] Tips from the Help menu.

About the Lightroom Print module

In the Print module you'll find tools and controls for each step in the printing workflow. Change the order of your photos, choose a print template and refine the layout, add borders, text, and graphics, and then adjust the output settings; everything you need to produce professional-looking prints is at your fingertips.

The left panel group contains the Preview, Template Browser, and Collections panels. Move the pointer over the list in the Template Browser to see a thumbnail preview of each layout template displayed in the Preview panel. When you choose a new template from the list, the Print Editor view—at center-stage in the workspace—is updated to show how the selected photos look in the new layout.

You can quickly select and rearrange the photos for your print job in the Filmstrip, where the source menu provides easy access to the images in your library, listing your favorites and recently used source folders and collections.

You'll use the controls in the right panel group to customize your layout template and to specify output settings.

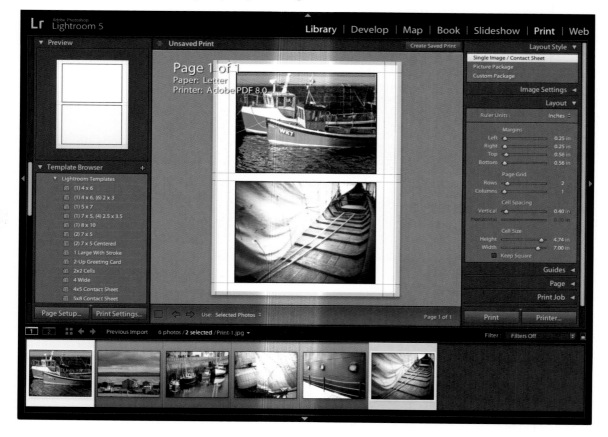

The Template Browser contains templates of three distinct types: Single Image / Contact Sheet layouts, Picture Package layouts, and Custom Package layouts.

Four of the first fifteen preset Lightroom templates in the menu are Picture Package layouts, which repeat a single image at a variety of sizes on the same page. The other eleven are Single Image / Contact Sheet layouts, which can be used to print multiple photos at the same size on a single sheet. Single Image / Contact Sheet layouts are based on an adjustable grid of image cells. They range from contact sheets with many cells to single-cell layouts such as the Fine Art Mat and Maximize Size templates. The Custom layout templates further down the menu enable you to print multiple images at any size on the same page. All of the templates can be customized; you can save your modified layouts as user-defined templates, which will be listed in the Template Browser.

Once you've chosen a layout from the Template Browser, the Layout Style panel at the top of the right panel group indicates which type of template you're working with. The suite of panels you see below the Layout Style panel will vary slightly, depending on which type of template you have chosen.

The controls in the Image Settings panel enable you to add photo borders and to specify the way your pictures are fitted to their image cells.

For a Single Image / Contact Sheet template, you can use the Layout panel to adjust margins, cell size and spacing, and to change the number of rows and columns that make up the grid. For a Picture Package or Custom package template, you'll modify your layout with the Rulers, Grid & Guides panel and the Cells panel. Use the Guides panel to show or hide a selection of layout guides. The Page panel has controls for watermarking your images and adding text, graphics, or a background color to your print layout. In the Print Job panel you can set the print resolution, print sharpening, paper type, and color management options.

About layout styles and print templates

The Template Browser offers a wide choice of preset Lightroom print templates that differ not only in basic layout but may also include a variety of design features such as borders and overlaid text or graphics.

Templates may also differ in their output settings: the preset print resolution setting for a contact sheet, for example, will be lower than the resolution set for a template designed for producing finished prints.

You can save time and effort setting up your print job by selecting the print template that most closely suits your purpose. In this exercise you'll be introduced to the different types of templates and use the panels in the right panel group to examine the characteristics of each layout.

1   In the left panel group, make sure that the Preview and Template Browser panels are expanded. If necessary, drag the top border of the Filmstrip down so that you can see as many of the templates in the Template Browser as possible. In the right panel group, expand the Layout Style panel and collapse the others.

2   Choose Edit > Select None, and then select any one of the images in the Filmstrip. The Print Editor view at the center of the workspace is updated to display the selected photo in the current layout.

3   If necessary, expand the Lightroom Templates folder in the Template Browser panel. Move the pointer slowly over the list of preset templates to see a preview of each layout in the Preview panel.

4   Click the second template in the Template Browser: "(1) 4 × 6, (6) 2 × 3." The new template is applied to the image in the Print Editor view. Scroll up in the right panel group, if necessary, and inspect the Layout Style panel. You'll see that the Layout Style panel indicates that this template is a Picture Package layout. In the Template Browser, click the sixth Lightroom template "(2) 7 × 5." The Layout Style panel indicates that this is also a Picture Package layout.

5   Now choose the ninth preset template in the Template Browser: "2-Up Greeting Card." The Layout Style panel indicates that the template "2-Up Greeting Card" is a Single Image / Contact Sheet layout, and the Print Editor view at the center of the workspace displays the new template.

6   In the Layout Style panel, click Picture Package. The Print Editor is updated to display the last selected Picture Package layout: "(2) 7 × 5." Click Single Image / Contact Sheet in the Layout Style panel and the Print Editor view returns to the last selected Single Image / Contact Sheet layout: "2-Up Greeting Card."

You'll notice that different control panels become available in the right panel group as you move between the Single Image / Contact Sheet and Picture Package layout styles. Panels common to both layout styles may differ in content for each.

7 In the right panel group, expand the Image Settings panel. In the Layout Style panel, click Picture Package and expand the Image Settings panel again. Toggle between the Picture Package and Single Image / Contact Sheet layouts and notice how the options available in the Image Settings panel change.

You can see that the selected photo fits to the image cell differently for each of these templates. In the Picture Package layout "(2) 7 × 5," the Zoom To Fill option is activated in the Image Settings panel so that the photo is zoomed and cropped to fill the image cell. In the Single Image / Contact Sheet "2-Up Greeting Card," the Zoom to Fill option is disabled and the photo is not cropped. Take a moment to examine the other differences in the Image Settings panel.

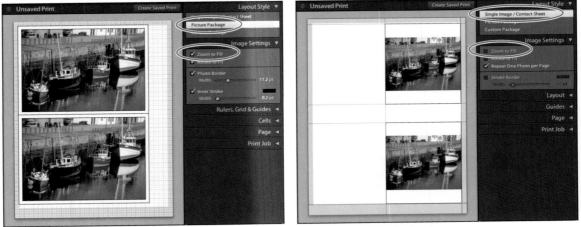

(2) 7 × 5 template   2-Up Greeting Card template

8 Select the Single Image / Contact Sheet layout style. Look at the page count at the right of the Toolbar below the Print Editor view: it reads "Page 1 of 1." Press Ctrl+A / Command+A or choose Edit > Select All to select all six images in the Filmstrip. The page count in the Toolbar now reads "Page x of 6." The template "2-Up Greeting Card" is now applied to all six photos, resulting in a print job of six pages. Use the navigation buttons at the left the Toolbar to move between the pages and see the layout applied to each image in turn.

Show first page

► **Tip:** You can also navigate your multi-page print document by using the Home, End, Page Up, Page Down, and left and right arrow keys on your keyboard, or choosing from the navigation commands in the Print menu.

9 For the last step in this exercise, collapse the Image Settings panel and expand the Print Job panel. You'll notice that in the Print Job panel, the Print Resolution for the "2-Up Greeting Card" template is set to 240 ppi. Select the template "4×5 Contact Sheet" in the Template Browser. The Print Resolution option in the Print Job panel is disabled and the Draft Mode Printing option is activated.

Selecting a print template

Now that you've explored the Template Browser, it's time to choose the template that you'll customize in the next exercise.

1 In the Template Browser, click the template "4 Wide." Later in this lesson you'll customize your identity plate, but for now, uncheck the Identity Plate option in the Page panel to hide the default design.

2 Choose Edit > Select None. In the Filmstrip, select the images Print-1.jpg, Print-2.jpg, and Print-3.jpg. The images will be arranged in the template in the same order in which they appear in the Filmstrip. Drag the images inside their grid cells to reposition them as shown in the illustration below.

▶ **Tip:** By default, each photo will be centered in its own image cell. To expose a different portion of an image that is cropped by the boundaries of its cell, simply drag the photo to reposition it within its image cell.

▶ **Tip:** Lightroom automatically scales your photos in the print layout template to fit the paper size you have specified. In the Print Setup / Page Setup dialog box, leave the scale setting at the default 100% and let Lightroom fit the template to the page— that way, what you see in the Print Editor view will be what you'll get from your printer.

Specifying the printer and paper size

Before you customize the template, you'll need to specify the paper size and page orientation for your print job. Doing this now may save you the time and effort of readjusting the layout later.

1 Choose File > Page Setup.

2 In the Print Setup / Page Setup dialog box, choose the desired printer from the Name / Format For menu. From the Paper Size menu, choose Letter (Windows) / US Letter > US Letter (Mac OS). Under Orientation, choose the portrait format (vertical) thumbnail, and then click OK.

Customizing print templates

Having established the overall layout of your print job, you can use the controls in the Layout panel to fine-tune the template so that the images fit better to the page.

Changing the number of cells

For the purposes of this exercise, we need only three of the four preset image cells.

1　If necessary, expand the Layout panel in the right panel group. Under Page Grid, drag the Rows slider to the left or type **3** in the text box to the right of the slider.

2　Experiment with the Margins, Cell Spacing, and Cell Size sliders—making sure to undo (Ctrl+Z / Command+Z) after each change. Activate the Keep Square option below the Cell Size sliders. The Cell Width and Cell Height sliders are locked together at the same value. Disable the Keep Square option.

3　The black lines you might see around the photos are merely guides indicating the image cell boundaries; they will not appear on your printed page. These guides are helpful while you're adjusting the cell size and spacing but they'll be distracting when you add printable borders to your layout in the next exercise.

> ▶ **Tip:** If you don't see the guides referred to in this step, activate the Show Guides check box at the top of the Guides panel and toggle each option to see the effect.

If necessary, expand the Guides panel below the Layout panel and disable the Image Cells option; then collapse the Layout and Guides panels.

Modifying the page layout of a print template

Layout controls for Single Image / Contact Sheet and Picture Package templates

Depending on which type of print template you are working with, you'll find a slightly different suite of panels in the right panel group. The Image Settings, Page, and Print Job panels are available for all template types but the controls for modifying the page layout differ. If you've chosen a Single Image / Contact Sheet template, you'll customize your layout using the Layout and Guides panels. For a Picture Package template, you'll use the Rulers, Grids & Guides panel and the Cells panel. For Custom Package layouts you'll also use the Rulers, Grids & Guides panel and the Cells panel—where you'll find a few minor differences from the options offered in the same panels for a Picture Package.

Picture Package templates and Custom Package layouts and are not grid-based so they are very flexible to work with; you can arrange the image cells on the page either by simply dragging them in the Print Editor view or by using the controls in the Cells panel. You can resize a cell using the width and height sliders or simply drag the handles of its bounding box. Add more photos to your layout with the Cells panel controls or Alt-drag / Option-drag a cell to duplicate it and resize it as you wish.

Lightroom provides a variety of guides to help you adjust your layout. Guides are not printed: they appear only in the Print Editor view. To show or hide the guides, activate Show Guides in the Guides panel, or choose View > Show Guides (Ctrl+Shift+H / Command+Shift+H). In the Guides panel you can specify which types of guides will be displayed in the Print Editor view.

Note: The Margins and Gutters guides and Image Cells guides—available only for Single Image / Contact Sheet layouts—are interactive; you can adjust your layout directly by dragging the guides themselves in the Print Editor view. When you move these guides, the Margins, Cell Spacing and Cell Size sliders in the Layout panel will move with them.

Using the Layout panel to modify a Contact Sheet / Grid layout

Ruler Units sets the units of measurement for most of the other controls in the Layouts panel and for the Rulers guide in the Guides panel. Click the Ruler Units setting and choose Inches, Centimeters, Millimeters, Points or Picas from the menu. The default setting is Inches.

Margins sets the boundaries for the grid of image cells in your layout. Most printers don't support borderless printing, so the minimum value for the margins is dependent on the capabilities of your printer. Even if your printer does support borderless printing, you may first need to activate this feature in the printer settings before you can set the margins to zero.

Page Grid specifies the number of rows and columns of image cells in the layout. The grid can contain anything from one image cell (Rows: 1, Columns: 1) to 225 image cells (Rows: 15, Columns: 15).

Cell Spacing and Cell Size settings are linked so that changes you make to one will affect the other. The Cell Spacing sliders set the vertical and horizontal spaces between the image cells in the grid; the Cell Size controls change the height and width of the cells. The Keep Square option links the height and width settings so that the image cells remain square.

Using the Guides panel to modify a Contact Sheet / Grid layout

Rulers are displayed across the top and at the left of the Print Editor view. If Show Guides is activated, you can also show the rulers by choosing View > Show Rulers (Ctrl+R / Command+R). To change the ruler units, click the setting in the Layout panel.

Page Bleed shades the non-printable edges of the page, as defined by your printer settings.

Margins and Gutters guides reflect the Margins settings in the Layout panel; in fact, dragging these guides in the Print Editor view will move the respective sliders in the Layout panel.

Image Cells shows a black border around each image cell. When the Margins and Gutters guides are not visible, dragging the Image Cells guides in the Print Editor view will change the Margins, Cell Spacing, and Cell Size settings in the Layout panel.

Dimensions displays the measurements of each image cell in its top left corner, expressed in whatever units of measurement you have chosen for the Ruler Units.

Using the Rulers, Grids & Guides panel to modify a Picture Package layout

Rulers shows the rulers and lets you set the units of measurement just as you would in the Layout panel when you're working with a Contact Sheet / Grid template.

Grid displays a grid guide behind the image cells in the Print Editor view. As you drag the cells, you can have them snap to each other or to the grid (or turn the snap behavior off) by choosing Cells, Grid, or Off from the Snap menu options. The grid divisions are affected by your choice of ruler units.

Note: The snap behavior helps you to position the image cells accurately on the page. If you accidentally overlap your photos, Lightroom will let you know by showing a triangular yellow warning icon (!) in the top right corner of the page.

Bleeds and **Dimensions** are the Picture Package equivalents of the Page Bleed and Dimensions guides.

Using the Cells panel to modify a Picture Package layout

Add To Package offers six preset image cell sizes that can be placed in your layout at the click of a button. You can change which of the presets is assigned to each button by clicking its menu triangle. The default presets are standard photo sizes but you can edit them if you wish.

New Page adds a page to your layout, though Lightroom automatically adds pages if you use the Add to Package buttons to add more photos than fit on a page. To delete a page from your layout, click the red X in its upper left corner of the page in the Print Editor view.

Auto Layout optimizes the arrangement of the photos on the page for the fewest cuts.

Clear Layout removes all the image cells from the layout.

Adjust Selected Cell lets you change the height and width of an image cell using sliders or numerical input.

Rearranging the photos in a print layout

Lightroom places your photos in the cells of a multiple-image print layout in the order in which they appear in the Filmstrip (and the Library module Grid view).

If your image source is a Collection, or a folder without subfolders nested inside it, you can change the placement of your images in the print job by simply dragging their thumbnails to new positions in the Filmstrip. Rearranging photos in this way is not possible if either the All Photographs folder or Previous Import folder is the selected image source.

1   In the header bar of the Filmstrip, the Lesson 9 folder is listed as the source of the images displayed. Click the white triangle to the right of the image source information in the header bar of the Filmstrip to see the options available in the source menu.

If you enter the Print module with the Previous Import folder selected as the image source, making it impossible to reorder the photos for your print job, you can choose from recently opened folders and collections in the Filmstrip source menu.

2   Choose Edit > Select None, or press Ctrl+D / Command+D on your keyboard; then, drag the thumbnails in the Filmstrip to reverse the order of the first three photos, Print-1, Print-2, and Print-3.

3   Ctrl-click / Command-click to group-select the three reordered photos in the Filmstrip.

The three photos are rearranged in your modified layout template to reflect the new sorting order in the Filmstrip.

For a Picture Package layout, which repeats a single photo at various sizes on the same page, a new page is added to the print job for each selected photo; reordering the photos in the Filmstrip will affect only the page order.

Creating stroke and photo borders

For our Single Image / Contact Sheet layout, the Image Settings panel offers options that affect the way your photos are placed in the image cells, and a control for adding borders. In this exercise you'll add a stroke border around each of the three images and adjust the width of the stroke.

▶ **Tip:** You can change the color of the border by clicking the Stroke Border color swatch and choosing a color from the Color Picker.

1   Expand the Image Settings panel. For the 4 Wide template, the Zoom To Fill option is activated. This means that our photos are cropped in height to fit the proportions of the image cells.

2   Click the check box to activate the Stroke Border option, and then drag the Width slider to the right or type **2.0** in the text box to the right of the slider. For your reference, one inch is equivalent to 72 points (pt).

3   In the Layout Style panel, click Picture Package. In the Rulers, Grid & Guides panel, activate the Image cells option to see the borders of the cells. For a Picture Package template, the Image Settings panel offers two controls for borders. An Inner Stroke border is the Picture Package equivalent of a Stroke Border. The Photo Border control lets you set the width of a blank frame between the edge of each photo and the boundary of its image cell.

4   Experiment with the Inner Stroke and Photo Border settings.

5   Disable the Image Cell guides. In the Layout Style panel, click Single Image / Contact Sheet to return to your modified 4 Wide template.

Using the Rotate To Fit option

By default, Lightroom will place photos so that they are upright within their image cells. The Rotate To Fit option in the Image Settings panel will override this behavior so that your photos are rotated to match the orientation of the image cells. For presentation layouts you would not wish to have images displayed in different orientations on the same page but in some situations this feature can be very helpful and save on expensive photo paper too! The Rotate To Fit option is particularly useful when you wish to print photos in both portrait and landscape formats on the same sheet, as large as possible and without wasting paper, as shown in the illustration on the right.

Another situation where you might choose to use the Rotate To Fit setting is when you are printing contact sheets. As you can see in the next illustration, Rotate To Fit enables you to see all the photos at the same size regardless of the image orientation.

Customizing your identity plate

In the Page panel you'll find controls for adding an identity plate, crop marks, page numbers, and text information from your photos' metadata to your layout. To begin with, you'll edit the identity plate to suit your layout.

1 Expand the Page panel; then click the check box to activate the Identity Plate option. The illustration at the right shows a preview of the default Identity Plate on Windows; on Mac OS, the default design will feature your user name. Click the triangle in the lower right corner of the identity plate preview pane and choose Edit from the menu.

2 In the Identity Plate Editor dialog box, activate the Use A Styled Text Identity Plate option. Choose Arial, Regular, and 36 point from the font menus. To change the text color, swipe over the text in the text box to select it, and then click the color swatch to the right of the font size menu; we chose a slightly darker gray than the default. Swipe to select the text again, if necessary, and type **Manneken Photography** (or a name of your own choice); then click OK.

▶ **Tip:** If your text is too long to be fully visible in the text box, either resize the dialog box or reduce the font size until you've finished editing.

3 In the Page panel, drag the Scale slider to the right so that the identity plate text is the same width as the image. You can also scale the identity plate by clicking it in the Print Editor view and dragging the handles of its bounding box.

▶ **Tip:** By default the identity plate will be oriented horizontally. This setting (0°) is indicated at the top right of the Identity Plate pane in the Page panel. To re-orient your identity plate on the page, click on the 0° indicator and choose 90°, 180°, or −90° from the menu. To move your identity plate, simply drag it in the Print Editor view.

4   Now you'll change the color of the identity plate. Click the Override Color check box to set the color of the identity plate for this layout only—without affecting the defined color settings for the identity plate.

5   Click the Override Color swatch to open the Color Picker. Set the RGB values: R: **10%**, G: **25%**, B: **20%**, and then close the Color Picker. The color of the text identity plate is now a deep sea green.

▶ **Tip:** If you see a hexadecimal value displayed in the lower right corner of the Color Picker rather than RGB values, click RGB below the color slider.

6   In the Identity Plate pane, use the Opacity slider or type **75** in the text box beside it to set an opacity value of 75% for the identity plate. This feature can be particularly effective if you wish to position your identity plate over an image.

Printing captions and metadata information

In this exercise, you will add a caption and metadata information—in this case, titles for the images—to your print layout using the Page panel and the Text Template Editor.

1   At the bottom of the Page panel, click the check box to activate the Photo Info overlay option, and then choose Edit from the menu to the right. Most of the other options in the Photo Info menu are drawn from the images' existing metadata.

The Text Template Editor enables you to combine custom text with the metadata embedded in your image files, and then save your edited template as a new preset, making it easy to add the same items of text information to future print jobs.

The capture locations of our lesson photos have been entered in the Caption field of the images' metadata; you'll base your text captions on this metadata.

▶ **Tip:** You'll find more detailed information on the Text Template Editor in the section "Using the Text Template Editor" in Lesson 8.

2   Choose Caption from the Preset menu at the top of the Text Template Editor dialog box.

3   Click to place the insertion cursor just before the Title token in the Example text box. Type **Down to the sea in ships...** (including the periods); then, type a space between your text and the token.

4   Click to place the cursor after the Caption token in the Example box. Type a comma, and then a space; then, choose Date (Month) from the second Numbering menu. If the Date (Month) token does not appear in the Example box, click the Insert button to the right of the Date menu.

5   Add a space after the Date (Month) token; then, choose Date (YYYY) from the second Numbering menu and click the Insert button if necessary.

6   Click Done to close the Text Template Editor dialog box. The images in the Print Editor view are now captioned and dated.

7   Click the triangle beside the Font Size menu at the bottom of the Page panel and choose 12 pt; then collapse the Page panel.

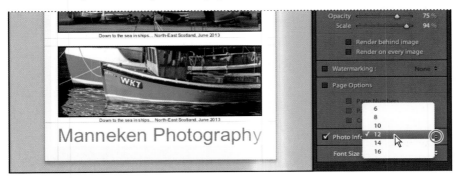

Saving your customized print template

Having started with a preset print template, you've created your own page design by modifying the layout and adding borders, an identity plate, and caption text to the images. You can now save your customized layout for future use.

1   Click the Create New Preset button (+) in the header of the Template Browser panel header, or choose Print > New Template.

2   In the New Template dialog box, type **My Wide Triptych** in the Template Name text box. By default, new templates are saved to the User Templates folder. For this exercise, accept the default User Templates as the destination folder and click Create.

3   Your saved template appears in the User Templates folder in the Template Browser panel where you can access it quickly for use with a new set of images. With your new template selected in the Template Browser, select the last three images in the Filmstrip, Print-4.jpg, Print-5.jpg, and Print-6.jpg.

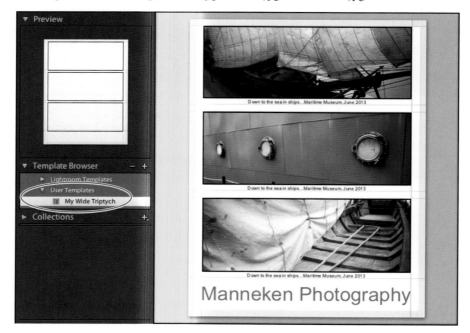

Creating a Custom Package print layout

Every Single Image / Contact Sheet template is based on a grid of image cells that are all the same size. If you want a more free-form layout, or you prefer to create your own page layout from scratch, without using any of the preset templates as a starting point, you can use the Custom Package option in the Layout Style panel.

▶ **Tip:** If you'd prefer to work without using a template, start by clicking Custom Package in the Layout Style panel; then, click Clear Layout in the Cells panel and drag photos from the Filmstrip directly onto the page preview.

1   Choose Edit > Select None, or press Ctrl+D / Command+D on your keyboard. In the Template Browser, select the layout Custom Overlap × 3 Landscape from the list of Lightroom templates.

2   In The Rulers, Grid & Guides panel, activate the Show Guides option, if necessary; then, disable all but the Page Bleed and Page Grid guides.

The images in a Custom Package layout can be arranged so that they overlap. The selected template includes three overlapping image cells spread diagonally over a fourth that occupies most of the printable page area.

3   Click to select the central image cell in the layout, and then right-click / Control-click inside the selected cell. Note the options in the context menu; the first four commands enable you to move an image forwards or backwards in the stacking order.

4   For now, choose Delete Cell from the context menu; then, delete the small cell at the lower left.

5   At the bottom of the Cells panel, activate the Lock To Photo Aspect Ratio option. Drag the image Print-4.jpg from the Filmstrip into the smaller image cell; then, drag the photo Print-5.jpg into the larger cell behind it.

6   Click away from the large photo cell to deselect it; then re-select the image and use the controls in the Cells panel to set the Width to **9.5** inches. The Height value is adjusted automatically, maintaining the photo's original proportions.

7 In the Cells panel, disable Lock To Photo Aspect Ratio; then, drag the handle at the top of the large cell's bounding box downwards, or use the slider to set the Height to **2.45** inches. With the Lock To Photo Aspect Ratio option disabled, the image is cropped to fill the altered proportions of its cell.

8 Select the smaller image on the page and set both the Width and Height values to **4.6** inches. Hold down the Alt / Option key and drag the square-cropped image to produce a copy; then, replace the photo in the copied cell by dragging the image Print-6.jpg from the Filmstrip.

● **Note:** Depending on your printer, the printable (non-bleed) area may not be centered on the page, as is the case in these illustrations.

9 Drag the three images to arrange them on the page as shown in the illustration below. Be sure to center the arrangement within the printable area of the page; that is, inside the area defined by the gray border of the Page Bleed guide. To refine the way each image is cropped, hold down the Ctrl / Command key as you drag to reposition the photo within the frame of its image cell.

Changing the page background color

1. In the Image Settings panel, activate the Inner Stroke option. Use the slider or type over the current value to set the width of the stroke to **1.0** pt. Leave the stroke color set to the default white; the white stroke borders will become visible when you set a background color in step 4.

2. In the Rulers, Grid & Guides panel, disable Show Guides.

3. In the Page panel, click the check box to activate the Page Background Color option. Click the Page Background Color color swatch to open the Color Picker.

4. In the Color Picker, click the black swatch at the top of the Page Background Color picker to sample it with the eyedropper cursor, and then click the Close button (x) or click outside the Color Picker to close it.

Tip: To save on printer ink, you may prefer not to print a page with large areas of bold color or black in the background on your home printer, but when you're ordering professional prints this can be a striking choice.

The new color appears in the Page Background Color color swatch and in the page preview in the Print Editor view.

Soft proofing photos before printing

Each type of monitor and printer operates within its own *color gamut* or *color space*, which defines the range of colors that can be reproduced accurately by that device. By default, Lightroom uses your monitor's *color profile*—a mathematical description of its color space—to make your photos look as good as possible on screen. When you print an image, the image data must be reinterpreted for the printer's color space, which can sometimes result in unexpected shifts in color and tone.

You can avoid such unpleasant surprises by soft proofing your photos in the Develop module before you bring them into the Print module. Soft proofing lets you preview how your photos will look when they're printed; you can have Lightroom simulate the color space of your printer, and even the inks and paper you're using, giving you the opportunity to optimize your photos before printing them. To activate soft proofing, open a photo in the Develop module and click the Soft Proofing check box in the Toolbar, or press the S key on your keyboard. The background surrounding the image changes to white "paper" and a Proof Preview label appears in the corner of the work area. Use the view button in the Toolbar to switch between the Loupe view and a choice of before and after views.

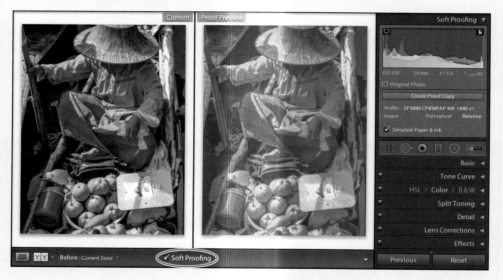

When you activate soft proofing, the Histogram panel changes to the Soft Proofing panel, which provides access to proofing options. The tonal distribution graph is updated according to the currently selected color profile. In the illustration at the right, the graph in the Histogram panel corresponds to the Before image in the illustration above. The graph in the Soft Proofing panel reflects the comparative flatness of the Proof Preview.

To soft proof your photo for a different printer, choose another color profile from the Profile menu in the Soft Proofing panel. If you don't see the profile you want in the menu, choose Other, and then select from the list of installed color profiles in the Choose Profiles dialog box.

The Intent setting determines the rendering intent, which affects how colors are converted from one color space to another. The Perceptual rendering intent aims to preserve the visual relationship between colors so they look natural, though the color values may change. Relative rendering prints in-gamut colors as they are and shifts out-of-gamut colors to the closest printable approximations, retaining more of the original colors, though the relationships between some of them may be altered.

Once you've chosen a printer profile, you can activate the Simulate Paper & Ink option to simulate the off-white of real paper and the dark gray of real black ink. This option is not available for all profiles.

To check if your colors are in-gamut for the selected profile and rendering intent, use the buttons in the upper corners of the histogram in the Soft Proofing panel. Move the pointer over the Show /Hide Monitor Gamut Warning button on the left; colors that are outside your display's capabilities turn blue in the Proof Preview. Move the pointer over the Show/Hide Destination Gamut Warning button on the right; colors that cannot be rendered by your printer turn red in the preview. Colors that are out-of-gamut for both the monitor and the printer turn pink. Click the buttons to show the gamut warning colors permanently; click again to hide them.

Click Create Proof Copy to generate a virtual copy that you can adjust without affecting your master settings. If you start adjusting a photo while soft proofing is on without first creating a proof copy, Lightroom asks if you want to create a virtual copy for soft proofing or make the master image a proof.

Configuring the output settings

The final step before you're ready to print your layout is to adjust the output settings in the Print Job panel.

1 Expand the Print Job panel in the right panel group.

From the Print To menu at the top of the Print Job panel you can choose to send the job directly to your printer or generate a JPEG file, which you can print later or send out for professional printing. The controls in the Print Job panel vary slightly depending on which option is selected in the Print To menu.

2 Choose Printer from the Print To menu at the top of the Print Job panel.

Note: The terms "print resolution" and "printer resolution" have different meanings. "Print resolution" refers to the number of printed pixels per inch (ppi); "printer resolution" refers to the capability of the printer, called dots per inch (dpi). A printed pixel of a particular color is created by patterns of tiny dots of the few ink colors available.

Activating the Draft Mode Printing option will disable the other options in the Print Job panel. Draft Mode Printing results in high speed output at a relatively low quality, which is an efficient option for printing contact sheets or for assessing your layout before you commit it to high quality photo paper. The 4 × 5 Contact Sheet and the 5 × 8 Contact Sheet templates are preset for Draft Mode Printing.

The Print Resolution setting that is appropriate for your print job depends on the intended print size, the resolution of your image files, the capabilities of your printer, and the quality of your paper stock. The default print resolution is 240 ppi, which generally produces good results. As a rule of thumb, use a higher resolution for smaller, high quality prints (around 360 ppi for letter size). You can use a lower resolution setting for larger prints (around 180 ppi for 16″ × 20″) without compromising too much on quality.

3 The Print Resolution control has a range of 72 ppi to 1440 ppi. For this exercise, type **200** in the Print Resolution text box.

Note: The purpose of the Sharpening feature in the Develop module is to compensate for blurriness in the original photo, while Print Sharpening improves the crispness of printed output on a particular paper type.

Images tend to look less sharp on paper than they do on screen. The Print Sharpening options can help to compensate for this by increasing the crispness of your printed output. You can choose between Low, Standard, and High Print Sharpening settings, and specify a Matte or Glossy Media Type. You won't notice the effects of these settings on screen so it's useful to experiment by printing at different settings to familiarize yourself with the results.

4 If it's not already selected, choose Low from the Print Sharpening menu.

Working with 16 Bit Output on Mac OS

If you are running Mac OS and are using a 16-bit printer, you can activate the 16 Bit Output setting in the Print Job panel. This will result in less image degradation and color artifacts in files that have been extensively edited.

Note: If you select 16 Bit Output and print to a printer that does not support it, print performance is slowed, but quality is not affected.

For detailed information on working with 16-bit output, consult the documentation for your printer or check with your output center.

Using color management

Printing your digital images can be challenging: what you see on screen is not always what you get on paper. Lightroom is able to handle a very large color space but your printer may operate within a much more limited gamut.

In the Print Job panel, you can choose whether to have Lightroom handle color management or leave it up to your printer.

Color managed by your printer

The default Color Management setting in the Print Job panel is Managed By Printer. This can be the easiest option and, given the continuing improvement of printing technology, will generally produce satisfactory results. In the Print Setup / Print dialog box (File > Print Settings), you can specify the paper type, color handling, and other print settings. On Windows, click Properties in the Print Setup dialog box to access additional printer specific settings.

● **Note:** For Draft Mode Printing, color management is automatically assigned to the printer.

● **Note:** The options available in the Print Setup / Print dialog box may vary depending on your printer.

Tip: If you choose a custom printer color profile rather than Managed By Printer from the Profile menu in the Color Management panel, make sure color management is turned off in the printer driver software; otherwise, your photos will be color managed twice, and the colors might not print as you expect them to.

If you choose Managed By Printer, enable the ICM Method for Image Color Management (Windows) or activate the ColorSync option in the Color Management settings for the printer driver software (Mac OS) so that the correct profile is applied before printing. Depending on the printer driver software, you can usually find the color settings in the Print Document dialog box under Setup / Properties / Advanced (Windows), or in the menu below the Presets in the Print dialog box (Mac OS).

Color management controlled by Lightroom

Letting your printer manage color may be acceptable for general printing purposes but to achieve really high quality results it's best to have Lightroom do it. If you choose this option you can specify a printing profile tailored to a particular type of paper or custom inks.

1   In the Print Job panel, choose Other from the Color Management Profile menu.

You can choose this option when the profile you want isn't listed in the Profile menu. Lightroom searches your computer for custom printer profiles, which are usually installed by the software that came with your printer. If Lightroom is unable to locate any profiles, choose Managed By Printer and let the printer driver handle the color management.

Tip: The Include Display Profiles at the bottom of the Choose Profiles dialog box enables you to load color profiles for devices other than printers. This can be useful when you need to save your images to a different color space for use on the Internet.

2   Depending on your printer and paper stock, choose one or more printer profiles. In this illustration a profile for the Epson Stylus Pro R800 using glossy photo paper has been selected. Each profile you choose will be added to the Profile menu under Color Management in the Print Job panel for easy access next time you print.

Once you've chosen a printer profile from the Profile menu, the Rendering Intent options become available in the Print Job panel. The color space of an image is usually much larger than that within which most printers operate, which means that your printer may not be able to accurately reproduce the colors you see on screen. This may result in printing artifacts such as posterization or banding in color gradients as the printer attempts to deal with out-of-gamut colors. The Rendering Intent options help to minimize these problems. You can choose between two settings:

- **Perceptual** rendering aims at preserving the visual relationship between colors. The entire range of colors in the image will be re-mapped to fit within the color gamut your printer is able to reproduce. In this way, the relationships between all the colors are preserved but in the process even colors that were already in-gamut may be shifted as the out-of-gamut colors are moved into the printable range. This may mean that your printed image will be less vivid than it appeared on screen.

- **Relative** rendering prints all the in-gamut colors as they are and shifts out-of-gamut colors to the closest printable colors. Using this option means that more of the original color of the image is retained but some of the relationships between colors may be altered.

In most cases the differences between the two rendering methods are quite subtle. As a general rule, perceptual rendering is the best option for an image with many out-of-gamut colors and relative rendering works better for an image with only a few. However, unless you are very experienced it may be hard to tell which is which. The best policy is to do some testing with your printer. Print a very colorful, vivid photo at both settings and then do the same with a more muted image.

3   For the purposes of this exercise, choose Relative rendering.

Tweaking printed color manually

Printed results don't always match the bright and saturated look of the colors you see on-screen in Lightroom—even when you've spent time setting up the color management for your print job.

The problem may be related to your printer, the inks or paper stock you're using, or an incorrectly calibrated monitor; whatever the cause, you can make quick and easy adjustments with the Brightness and Contrast sliders in the Color Management pane of the Print Job panel.

Tip: The tone curve adjustments produced by the Print Adjustment sliders do not appear in the on-screen preview. You may need to experiment a little to find the settings that work best for your printer.

Your Print Adjustment settings are specific to the combination of printer, paper, and ink that you're using—they'll stay in place as long as you're working with the same output settings, and will be saved in the Lightroom catalog file with your custom template or saved print job.

Saving print settings as an output collection

Since you entered the Print module, you've been working with an *unsaved print*, as is indicated in the bar across the top of the Print Editor view.

> **Unsaved Print**   Create Saved Print

Until you save your print job, the Print module works like a scratch pad. You can move to another module, or even close Lightroom, and find your settings unchanged when you return, but if you click a new layout template—or even the one you started with—in the Template Browser, the "scratch pad" will be cleared and all your work will be lost.

▶ **Tip:** Once you've saved your print job, any changes you make to the layout or output settings are auto-saved as you work.

Converting your print job to a Saved Print not only preserves your layout and output settings, but also links your layout to the particular set of images for which it was designed. Your print job is saved as a special kind of collection—an *output collection*—with its own listing in the Collections panel. Clicking this listing will instantly retrieve the images you were working with, and reinstate all of your settings, no matter how many times the print layout scratch pad has been cleared.

Depending on the way you like to work, you can save your print job at any point in the process; you could create a Saved Print as soon as you enter the Print module with a selection of images or wait until your layout is polished.

A print output collection is different from a normal photo collection. A photo collection is merely a grouping of images to which you can apply any template or output settings you wish. An output collection links a photo collection (or a selection of images from that collection) to a particular template and specific output settings.

For the sake of clarity: an output collection also differs from a custom template. A template includes all your settings but no images; you can apply the template to any selection of images. An output collection links the template and all its settings to a particular selection of images.

1   Click the Create Saved Print button in the bar at the top of the Slideshow Editor view, or click the New Collection button (⊕) in the header of the Collections panel and choose Create Print.

▶ **Tip:** The Make New Virtual Copies option (Windows only) is useful if you wish to apply a particular treatment, such as a developing preset, to all the pictures in your print job, without affecting the photos in the source folder or collection.

2   In the Create Print dialog box, type **Boat Prints** as the name for your saved print job. Make sure that the Location option is disabled, and then click Create.

Your saved print appears in the Collections panel, marked with a Saved Print icon () to differentiate it from an image collection, which has a stacked photos icon. The image count shows that the new output collection contains three photos.

Tip: Adding more photos to a saved print job is easy: simply drag images to the gallery's listing in the Collections panel. To open your layout in the Print module from the Library, click the white arrow that appears to the right of the image count when you move the pointer over your saved layout in the Collections panel.

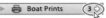

The title bar above the Print Editor now displays the name of your saved print job, and no longer presents the Create Saved Print button.

Printing your job

1   Click the Print button at the bottom of the right panel group or choose File > Print.

2   Verify the settings in the Print dialog box and click OK / Print to print your page, or click Cancel to close the Print dialog box without printing.

Clicking the Print One button will send your print job to the printer queue without opening the Print dialog box. This is useful if you print repeatedly using the same settings and don't need to confirm or change any settings in the Print dialog.

To achieve the best results when you print, calibrate and profile your monitor regularly, always verify that print settings are specified correctly, and use quality papers. However, there is no substitute for experience. Experiment with a variety of settings and options—and if at first you do succeed, consider yourself very lucky!

Congratulations! You've completed another Lightroom lesson. In this lesson you learned how to set up your own sophisticated print layouts.

In the process, you've explored the Print module and used the control panels to customize a print template—refining the layout and output settings and adding a background color, text, borders, and an identity plate to your printed page.

In the next chapter you'll look at ways to publish and share your photos, but before you move on, take a few moments to refresh your new skills by reading through the review questions and answers on the following pages.

Review questions

1   How can you quickly preview the preset print templates, and how can you see how your photos will look in each layout?

2   What are the three print template layout styles, and how can you check which type of template you have chosen?

3   When you're working with the Print Setup / Page Setup dialog box, why is it better to leave the Scale setting at 100%?

4   For what purposes is Draft Mode Printing appropriate?

5   What is the difference between a Saved Print collection, a photo collection, and a saved custom print template?

6   What is Soft Proofing?

Review answers

1   Move the pointer over the list of templates in the Template Browser to see a thumbnail preview of each layout displayed in the Preview panel. Select your images in the Filmstrip and choose a template from the list; the Print Editor view shows how your photos look in the new layout.

2   Single Image / Contact Sheet layouts can be used to print multiple photos at the same size on a single sheet. Based on an adjustable grid of image cells that are all the same size, they range from contact sheets with many cells to single-cell layouts such as the Fine Art Mat and Maximize Size templates. Picture Package layouts repeat a single image at a variety of sizes on the same page in cells that can be moved and resized. Custom Package layouts are not based on a grid; they enable you to print multiple images at any size on the same page, and even to arrange them so that they overlap.

The Layout Style panel indicates whether a layout selected in the Template Browser is a Custom Package, Picture Package, or Single Image / Contact Sheet template.

3   Lightroom automatically scales your photos in the print layout template to fit the specified paper size. Changing the scale in the Print Setup / Page Setup dialog will result in the layout being scaled twice so your photos may not print at the desired size.

4 Draft Mode Printing results in high speed output at a relatively low quality, which is an efficient option for printing contact sheets or for assessing your layout before you commit it to high quality photo paper. The contact sheet templates are preset for Draft Mode Printing.

5 A photo collection is merely a virtual grouping of images to which you can apply any template or output settings you wish, whereas a Saved Print output collection links a selection of images to a particular template and specific layout and output settings. A saved print template preserves your customized layout and output settings but includes no images; you can apply the template to any selection of images. A Saved Print collection links the template and all its settings to a particular set of images.

6 Soft Proofing is a way to check on-screen how your photos will look when printed, or perhaps output for use on the Web. Lightroom uses color profiles to simulate the result of printing to specific printers with particular types of ink and paper—or of saving your images to a different color space as you might do with pictures intended for the Internet—enabling you to make the appropriate adjustments to your photos before exporting copies or committing to printing.

PHOTOGRAPHY SHOWCASE
COLBY BROWN

"I hope that my images resonate with others,
giving me the opportunity to share the world I love
and hopefully helping others to learn to appreciate
the beauty found all around us."

As a photographer I believe that the artistic process of an image doesn't stop once the shutter has been released, but continues into the digital darkroom. By blending various exposures together and increasing the dynamic range of details that I can preserve in a given scene, I am able to more accurately recreate and showcase moments frozen in time as I witnessed them, rather than limit myself based on current camera technology.

One of the most prolific aspects of the digital revolution of photography is the sheer fact that more people today, have the ability to digitally express themselves than ever before. Billions of people, all across this planet, are capturing the world around them and sharing those experiences with others. This is helping to push the boundaries of what we think is artistically possible as individuals begin to test the limits of their own creativity and passion.

As human beings I feel that we are all looking for inspiration as we move through life. We all want to be inspired to be more then we are, see more of the world, and experience more with the limited time that we have. I hope that my images resonate with others, giving me the opportunity to share the world I love and hopefully help others to learn to appreciate the beauty found all around us.

www.colbybrownphotography.com

PETRA BY NIGHT

FOCUSED

MIRRORED REFLECTIONS

YOSEMITE FALLS AMIDST THE STORM

THE SUBWAY

LOST INNOCENCE

10 PUBLISHING YOUR PHOTOS

Lesson overview

Lightroom offers several easy-to-use options for sharing your photos. Publish Services enable you to share images directly from the Library module. You can create a Publish Collection to help you manage the files you've handed off to a client, to sync photos to your iPhone, or to upload images directly to a photo sharing website. The Web module provides a range of customizable gallery templates and all the tools you need to build a striking website and upload it to your web server.

In this lesson, you'll learn the techniques and skills you need to publish photos from the Library and to create your own web gallery:

- Publishing images to a photo sharing website
- Using Publish Collections and republishing updated images
- Distinguishing between HTML and Flash gallery templates
- Choosing and customizing a gallery layout template
- Rearranging the order of the images in your gallery
- Specifying the output settings and adding a watermark
- Saving your customized templates and presets
- Uploading your gallery to a web server

You'll probably need between one and two hours to complete this lesson. If you haven't already done so, download the Lesson 10 work files from the Lesson & Update Files tab of your Account page at www.peachpit.com.

Use integrated Publish Services to share your photos online, directly from the Lightroom Library module, or choose from HTML and Flash templates in the Web module to quickly generate sophisticated interactive web galleries. Post images to a photo sharing site, sync photos to your iPhone, or upload an interactive gallery directly to a web server—all without leaving the Lightroom workspace.

Getting started

Note: This lesson assumes that you already have a basic working familiarity with the Lightroom workspace. If you find that you need more background information, refer to Lightroom Help, or review the previous lessons.

Before you start on this lesson, make sure you've set up the LR5CIB folder for your lesson files and created the LR5CIB Catalog file to manage them, as described in "Setting up a work folder" and "Creating a catalog file for working with this book" in the Getting Started chapter at the beginning of this book.

If you haven't already done so, download the Lesson 10 folder from your Account page at www.peachpit.com to the LR5CIB/Lessons folder, as detailed in the section "Accessing the Classroom in a Book files" in the chapter "Getting Started."

1   Start Lightroom.

2   In the Adobe Photoshop Lightroom - Select Catalog dialog box, make sure that the file LR5CIB Catalog.lrcat is selected under Select A Recent Catalog To Open, and then click Open.

Adobe Photoshop Lightroom – Select Catalog

Select a recent catalog to open

Lr	LR5CIB Catalog.lrcat	/Users/John/Documents/LR5CIB/LR5CIB Catalog
	Lightroom 5 Catalog.lrcat	/Users/John/Pictures/Lightroom/Lightroom 5 Catalog

☐ Always load this catalog on startup   ☐ Test integrity of this catalog

Note: Lightroom Catalogs cannot be on network volumes or in read-only folders.

Choose a Different Catalog...   Create a New Catalog...   Quit   Open

Tip: If you can't see the Module Picker, choose Window > Panels > Show Module Picker, or press the F5 key. If you're working on Mac OS, you may need to press the fn key together with the F5 key, or change the function key behavior in the system preferences.

3   Lightroom will open in the screen mode and workspace module that were active when you last quit. If necessary, switch to the Library module by clicking Library in the Module Picker at the top of the workspace.

  Lightroom   File   Edit   Library   Photo   Metadata   View   Window   Help
  ● ● ●   🔲 LR5CIB Catalog.lrcat – Adobe Photoshop Lightroom – Library

  Lr Adobe Photoshop
      Lightroom 5   (Library) Develop | Map | Book | Slideshow | Print | Web

Importing images into the library

The first step is to import the images for this lesson into the Lightroom library.

1   In the Library module, click the Import button below the left panel group.

► Folders   +
► Collections   +
► Publish Services   +
        Import...   Export...

2   If the Import dialog box appears in compact mode, click the Show More
    Options button at the lower left of the dialog box to see all the options in the
    expanded Import dialog box.

3   At the top of the Source panel at the left of the Import dialog box, activate the
    option Include Subfolders; then, navigate to and select the LR5CIB / Lessons /
    Lesson 10 folder. Ensure that all the Lesson 10 images are checked for import.

4   In the import options above the thumbnail previews, select Add so that the
    imported photos will be added to your catalog without being moved or copied.
    Under File Handling at the right of the expanded Import dialog box, choose
    Minimal from the Render Previews menu and ensure that the Don't Import
    Suspected Duplicates option is activated. Under Apply During Import, choose
    None from both the Develop Settings menu and the Metadata menu and type
    Lesson 10 in the Keywords text box. Make sure that your import is set up as
    shown in the illustration below, and then click Import.

The images are imported from the four subfolders nested inside the Lesson 10
folder, and now appear in the the Library module, in both the Grid view and the
Filmstrip across the bottom of the Lightroom workspace.

Publishing photos from the Library

We live in a connected world where, for many of us, posting images to photo sharing websites, or handing off photos online to a client are daily occurrences.

The Publish Services panel enables you to publish your images directly from the Library module, providing integrated connections to Behance, Facebook and Flickr, as well as a link to Lightroom Exchange where you can download third-party Publish Services plug-ins that will give you direct access to other sharing websites.

Use the Publish Services panel to create Publish Collections that will not only make sharing photos to your favorite website as simple as drag and drop, but also help you manage your shared images by keeping track of whether or not they've been updated to the most current versions. You can use a Publish Collection to manage and update the images you've handed off to a client or shared online, or to keep the photos on your iPhone in sync with the versions in your Lightroom library.

Setting up a Flickr account

In this exercise, you'll set up a Flickr account and publish a selection of photos.

▶ **Tip:** If you don't see the Publish Services panel, right-click / Control-click the header of any panel in the left group and choose its name from the menu.

1 Expand the Publish Services panel, if necessary, by clicking the triangle to the left of the panel's name; then, click Set Up in the Flickr header.

The Lightroom Publishing Manager dialog box opens.

2 Under Publish Service, type your name in the Description text box; then, click the Authorize button in the Flickr Account pane.

3 Lightroom asks your permission to upload images to Flickr; click Authorize.

Your default web browser opens. You will be asked to sign in to Yahoo, or through Google or Facebook, and then your browser will open the Flickr sign-in page.

4 Type a screen name for your Flickr account and click Create A New Account.

5   Flicker asks you to confirm the request from Lightroom to link to your Flickr account. Click "OK, I'll Authorize It" to authorize Lightroom to access all content in your Flickr account, to upload, edit, replace, and delete photos in your account, and to interact with other Flickr members.

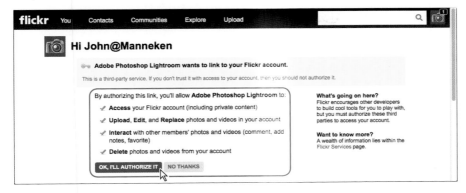

6   Click OK to establish the link between with Lightroom; then, click Done to return to the Lightroom Publishing Manager. In the Flickr Account pane, the Authorize button is now disabled; the account has been successfully authorized.

7   In the Lightroom Publishing Manager dialog box, set the Flickr Title to use the images' existing file names. Under File Settings, drag the Quality slider to set a value of 75. Scroll down, if necessary, to see the Output Sharpening options. Click the check box to enable sharpening, and then choose Screen from the Sharpen For menu and Standard from the Amount menu.

8   Make sure that Watermarking is disabled. Under Privacy and Safety, activate the Public setting, so that access to your photos will be unrestricted. Leave the options for renaming, resizing, video and metadata unchanged.

9   Click Save to close the Lightroom Publishing Manager dialog box.

In the Publish Services panel, your activated Flickr service displays the name you assigned in step 2. The service now contains a single Photostream; an image count of 0 at the right indicates that the new Photostream does not yet contain any photos.

Publishing photos to Flickr

In this exercise you'll add a selection of images to your Flickr Photostream.

1   In the left panel group, expand the Folders panel. Collapse other panels, if necessary, so that you can see the expanded Folders panel and the Publish Services panel at the same time, without scrolling.

2   In the Folders panel, expand the Lesson 10 folder and click to select the nested subfolder named Batch1.

3 Press Ctrl+A / Command+A to select all four images, and then drag the selected photos to your newly created Photostream in the Publish Services panel.

4 In the Publish Services panel, click the Photostream to see its contents; the four images are displayed in the work area under the header New Photos To Publish.

5 Click the Publish button at the bottom of the left panel group.

A progress bar appears in the upper left of the workspace as the images are uploaded to Flickr. While the upload is in progress, the work area is split horizontally, showing which images have been published and which have yet to be uploaded.

6 Wait until the publish process is complete and all four photos are listed as published; then, right-click / Control-click the entry for your new Photostream in the Publish Services panel and choose Show In Flickr from the menu.

Publishing photo comments

Your Publish Services connection allows for two-way interaction between Flickr and Lightroom, so you can keep up to date with—and respond to—any comments that are posted on your images.

1   On your Flickr web page, click the photo Lighthouse-1.jpg to see the image enlarged. Type a comment in the text box below the enlarged image and click Post Comment.

2   Switch back to Lightroom and click the Refresh Comments button (⟳) at the left of the header of the Comments panel in the right panel group. Watch the progress bar at the top left of the workspace as Lightroom connects to Flickr and updates your Publish Collection.

3   Click to select the image Lighthouse-1.jpg under the Published Photos header in the work area. If necessary, expand the Comments panel; the comment you posted on your Flickr page has been downloaded to Lightroom.

▶ **Tip:** To post a comment to an image in your Flickr Photostream from within Lightroom, click the Flickr listing in the Publish Services panel, select a published photo, type your comment in the Comments panel, and then press Enter / Return.

Republishing a photo

Publish Services helps you keep track of images that have been modified since they were published, so you can easily make sure that you are sharing the latest versions.

1   With your Flickr Photostream selected in the Publish Services panel, and the image Lighthouse-1.jpg selected in the work area, expand the Quick Develop panel in the right panel group.

2 From the Saved Preset menu at the top of the Quick Develop panel, choose Lightroom B&W Presets > B&W Contrast High. In the work area, the edited image is now displayed under the header Modified Photos To Re-Publish.

3 Click the Publish button in the bar at the top of the work area to re-publish the modified photo. A dialog box appears asking if you wish to replace the photo on Flickr, and warning that any ratings or comments attached to an image will be deleted when the image is replaced. Click Replace.

4 Right-click / Control-click your Photostream under Flickr in the Publish Services panel and choose Show In Flickr from the menu.

You may need to wait a few moments while your Flickr page is updated to show the re-published, black and white version of the image Lighthouse-1.jpg. If you don't see your re-published photo, try reloading the page in your browser.

Creating a new Photoset on Flickr

The Publish Services panel offers several options for working with your Flickr account from within Lightroom; let's look at another of them.

1 In the Folders panel in the left panel group, expand the Lesson 10 folder, if necessary, and then click to select the subfolder named Batch2.

2 Choose Edit > Select All or Ctrl-click / Command-click to select all six images in the Batch2 folder.

3 Right-click / Control-click your new Photostream in the Publish Services panel and choose Create Photoset from the context menu.

4 In the Create Photoset dialog box, type **Littoral** as the name for the new set. Ensure that the Include Selected Photos option is activated and the option Make New Virtual Copies is disabled, and then click Create.

A listing for your new Photoset appears, nested inside the Flickr service in the Publish Services panel, and the central work area displays the six Littoral images under the header New Photos To Publish.

5 Click the Publish button below the left panel group, or in the bar above the work area, and then wait while the new set of images is uploaded to Flickr.

6 To view the newly published set of images online, right-click / Control-click your new Photoset in the Publish Services panel and choose Show In Flickr from the menu. When you're done, return to Lightroom.

▶ **Tip:** The context menu for your Flickr Photostream also offers the option to create a Smart Photoset: a publish collection which will update itself to include any new photos imported to Lightroom that match its search criteria.

Sharing images to Facebook

The Publish services panel also incorporates a direct connection to Facebook.

1 In the Publish Services panel, click the Facebook connection Set Up button.

2 Under Facebook Account in the Lightroom Publishing Manager dialog box, click Authorize On Facebook. Click OK.

Your default web browser opens. If you are already logged in to Facebook, your Home page opens. If you are not logged in, you'll see the Facebook Login page. If you don't have a Facebook account, you can get started by clicking the Sign Up For Facebook link at the bottom of the login page.

3 Sign up or log in to Facebook, and then follow the prompts to allow Facebook to communicate with Lightroom. When you're done, return to the Lightroom Publishing Manager.

4 Type **Albums** in the Description text box under Publish Service. Under the Facebook Album header, click Create New Album. Type **Scotland Trip** as the name of the new album; then, click OK. Choose the new album from the pop-out Album menu. Leave the rest of the default settings as they are and click Save to dismiss the Lightroom Publishing Manager.

5 In the Folders panel, click to select the subfolder Batch3, nested inside the Lesson 10 folder. Choose Edit > Select All, or Ctrl-click / Command-click to select all the images in the Grid view or Filmstrip. Drag the six selected photos to your newly created Scotland Trip album, listed under the Facebook connection in the Publish Services panel.

6 Click the Scotland Trip album under Facebook in the Publish Services panel; then, click the Publish button below the left panel group, or in the header bar.

A progress bar appears in the upper left of the workspace as the files are uploaded to your Facebook page and the work area becomes a split screen that shows which images have already been published and which have yet to be uploaded.

7 Wait until the publish process is complete and all six photos are listed as published; then, right-click / Control-click your new album in the Publish Services panel and choose Show Album In Facebook from the menu.

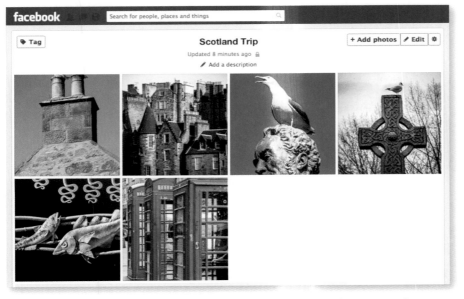

Your Facebook publish service allows two-way communication between Lightroom and Facebook. Select a published image in your Facebook collection and click the Refresh Comments button (G) in the header of the Comments panel to download comments. Type in the Comments panel to post a comment to your album.

8 When you're done, return to Lightroom.

Sharing work in progress on Behance

The latest addition to the integrated sharing services in the Publish Services panel, Behance (www.behance.net) is a popular online showcase for creative work across disciplines. Behance also powers portfolio display for many other websites.

The Lightroom publish service links to the Work In Progress (WIP) area on the Behance site, where you can showcase photos that you're working on, get collaborative feedback from a private network or the entire Behance creative community, and then post updates of your work in progress to be displayed as revisions.

In order to use the Behance service, you first need to set up your free account. In the Publish Services panel, click Set Up, at the right of the Behance header. Enter a name for your Behance service in the Lightroom Publishing Manager, and then click Sign Up in the Behance Account pane. Your web browser will open to the Behance signup page, where you can sign up using your email address, sign in through Facebook or Google, or log in with an Adobe ID.

You'll be offered the chance to begin establishing your own network—known in Behance as a Feedback Circle—by searching your Facebook, Google, or Twitter contacts. On the same screen, you can browse and choose to follow the work of other creatives. When you're done, verify your e-mail address, establish a user name and password; then, return to Lightroom. In the Lightroom Publishing Manager, enter your Behance user name and password in the Behance Account pane; then, click Log In to authorize the service. Set up your sharing preferences, and then click Save to close the Publishing Manager.

Now, simply drag the photos you wish to publish to the new listing in the Publish Services panel, and then click Publish; you'll be given the opportunity to tag and title each image, specify whether your post will be visible to the public, or only to your Feedback Circle, and post a comment to start the conversation. When you edit a photo you've shared to Behance, click your service in the Publish Services panel; the image is listed under the header Modified Photos To Republish. Click the Publish button in the header. Right-click / Control-click the published collection and choose Go To Published Collection; on Behance your photo is listed as having two revisions and the edited version of the photo is displayed beside your original post.

Publishing photos to your hard disk

The Publish services panel also enables you to create publish collections on your hard disk; then, Lightroom will keep track of which images have been updated since the collection was published, just as it does for a collection published online.

You can create a new publish collection for each of your clients, making it easy to check whether they have the most current versions of the photos you hand off, or set up a publish collection that will enable you to publish images to your iPhone sync folder with drag and drop convenience.

1   In the Publish Services panel, click Set Up at the right of the Hard Drive header. Type **Sync to iPhone** in the Description text box under Publish Service in the Lightroom Publishing Manager dialog box.

2   Under Export Location, click Choose and specify your My Pictures Folder / Pictures Folder as the destination. Activate the Put In Subfolder option and type **iPhone** as the name for the new subfolder.

3   Under File Settings, set a Quality value of 50. Review the other options in the Lightroom Publishing Manager dialog box, leaving the settings unchanged for the moment, and then click Save.

A listing for your new iPhone publish collection appears under the Hard Drive header; the image count shows that the collection does not yet contain any photos.

4   In the Folders panel in the left panel group, Ctrl-click / Command-click to select the four "Batch" subfolders nested inside the Lesson 10 folder, leaving the Extras folder unselected. Choose Edit > Select All to select all twenty-five images in the four subfolders, and then drag the selected photos to your newly created iPhone entry in the Publish Services panel.

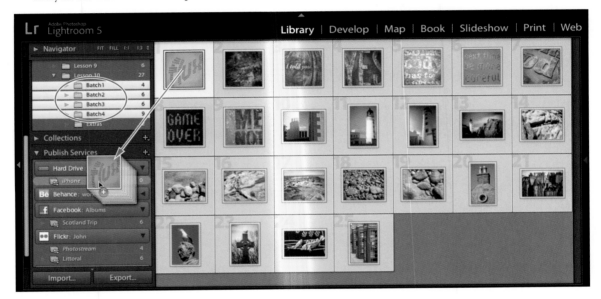

5   Click the iPhone entry in the Publish Services panel. The Lesson 10 photos in the new publish collection are displayed in the work area under the header New Photos To Publish. Click the Publish button at the bottom of the left panel group or in the header bar and wait while Lightroom processes the images.

6   Right-click / Control-click iPhone collection in the Publish Services panel and choose Go To Published Folder from the context menu. An Explorer / Finder window opens showing the twenty five published images in the new iPhone folder. Close the Explorer / Finder window and return to Lightroom.

The Lightroom Web module

Another great way to share and showcase your photos is to use the Lightroom Web module to design, preview, and upload your own web gallery.

In the Web module, you'll start by using the Template Browser in the left panel group to preview the wide range of gallery layout templates. When you've made your choice from the Template Browser, the Gallery Editor view in the central work area shows how your images look in the selected gallery layout.

In the Gallery Editor view, your gallery is fully interactive, performing exactly as it will on the web.

You'll use the panels in the right group to customize the gallery template. You can change the layout, the color scheme, or the background, and add text, borders, or effects. With a single click, you can preview your gallery in a web browser or upload it to your web server without leaving Lightroom.

Assembling photos for an online gallery

In the exercises to follow, you'll create an interactive web portfolio based on one of the Lightroom Flash templates to showcase some photographs of paintings. The first step in creating a web gallery is to isolate the images you want to use from the rest of your catalog.

1   In the Folders panel, select the folder Batch4, nested inside the Lesson 10 folder.

The fact that the selected image source is a folder without subfolders means that you'll be able to rearrange photos in the Grid view or the Filmstrip to create a custom order for your gallery, but you won't be able to exclude an image from the selection without removing it from the catalog.

The solution is to create a collection to group the photos for your project, where you can rearrange the image order—just as you can with a single folder—and also remove an image from the virtual grouping, without deleting it from your catalog.

A collection has a permanent listing in the Collections panel, making it easy to retrieve a selection of images at any time, even if they're stored across multiple folders, as could have been the case if you had assembled the images for your gallery by means of a multiple-criteria search of your library.

Tip: You can reorder photos in a collection by simply dragging the thumbnails in the Grid view or in the Filmstrip. Your custom display order will be saved with the collection.

2   Check that the Lesson 10 / Batch4 folder is still selected in the Folders panel; then, press Ctrl+A / Command+A or choose Edit > Select All.

3   Click the New Collection button (➕) in the header of the Collections panel and choose Create Collection from the menu. In the Create Collection dialog box, type **Paintings** as the name for the collection, and make sure that the Location option is disabled. Under Collection Options, activate Include Selected Photos and disable Make New Virtual Copies; then, click Create.

In the Collections panel, your new collection automatically becomes the active image source; the image count to the right shows that it contains nine photos.

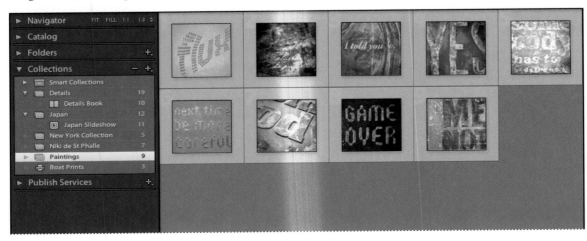

Choosing a template in the Web module

► **Tip:** The first time you enter any of the Lightroom modules, you'll see module tips that will help you get started by identifying the components of the Lightroom workspace and stepping you through the workflow. Dismiss the tips by clicking the Close button. To reactivate the tips for any module, choose [*Module name*] Tips from the Help menu.

1   Keeping the Paintings collection selected in the Collections panel, choose Edit > Select None; then, press Ctrl+Alt+7 / Option+Command+7, or click Web in the Module Picker to switch to the Web module.

2   In the Layout Style panel at the right, select the Lightroom HTML Gallery. In the Template Browser at the left, the default HTML gallery template is activated, the Preview panel shows a thumbnail of the selected design, and the Gallery Editor view shows how your images will look in that layout. From the Use menu in the Toolbar below the Gallery Editor, choose All Filmstrip Photos.

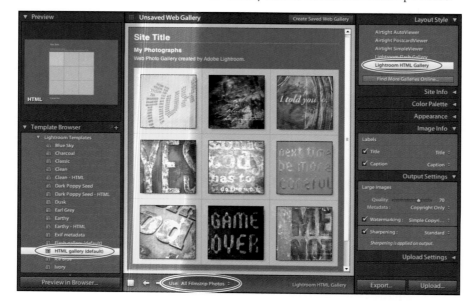

3   Hide the Filmstrip, if necessary, so that you can see the Preview panel and as much as possible of the list of templates in the Template Browser. Move the pointer down the list to preview the different template designs in the Lightroom Templates folder. Note the HTML or Flash icon in the lower left corner of the layout preview indicating the gallery type for each template.

4   When you've finished previewing the gallery templates in the Template Browser, click to select the template Flash Gallery (Default).

The Gallery Editor view in the work area shows your images displayed in the new template layout.

Distinguishing between HTML and Flash templates

In the Template Browser you'll find both HTML and Flash templates. As you move the pointer down the list of gallery templates, you'll see a preview of each template layout in the Preview panel.

An icon in the lower left corner of the layout preview indicates the gallery type. Once you click to select a template in the Template Browser, the gallery type is also shown in the Layout Style panel in the right panel group and at the right of the Toolbar below the Gallery Editor view.

Templates of either type can be customized to show your work in its best light. You can add text and effects to your layout and change the color scheme, the background, and the image size.

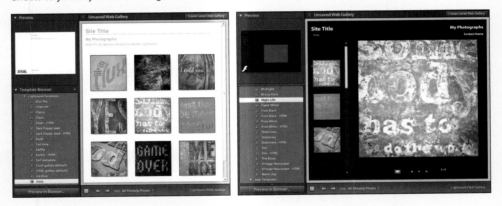

The HTML gallery templates enable you to produce simple websites that are compatible with most browsers. The HTML pages generated can be customized further in an HTML editor.

Flash templates can produce more sophisticated web galleries, including animations, slideshows with smooth transitions, and other special effects. However, Flash galleries require that the viewer has the appropriate Adobe Flash Player plug-in installed. Should security settings be in place to block scripts and ActiveX controls, your audience may have to click through warning messages in the web browser before being able to see the gallery.

5 In the Gallery Editor view you'll notice that the default Lightroom Flash gallery has its own navigation controls below the large image. Click the Play button to view the gallery slideshow.

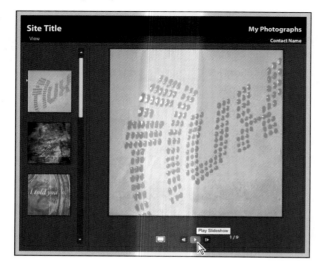

6 To stop the slideshow, click the Pause button.

Rearranging the order of your images

● **Note:** The order of the images in the Grid view and the Filmstrip determines their display order in a Web gallery.

After seeing your slideshow in action, you may wish to change the order in which the images appear in the web gallery. In this exercise, you'll move two of the images so that the slideshow alternates between cool and warm colors.

1 Click the Library Grid button (⊞) at the top left of the Filmstrip, or press G on your keyboard, to return to the Grid view in the Library module.

2 Make sure that the Paintings collection is still selected in the Collections panel; then, choose Edit > Select None.

● **Note:** Dragging an image that is part of a multiple selection will move all the selected images. If all images in a collection are selected you will not be able to rearrange their order.

3 In the Grid view, drag the image Art-8.jpg to position it between the first two thumbnails. Release the mouse button when the vertical black line appears to indicate an insertion point between the images Art-1.jpg and Art-2.jpg.

4   In the Filmstrip, drag the image Art-2.jpg, now in the third position, to the right. Release the mouse button when a vertical black line appears to indicate an insertion point between the last two images Art-7.jpg and Art-9.jpg.

5   Click Web in the Module Picker. Click the Play button to review the slideshow in the Gallery Editor view. Click the Pause button to stop the slideshow.

You can rearrange the order of images in the Filmstrip while you're working in any of the Lightroom modules, as long as your image source is a collection or a folder without subfolders. When you re-order photos in the Filmstrip in the Web module, the Gallery Editor view in the work area may be slow to reflect the changes. If necessary, you can refresh the Gallery Editor view by choosing Web > Reload.

Customizing your web gallery

You can save time when creating your web gallery by starting with the layout template closest to the design you have in mind. Once you've made your choice, you can use the Site Info, Color Palette, Appearance, Image Info, and Output Settings panels in the right panel group to customize the template. You can add text, choose backgrounds and color schemes, and tweak the layout to change the look and feel of your gallery. In the following exercises, you'll customize the text in your gallery template, adjust the layout, place a logo, and add a watermark to the images.

Replacing text

In the Site Info panel you can add a website title, a collection description, contact information, and web or e-mail links. The information you enter in the Site Info panel will appear on your website.

1   If the Site Info panel is currently collapsed in the right panel group, expand it by clicking the triangle beside its name.

2 Click the default Site Title text in the Site Info panel and type a title for your site. Press Enter on your keyboard to update the title displayed in your layout in the Gallery Editor view. In a web browser, the site title will also appear in the title bar of the browser window.

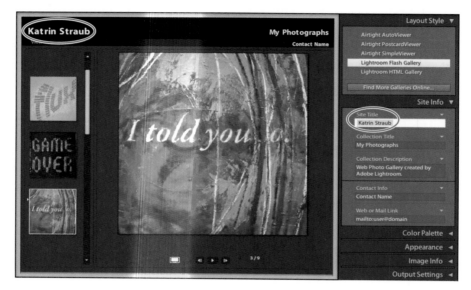

3 Click the triangle beside Site Title and note the entries in the Site Title menu. Lightroom keeps track of your entries for each of the text boxes in the Site Info panel. Instead of retyping information each time you create a new web gallery, you can choose previously entered details from this list.

4 As an alternative to working with the Site Info panel, you can edit the text in your gallery directly in the Gallery Editor view in the work area. Click the Collection Title (My Photographs) in the top right corner of the Gallery Editor view and type a new title. Press Enter and both the gallery preview and the corresponding entry in the Site Info panel will be updated.

5 In the Site Info panel, delete the default text under Collection Description. Additional information about the images in your web gallery can be entered here. In this particular template, the viewer can access those details by clicking View below the site title and choosing About These Photos from the menu.

The last two items in the Site Info panel let you to set up a clickable Contact Info message connected to a Web Or Mail Link, so that when the viewer clicks the contact message—which may be "Home," "Purchase," or "Enquiries"—the web browser will either jump to the specified web page or open a new message in their default e-mail application.

Enter an e-mail address like this: mailto:user@domain.com, or a web address in the following format: http://www.domain.com.

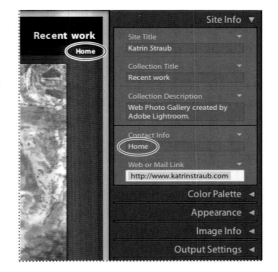

▶ **Tip:** As illustrated here, you could use the Contact Info pane to set up a link to your Home page where you can offer the viewer links to other galleries you've created in Lightroom.

Changing colors

The controls in the Color Palette panel enable you to change the color scheme for your website. You can set the color for every element in your layout: background, borders, header, menu bar, and text.

Choosing colors that work well together and look good on any system may seem a major challenge, but keeping just a few simple rules in mind should help you to stay within a safe color palette:

- Use dark text on a light background and light text on a dark background.
- Text that stands out from the background due to color, rather than light-dark contrast, may be hard to see if the colors are shifted on the viewer's browser.

In this exercise you'll change the color of the text for the site and collection titles, but the same technique applies to any of the color settings.

● Note: For base elements such as the background, borders, and headers, neutral, muted colors will compete less with your images. If you want to get serious about designing color schemes, Kuler® from the Adobe labs can be an invaluable reference. Go to kuler.adobe.com.

1 Expand the Color Palette panel by clicking the triangle next to its name. If necessary, you can collapse other panels to make more space.

2 In the Color Palette, click the Header Text color swatch to open the Lightroom Color Picker.

▶ Tip: You can simplify the way you work with the side panel groups by setting the panels to Solo Mode, which automatically collapses all the panels in the group other than the one you're working with. Right-click / Control-click any panel header, and toggle Solo Mode in the context menu.

3 In the Color Picker, drag the slider at the right almost to the top, and then click a bright red in the large color field on the left. We chose a color with RGB values of R: 90%, G: 10%, B: 15%. You can enter these RGB values directly by clicking the number and typing a new value. The new color appears in the Header Text color swatch in the Color Palette panel and is applied to both the site and collection titles in the Gallery Editor view.

4 Close the Color Picker and collapse the Color Palette panel.

Tweaking the layout of a web gallery

You can adjust your gallery layout using the Appearance panel. The options available in the Appearance panel differ for Flash and HTML galleries.

For an HTML gallery, the Appearance panel offers the options shown in the illustration to the right. You can add borders or drop shadows to your images and display an index number in the background of each image cell. Change the number of rows and columns used on the index page with the Grid Pages controls, which will indirectly determine the size of the thumbnail images in the grid. The minimum grid is three by three—if your gallery contains more than nine images additional index pages will be generated. You can also set the size of the page and the width of a photo border for the enlarged view of an image.

These options give you great flexibility in customizing the look and feel of your HTML gallery. For a Flash gallery the options in the Appearance panel are more restricted.

1 In the right panel group, expand the Appearance panel; then click the double triangle beside Layout, and choose the Scrolling layout option from the menu.

The Scrolling layout displays a scrollable row of index thumbnails beneath an enlarged image view.

2 In the Appearance panel, click the double triangle beside Layout, and choose the Paginated layout option from the menu.

The Paginated layout displays thumbnails organized as an index beside an enlarged image view. Navigation controls below the thumbnails provide easy access to additional index pages.

3   Under Thumbnail Images in the Appearance panel, click the double triangle beside Size and choose Medium from the menu.

The gallery preview is updated in the Gallery Editor view. Depending on the number of images in your collection and the size of your Lightroom workspace window, the new thumbnail size may affect the number of index pages for your gallery.

4   In the Appearance panel, click the double triangle beside Layout, and choose the Slideshow Only layout option from the menu.

The Slideshow Only layout displays only the enlarged image with controls for navigating through the collection and playing a gallery slideshow.

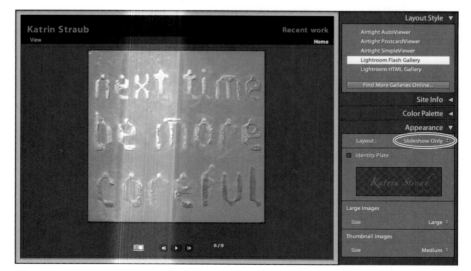

5 In the Appearance panel, click the double triangle beside Layout, and choose the Left layout option from the menu to return to the default layout for this gallery template, with a scrolling column of thumbnails to the left of the enlarged image view.

6 Click the View Slideshow button () below the enlarged image view to hide the index thumbnails and view a slideshow that will display only the enlarged images.

The View Slideshow button switches the gallery temporarily to Slideshow Only mode—it is available in all of the Flash gallery layout options except the Slideshow Only layout. When the View Slideshow button is clicked, it changes to the View Gallery button (⊞).

7 Click the View Gallery button (⊞) to return to the selected gallery layout, complete with index thumbnails.

Personalizing your web gallery

Next, you'll personalize your web gallery by placing a logo in the header area.

1 In the Appearance panel, activate the Identity Plate option; then click the white triangle at the lower right of the Identity Plate preview pane and choose Edit from the menu.

2 In the Identity Plate Editor dialog box, activate the option Use A Graphical Identity Plate, and then click the Locate File button.

3 In the Locate File dialog box, navigate to the Extras folder inside the Lesson 10 folder and select the file Web_Identityplate.png. Click Choose; then, click OK.

▶ **Tip:** For best results use an image that is no more than 60 pixels high so that it will not need to be scaled to fit your layout template. In this case we used an image with a height of 46 pixels.

The new identity plate appears in the gallery preview and in the Identity Plate preview in the Appearance panel. The identity plate will replace the site title on your web page, but when the gallery is viewed in a web browser, the text you entered as the Site Title will still be displayed in the title bar of the browser window.

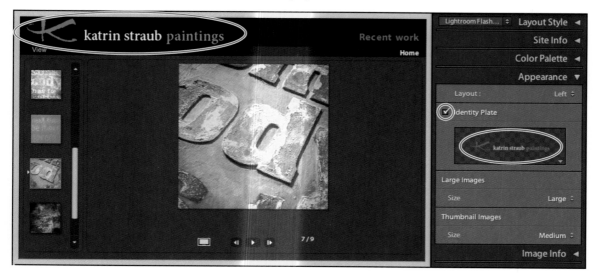

Working with identity plates

You can personalize your slideshows, Web presentations, and print layouts—and the Lightroom workspace itself—by adding your own identity plate.

A **Styled Text Identity Plate** will display the text you enter in the Identity Plate Editor dialog box. You can choose from the menus below the text box to specify the font characteristics.

A **Graphical Identity Plate** uses a graphic that is no more than 60 pixels high, in any of the following file formats: PDF, JPG, GIF, PNG, TIFF, or PSD (Windows) and JPG, GIF, PNG, TIFF, or PSD (Macintosh). The resolution of graphical identity plates may be too low for printed output. Choose Save As from the Enable Identity Plate menu, and give your identity plate a name.

To display your identity plate in the Lightroom workspace, choose Edit > Identity Plate Setup / Lightroom > Identity Plate Setup. In the Identity Plate Editor dialog box, activate the Enable Identity Plate option and choose one of your saved identity plates from the menu to the right.

Choose from the pop-up menus on the right side of the dialog box to change the font style, size and color for the Module Picker. The first color swatch sets the text color for the active module; the second swatch sets the text color for the others.

—From Lightroom Help

Providing more information

You can display information about the images in your web gallery by choosing from a range of options in the Title and Caption menus in the Image Info panel. Show specific details retrieved from the metadata of each image, apply the same text to all the images at once, or display your images without any text information at all.

You can also set up a text template that will combine information drawn from different sources to compose titles and captions for your images automatically. In this exercise, you'll add a title and caption to the first image in the collection.

1   Expand the Image Info panel in the right panel group. Make sure that both the Title and Caption options are activated.

2   Click on the double triangle beside Title to see the list of options. The same choices are available in the Caption menu. Most of the options display information retrieved from an image's metadata.

3   From the Title menu, choose Title. From the Caption menu, choose Caption.

Note: The title text will be displayed immediately below the enlarged image view. The caption appears below the title in a smaller font size.

Tip: Choose the Custom Text option to add "boilerplate" text that will be displayed with every image.

Next, you'll need to edit the image metadata from which the Title and Caption information will be drawn. You can do this in the Library module.

4 Press G to switch to the Grid view in the Library module.

5 Choose Edit > Select All or press Ctrl+A / Command+A. Expand the Metadata panel in the right panel group. In the Title text box, type **Token**, and then press Enter / Return. Click to confirm that you want to apply the change in metadata to all the selected images. In the Caption box, type **mixed media on canvas**; then, press Enter / Return and click to confirm the changes.

6 Choose Edit > Select None or press Ctrl+D / Command+D; then, select the first image in the series. In the Metadata panel, change the Title to **Token 1**. Select each of the other eight images in turn and add sequential numbers to their Title metadata.

7 To switch to the Web module, press Ctrl+Alt+7 / Command+Option+7.

The title and caption details drawn from the images' metadata are now displayed under the enlarged view of each painting.

Specifying output settings

In the Output Settings panel you can control the image quality and the sharpness of the JPEG images generated for your web gallery. You can also choose to add a watermark to your images—a minimal protection when publishing your work.

▶ **Tip:** It's always worth experimenting with the image quality settings; for some images a lower setting might be sufficient, resulting in a website that loads faster.

1 In the right panel group, collapse the Image Info panel and expand the Output Settings panel. Drag the Quality slider to set the image quality to 70%, or alternatively, click the value to the right, type **70** and press Enter. In most cases, an image quality setting of 70% to 80% strikes a good balance between file size and image quality.

2 Activate the Sharpening option at the bottom of the Output Settings panel. Click the double arrow to open the Sharpening menu and choose Standard.

You won't see the changes to these settings reflected in the images in the gallery preview; both the image quality and sharpening settings will not be applied until Lightroom exports the image files for your website.

Watermarking images

With the Watermark Editor interface, Lightroom makes it easy to watermark your images for export, printing, publishing, or for a web gallery.

You have the choice of applying a simple text watermark—ideal for a copyright message or your business name—or importing an image file such as your company logo to be applied as a graphic watermark.

For a text watermark you can specify a font and the text color, and for both watermark styles you can adjust the opacity and either use precise scaling and positioning controls or work directly with your watermark in the watermarking preview.

1   In the Filmstrip, select all the images in your web gallery. In the Output Settings panel, activate the Watermarking option. Click the double arrow to open the Watermarking menu and choose Edit Watermarks to open the Watermark Editor dialog box.

The default watermark style is a simple text copyright watermark. In the Watermark Editor dialog box you have the opportunity to enter your own message and specify the font, style, alignment, and color of your text. On Mac OS, you also have the option to set up a drop-shadow effect for your watermark text.

▶ **Tip:** For both watermark styles you can use the Watermark Effects controls at the right of the dialog box, where you can adjust the opacity of your watermark as well as its size and placement. Alternatively, you can move or resize your watermark directly in the watermarking preview; a bounding box and handles will appear around the watermark when you move the pointer over the preview. Use the left and right arrows at the top of the dialog box to change the image in the preview pane.

2 Under Image Options at the top right of the Watermark Editor dialog box, click Choose to select an image file to be used as a graphic watermark.

3 In the Open / Choose A File dialog box, navigate to and open the Extras folder inside the Lesson 10 folder. Select the file watermark_K.png; then, click Choose.

4 At the right of the Watermark Editor dialog box, scroll down if necessary and expand the Watermark Effects controls. Use the sliders or type new values to set up the Watermark Effects controls as shown in the illustration below. Set the opacity value to 50, proportional sizing value to 25, and both the horizontal and vertical inset values to 3. Use the Anchor setting at the lower left to specify where the watermark will appear on the image. For our purposes, you won't need to use the Rotate buttons to reorientate the watermark image.

5 Use the left and right arrow buttons at the top of the Watermark Editor dialog box to cycle the image in the watermarking preview and decide whether the settings are effective for all the images in the collection. Make any adjustments you wish to make.

6 Choose Save Current Settings As New Preset from the Custom menu above the watermarking preview. In the New Preset dialog box, type **web portfolio** as the name for your new preset, and then click Create. You could now apply the same watermark settings to another collection of images quickly and easily.

7 Click Done to close the Watermark Editor dialog box. The watermark appears on the images in the gallery preview and the web portfolio preset is indicated beside Watermarking in the Output Settings panel.

This concludes the section on customizing the look and feel of your web gallery. You've changed the site title text, added a Home page link, learned how to adjust the color scheme and the layout, personalized your web page by placing a graphic identity plate, and finally added titles, captions and a watermark to the images.

It's time to save all these modifications as a custom template that you can use as a starting point the next time you create a web gallery, but first let's preview your gallery in your web browser.

Previewing the gallery

To enable you to preview your gallery as it will appear on the Web, Lightroom generates the web pages and all the necessary image files in a temporary folder on your hard disk, and then opens the main page of the gallery in your default web browser.

1   To preview the gallery in your default web browser, click the Preview In Browser button below the left panel group, or choose Web > Preview In Browser.

While Lightroom generates the necessary files, a progress bar appears in the upper left corner of the Lightroom workspace. You can cancel the Preview In Browser command at any time by clicking the small cross icon (x) at the right end of the progress indicator—but for this exercise, let the process run its course.

2   Once Lightroom has finished generating the necessary files, your web gallery opens in your default browser.

> **Tip:** You should always preview your gallery in this way before uploading it to your website. Check that the navigation controls work as expected, examine the image quality, and confirm that your photos appear in the correct order. Finally, you should resize the browser window to see how well the gallery layout adapts to different display sizes.

3   To check how your web gallery performs in the browser, run these simple tests:

- Click the Play button in the group of navigation controls below the large image to start the gallery slideshow.

- Click the Pause button to stop playback.

- If necessary, use the scroll bar to scroll down the list of thumbnail images on the left. Click a thumbnail to view the enlarged image on the right.

- Click the word View just below the identity plate at the upper left of the gallery layout, and then choose Slideshow from the menu.

- Click the Next Image and Previous Image buttons on either side of the Play button to move from one image to the next.

- Click the View Gallery button at the left of the navigation controls below the large image to leave the slideshow mode and return to the gallery layout with the column of thumbnail images on the left.

- Resize your browser window to see how the gallery works at different sizes.

- Examine the image quality.

- Make sure the titles, captions, and watermarks are displayed correctly.

- Click the Home (Contact Info) button to see if it links correctly to your home page. (You'll need an active Internet connection to test this.)

4   When you're done, close the browser window and return to Lightroom.

Saving your custom template

Having spent time and effort modifying the gallery layout, changing the color scheme and text style, adding titles, captions, an identity plate, and watermarks, you should save your design as a custom web gallery template. The new template will be listed under User Templates in the Template Browser panel, where you can access it easily in case you need to rework or extend your gallery, or should you wish to use your customized template as a starting point for creating a new layout. You can create additional folders in the Template Browser to help you manage your custom templates.

1   With your customized web gallery still open in the Web module, click the Create New Preset button (+) in the header of the Template Browser panel in the left panel group. Alternatively, choose Web > New Template.

2   In the New Template dialog box, type **My Flash Web Portfolio**. Leave the default User Templates folder selected in the Folder menu and click Create.

Your customized web gallery template is now listed under User Templates in the Template Browser panel.

3   In the Template Browser panel right-click / Control-click the User Templates folder and choose New Folder from the context menu. In the New Folder dialog box, type **My CIB Templates** as the name for the new folder; then click Create.

4   In the Template Browser panel, drag the My Flash Web Portfolio template from the User Templates folder into your new My CIB Templates folder.

► **Tip:** To delete a selected template, click the Delete Selected Preset button (-) in the header of the Template Browser. You cannot delete the Lightroom templates. To delete a folder from the Template Browser, first delete all the templates inside it—or drag them into another folder; then right-click / Control-click the empty folder and choose Delete Folder from the context menu. You cannot delete the default templates folders.

Creating a Saved Web Gallery

Since you entered the Web module, you've been working with an *unsaved web gallery*, as is indicated in the bar across the top of the Slideshow Editor view.

⠿ **Unsaved Web Gallery**   Create Saved Web Gallery

Until you save your gallery design, the Web module works like a scratch pad. You can move to another module, or even close Lightroom, and find your settings unchanged when you return, but if you click a new gallery template—or even the one you started with—in the Template Browser, the "scratch pad" will be cleared and all your work will be lost.

Converting your project to a Saved Slideshow not only preserves your layout and output settings, but also links your layout to the particular set of images for which it was designed.

Your web gallery is saved as a special kind of collection—an *output collection*—with its own listing in the Collections panel. Clicking this listing will instantly retrieve the images you were working with, and reinstate all of your settings, no matter how many times the web gallery scratch pad has been cleared.

1   Click the Create Saved Web Gallery button in the bar at the top of the Gallery Editor view, or click the New Collection button (🞧) in the header of the Collections panel and choose Create Web Gallery.

► **Tip:** Once you've saved your gallery, any changes you make to the layout or output settings are auto-saved as you work.

2 In the Create Web Gallery dialog box, type **Web Portfolio** as the name for your saved presentation. In the Location options, activate Inside and choose the collection Paintings from the menu; then, click Create.

▶ **Tip:** Adding more photos to a saved gallery is easy: simply drag images to the gallery's listing in the Collections panel. To open your gallery in the Web module from the Library, click the white arrow that appears to the right of the image count when you move the pointer over your saved gallery in the Collections panel.

Your saved web gallery appears in the Collections panel, marked with a Saved Web Gallery icon (⊞), and nested inside the original source collection, Paintings. The image count shows that the new output collection, like the source, contains nine photos. The title bar above the Slide Editor displays the name of your saved gallery.

Depending on the way you like to work, you can save your web gallery at any point in the process; you could create a Saved Web Gallery as soon as you enter the Web module with a selection of images or wait until your presentation is polished.

Exporting your gallery

Now that you're happy with your gallery and you've saved the template, you can export the website to your hard disk. You can run the exported website from your laptop if you need to present your work where there is no Internet connection, or burn the exported files to a CD-ROM as a working backup or to send to a client.

1 Select My Flash Web Portfolio from the My CIB Templates folder in the Template Browser panel and click the Export button below the right panel group, or choose Web > Export Web Photo Gallery.

2 In the Save Web Gallery dialog box, navigate to your Lesson 10 folder. Type **My Web Gallery** in the File Name / Save As text box, and then click Save.

▶ **Tip:** Before burning your web gallery to a CD-ROM for a client, create an alias of the index.html file, place it beside the folder containing the files for the website, and rename it **Start here**. This will make it easy for your client to launch your presentation.

Lightroom will create a folder named My Web Gallery inside the Lesson 10 folder and generate all the necessary image files, web pages, subfolders and support files within that folder. If you have many images in your gallery, this operation might take a while—a progress bar at the upper left of the Lightroom workspace provides feedback as Lightroom completes the process.

3 When the export is complete, double-click the file index.html in the folder My Web Gallery inside your Lesson 10 folder. Your gallery opens in your default web browser. When you're finished reviewing the exported gallery, close the browser window and return to Lightroom.

Uploading your gallery to a web server

In the last exercise of this lesson you'll learn how to upload your web gallery to a server from within Lightroom. To do this, you'll need to know your FTP server access information. You can get these details from your Internet service provider.

1   In the Web module, expand the Upload Settings panel in the right panel group.

2   From the FTP Server menu in the Upload Settings panel, choose Edit.

3   In the Configure FTP File Transfer dialog box, enter the server address, your username and password, and the server path.

> **Tip:** For security reasons, don't activate the Store Password In Preset option unless you are the only person with access to the computer you're using.

4   From the Preset menu, choose Save Current Settings As New Preset.

5   In the New Preset dialog box, enter a name for your FTP server preset, and then click Create.

6   Click OK to close the Configure FTP File Transfer dialog box. You'll notice that the name of your new FTP server preset now appears in the Upload Settings panel, where you can access it at any time from the FTP Server Presets menu.

Tip: To avoid possible compatibility issues with your web server, you should use only lowercase letters, the minus sign (-), and the underscore character (_) in the subfolder name. Avoid using spaces in the folder name.

7 To place the gallery inside a subfolder on your FTP server, activate the option Put In Subfolder and type a name for the subfolder that's relevant to the content of the gallery. This subfolder name will become part of the URL of your web gallery. For example, we used **tokens** as subfolder name, so the complete URL might look like this: http://www.katrinstraub.com/tokens.

8 Click the Upload button below the right panel group. If you didn't save your FTP server password in the Configure FTP File Transfer dialog box, you'll need to enter it now in the Enter Password dialog box, and then click Upload.

Uploading your web gallery to an FTP server generally takes much longer than exporting it to your local hard disk. You can watch the upload status in the progress bar at the upper left of the Lightroom workspace.

Once the upload is complete, you can enter the URL of your gallery in your web browser and admire your site live on the Internet. Don't send the URL to a client or friends before you've confirmed that everything works as expected!

Congratulations—you've completed this lesson on publishing images. You've learned how to use the new Publish Services feature to publish images to a photo sharing website or to your hard disk. You've built your own web gallery, saved a custom gallery template and created new watermarking and FTP upload presets. Finally, you learned how to export your web gallery or upload it to a web server.

Before you move on to the next lesson, take a moment or two to review some of your new skills by reading through the questions and answers on the facing page.

Review questions

1 Why would you use Publish Services to publish images to your hard disk?

2 Why is it useful to create a collection to group the images that you intend to use for a web gallery?

3 What is the difference between HTML and Flash galleries?

4 Which panels would you use to customize the Lightroom web templates?

5 How do you add a graphic watermark to the images in your web gallery?

Review answers

1 You can create a new publish collection on your hard disk for each client to whom you hand off photos, making it easy to check whether they have the most current versions, as Lightroom will keep track of which images have been updated since the collection was published. You can also set up a publish collection that will enable you to publish images to your iPhone sync folder with drag and drop convenience.

2 Grouping your images as a collection not only keeps them all in one place for easy reference—it will also make the process of updating and adjusting your web gallery much more efficient. Once a selection of photos has been saved as a collection it is possible not only to re-order images, as you can with a single-folder image source, but also to exclude an image without deleting it from the catalog.

3 HTML gallery templates produce simple websites that are compatible with most browsers. Flash templates can produce more sophisticated web galleries, including animations, slideshows with smooth transitions, and other special effects. However, Flash galleries require that the viewer has the appropriate Adobe Flash Player plug-in. Viewers may need to click through security messages in the web browser before being able to see the gallery.

4 The panels in the right panel group—the Site Info, Color Palette, Appearance, Image Info, Output Settings, and Upload Settings panels—contain controls for modifying the gallery layout templates available in the Template Browser.

5 In the Web module, activate the Watermarking option in the Output Settings panel. Click the double arrow to open the Watermarking menu and choose Edit Watermarks to open the Watermark Editor dialog box. Under Image Options in the Watermark Editor dialog box, click Choose to select an image file to be used as a watermark.

11 MAKING BACKUPS AND EXPORTING PHOTOS

Lesson overview

Lightroom makes it easy to back up and export all the data connected with your image library. You can create backup copies to external storage during import, have Lightroom schedule automatic backups of your catalog file, and perform full or incremental backups of both your photos and develop settings. Export files in a range of formats—from images optimized for on-screen viewing to archival copies.

In this lesson you'll learn a variety of techniques to help you streamline your workflow and minimize the impact of accidental data loss:

- Backing up the catalog file
- Backing your entire image library
- Making incremental backups
- Exporting metadata
- Exporting photos for on-screen viewing
- Exporting photos to be edited in another application
- Exporting photos for archival purposes
- Using export presets
- Setting up automated post-export actions

 You'll probably need between one and two hours to complete this lesson. If you haven't already done so, download the Lesson 11 work files from the Lesson & Update Files tab of your Account page at www.peachpit.com.

Safeguard your photographs and develop settings against loss using Lightroom's build-in backup tools. Back up just your catalog file, or your entire photo library, complete with develop settings and copies of your master files. Export photos in different file formats for multimedia presentations, for further editing in an external image editor, as e-mail attachments, or to be burned to CD or DVD for archival purposes.

Getting started

● **Note:** This lesson assumes that you already have a basic working familiarity with the Lightroom workspace. If you find that you need more background information, refer to Lightroom Help, or review the previous lessons.

Before you start on this lesson, make sure you've set up the LR5CIB folder for your lesson files and created the LR5CIB Catalog file to manage them, as described in "Setting up a work folder" and "Creating a catalog file for working with this book" in the Getting Started chapter at the beginning of this book.

If you haven't already done so, download the Lesson 11 folder from your Account page at www.peachpit.com to the LR5CIB/Lessons folder, as detailed in the section "Accessing the Classroom in a Book files" in the chapter "Getting Started."

1 Start Lightroom.

2 In the Adobe Photoshop Lightroom - Select Catalog dialog box, make sure the file LR5CIB Catalog.lrcat is selected under Select A Recent Catalog To Open, and then click Open.

▶ **Tip:** If you can't see the Module Picker, choose Window > Panels > Show Module Picker, or press the F5 key. If you're working on Mac OS, you may need to press the fn key together with the F5 key, or change the function key behavior in the system preferences.

3 Lightroom will open in the screen mode and workspace module that were active when you last quit. If necessary, switch to the Library module by clicking Library in the Module Picker at the top of the workspace.

Importing images into the library

The first step is to import the images for this lesson into the Lightroom library.

1 In the Library module, click the Import button below the left panel group.

2   If the Import dialog box appears in compact mode, click the Show More Options button at the lower left of the dialog box to see all the options in the expanded Import dialog box.

3   In the Source panel at the left of the expanded Import dialog box, navigate to and select the LR5CIB > Lessons > Lesson 11 folder. Ensure that all six images in the Lesson 11 folder are checked for import.

4   In the import options above the thumbnail previews, select Add so that the imported photos will be added to your catalog without being moved or copied. Under File Handling at the right of the expanded Import dialog box, choose Minimal from the Render Previews menu and ensure that the Don't Import Suspected Duplicates option is activated. Under Apply During Import, choose None from both the Develop Settings menu and the Metadata menu and type **Lesson 11** in the Keywords text box. Make sure that the Import dialog box is set up as shown in the illustration below, and then click Import.

The six images are imported from the Lesson 11 folder and now appear in both the Grid view of the Library module and in the Filmstrip across the bottom of the Lightroom workspace.

Preventing data loss

The importance of a good backup strategy is often only understood too late. How much damage would be done if your computer was stolen right now? How many files would be irrecoverably lost if your hard disk failed today? How much work and money would that cost you? You can't prevent a disaster from happening but it *is* in your power to reduce the risks and the cost of recovery. Backing up regularly will reduce the impact of a catastrophe and save you time, effort, and money.

Lightroom delivers a range of options that make it easy to safeguard your photo library; as for the rest of the files on your computer, you really should have your own backup strategy in place.

Backing up the catalog file

The Lightroom catalog file stores a great deal of information for the photos in your library—not only the locations of the image files, but the metadata attached to them, including titles, captions, keyword tags, flags, labels, and ratings, together with all your developing and output settings. Every time you modify a photo in any way, from renaming the file during import to color correction, retouching, and cropping—all your work is saved to the catalog file. It records the way your images are grouped and ordered in collections, and records the publishing history, slide-show settings, web gallery designs, and print layouts associated with them as well as your customized templates and presets.

Unless you back up your catalog, you could lose hundreds of hours of work in the event of a hard disk failure, accidental deletion, or a corrupted library file—even if you do have copies of your original images stored safely on removable media. You can set Lightroom to initiate a regular backup of your catalog file automatically.

1   Choose Catalog Settings from the Edit / Lightroom menu. On the General tab, choose When Lightroom Next Exits from the Back Up Catalog menu.

2   Click OK / the Close button (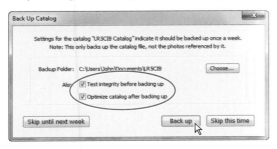) to close the Catalog Settings dialog box; then quit Lightroom.

3   In the Back Up Catalog dialog box, click the Choose button to change the folder where the backed up catalog will be stored. Ideally the backup should be located on a different disk than your original catalog file; for the purpose of this exercise you can select the LR5CIB folder on your hard disk. In the Browse For Folder / Choose Folder dialog box, select the LR5CIB folder as the backup directory and click Select Folder / Choose.

4   Make sure the options Test Integrity Before Backing Up and Optimize Catalog After Backing Up are activated. It's a good idea to keep these options activated whenever you back up your catalog; it would defy the purpose of a backup if your original catalog file was not in good working order. Click Back Up.

Each time you back up your catalog, Lightroom will create a complete copy of the catalog file in the directory you specified, inside a new folder with a name composed from the date and time of the backup. To save space on your backup drive, you can either delete your older backup files or compress them. Catalog files compress very effectively; you can expect a compressed catalog to be as small as 10% of the size of the original. Make sure to decompress the file before attempting to restore your catalog from the backup.

Should your catalog be accidently deleted or become corrupted, you can now restore it either by copying the backup file to your catalog folder or by creating a new catalog and importing the contents of your backup file. To avoid inadvertently modifying your backup file, it's preferable not to open it directly from the Lightroom File menu.

● **Note:** Backing up the catalog file in this way does not make backup copies of the original image files or the preview images that Lightroom displays in the workspace. The previews will be regenerated as your catalog file is restored from the backup, but you'll need to back up your original image files separately.

5   Start Lightroom. In the Adobe Photoshop Lightroom - Select Catalog dialog box, make sure that the file LR5CIB Catalog.lrcat is selected under Select A Recent Catalog To Open, and then click Open.

6   Choose Edit > Catalog Settings / Lightroom > Catalog Settings.

7   In the Catalog Settings dialog box, click the General tab and set your preferred backup frequency by choosing from the Back Up Catalog menu.

8   Click OK / the Close button (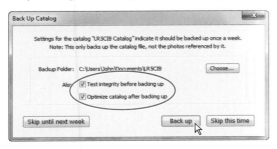) to close the Catalog Settings dialog box.

Exporting metadata

The catalog is a central storage location for all the information associated with every image in your library; exporting and distributing the catalog file's content is another strategy that will lessen the impact if your catalog file is lost or damaged. By saving the information from the catalog file that is specific to each photo to the respective image file on your hard disk—and keeping this exported information in sync with your catalog file, which can be done automatically—you have, in effect, a distributed backup of the metadata and develop settings for each of your photos.

When a photo has changes to its metadata that have not yet been saved to the original image file—such as the keyword tag you applied to the images for this lesson during the import process—its image cell in the Grid view and the Filmstrip is marked with the Metadata File Needs To Be Updated icon (≡⬇).

1   If you don't see the Metadata File Needs To Be Updated icon (≡⬇) in the Grid view image cells, choose View > View Options. On the Grid View tab in the Library View Options dialog box, activate the Unsaved Metadata option under Cell Icons. Click the Close button to close the Library View Options dialog box.

2   Select the first image in the Grid view. Right-click / Control-click the thumbnail and choose Metadata > Save Metadata To File from the context menu. Click Continue to confirm the operation: after a brief processing time, the Metadata File Needs To Be Updated icon disappears from the thumbnail cell.

3   Ctrl-click / Command-click to select the other five photos, and then click the Metadata File Needs To Be Updated icon (≡⬇) in the image cell of any of the selected images. Click Save to update the image files on your hard disk.

After a brief processing time, the Metadata File Needs To Be Updated badge disappears from each of the image cells.

If you edit or add to an image's metadata in another application, such as Adobe Bridge or the Photoshop Camera Raw plug-in, Lightroom will show the Metadata Was Changed Externally icon (≡⇧) above the thumbnail in the Grid view. To accept the changes and update your catalog file accordingly, choose Metadata > Read Metadata From Files. To reject the changed metadata and overwrite it with the information in your catalog file, choose Metadata > Save Metadata To Files.

You can update the metadata for a batch of modified images—or even for the entire catalog with all its folders and collections—by selecting the images or folders to be updated and choosing Metadata > Save Metadata To Files as you did in step 3.

You can use the Metadata Status filter in the Filter bar to quickly find those photos in your library with changes made externally to the master files on disk, any image with a metadata conflict—with unsaved changes made by both Lightroom and another application since the file's metadata was last updated, those with unsaved changes made in Lightroom, or images with metadata that is up to date.

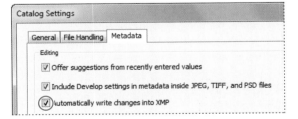

For DNG, JPEG, TIFF, and PSD file formats—which have defined spaces within the file structure where XMP information can be stored separately from the image data—Lightroom writes metadata into the image file itself. In contrast, changes made to camera raw images are written into a separate *XMP sidecar file* that records the metadata and develop settings exported to the image from Lightroom.

Many camera manufacturers use proprietary and undocumented formats for their Raw files, some of which become outdated as new ones appear. Because of this, storing the metadata in a separate file is the safest approach, avoiding the possibility of corruption in the Raw file or loss of the metadata exported from Lightroom.

You can configure the Catalog Settings (in the Edit / Lightroom menu) so that metadata is exported automatically whenever a Raw image is modified. Although you might notice some slowing in performance as Lightroom writes information to the hard disk, you'll always have an up-to-date copy of the metadata from your catalog stored in the sidecar file.

However, XMP information exported in this way contains only the metadata specific to the individual images: keywords, flags, labels, ratings, and develop settings. It does not include higher-level data relevant to the catalog as a whole such as information relating to stacks, virtual copies, and settings used in presentations.

Backing up the library

In the first exercise you backed up your catalog file without any images. In the second exercise, you updated your images files with metadata and develop information from the library catalog. This time, you'll export your entire Lightroom library: images, catalog, stacks, collections—the works!

Exporting images as a catalog

When you export your photos as a catalog, Lightroom creates a copy of the catalog file and gives you the option to make copies of the master files and the image previews at the same time. You can choose to export the entire library, or just a selection of your images, as a catalog. Exporting images in this way is ideal for moving your photos together with all the associated Lightroom catalog information from one computer to another. You can use the same technique to restore your entire library from a backup after a data loss.

1 In the Catalog panel, click All Photographs, and then choose File > Export As Catalog.

Ideally, you should save your backup files to a hard disk other than the one that stores your catalog and the master image files—but for this exercise, you can save the backup files to the LR5CIB folder on your hard disk.

2 In the Export As Catalog dialog box, navigate to the LR5CIB folder on your hard disk. Type **Backup** in the File Name / Save As text box. Disable Export Selected Photos Only and Build/Include Smart Previews, and activate Export Negative Files and Include Available Previews. Click Save / Export Catalog.

An initial progress bar is displayed while the new catalog is being created, which should only take a few seconds. Lightroom then begins copying all the image files associated with this catalog to the new location as a background task.

3   While you wait for the export to be completed, watch the progress bar in the upper left the Lightroom workspace.

4   When the export process is complete, switch to Windows Explorer / the Finder and navigate to the LR5CIB folder. Open the new Backup folder.

● **Note:** You may see a different set of folders than is shown in the illustration, depending on which lessons you've already completed.

You can see that the folder structure nested inside the Backup folder replicates the arrangement of folders you see in the Folders panel. All the master images in your Lightroom library have been copied into these new folders and the file Backup.lrcat is a fully functional copy of your original catalog.

5   In Lightroom, choose File > Open Catalog. In the Open Catalog / Open dialog box, navigate to the new Backup folder inside the LR5CIB folder. Select the file Backup.lrcat, and then click Open. If the Open Catalog dialog box appears, click Relaunch. Lightroom will open the backup catalog.

6   Other than the filename in the title bar of the workspace window, this catalog will be almost indistinguishable from your original. Only some minor status information has been lost. For example, you can see that the Previous Import folder in the Catalog panel is now empty.

7   Some of your preferences have been reset to defaults which may differ from the choices you've made for your LR5CIB catalog. Choose Catalog Settings from the Edit / Lightroom menu. Click the General tab in the Catalog Settings dialog box. You can see that the backup frequency has been reset to the default. Click Cancel / the Close button (⊜) to close the Catalog Settings dialog box.

8 Choose File > Open Recent > LR5CIB Catalog.lrcat. In the Open Catalog dialog box, click Relaunch. If the Back Up Catalog dialog box appears, click Skip Now.

Doing incremental backups

In the usual course of events, the majority of the images in your library will remain unchanged between backups. An incremental backup will save you time by replacing only the backup copies and catalog entries of images that have been modified since the last backup.

Although Lightroom does not have an incremental backup command, you can achieve the same effect by regularly updating your existing backup with just those files in your main catalog that have been modified since the last backup.

1 In the Folders panel, select the Lesson 11 folder. Apply star ratings to two or three of the images in the Grid view. This will be the incremental change to your library for the purposes of this exercise.

2 Choose File > Open Recent > Backup.lrcat to switch to the Backup catalog. If the Open Catalog dialog box appears, click Relaunch.

3 Choose File > Import From Another Catalog. In the Import From Lightroom Catalog dialog box, navigate to the LR5CIB folder. Drill down to the LR5CIB Library/LR5CIB Catalog folder. Inside that folder, select LR5CIB Catalog.lrcat, and then click Open / Choose.

4 In the Import From Catalog dialog box, make sure the Show Preview option is activated. Choose Metadata And Develop Settings Only from the Replace menu under Changed Existing Photos. Disable the option Preserve Old Settings As A Virtual Copy. Scroll down in the Preview panel to confirm that only the images you modified in step 1 are selected for import.

● **Note:** When you're adding new images to your backup library, choose Copy New Photos To A New Location And Import from the File Handling menu. Click the Choose button to specify your current Backup folder as the destination for the copied files.

5   Click Import. You can see that the modified images have been updated with the ratings you applied in the master catalog. You have just performed an incremental backup.

6   Click All Photographs in the Catalog panel, and then choose Edit > Select All or press Ctrl+A / Command+A. Choose Metadata > Save Metadata To Files or press Ctrl+S / Command+S; then, click Continue. This will export the metadata and develop settings for each photo in the backup library to the backup image file or its XMP sidecar, as an extra precaution against data loss.

▶ **Tip:** If you are asked whether Lightroom should overwrite the information embedded in the image files, click Overwrite Settings.

7   Choose File > Open Recent > LR5CIB Catalog.lrcat to return to your original catalog. If the Open Catalog dialog box appears, click Relaunch.

8   If the Back Up Catalog dialog box appears, click Skip This Time.

Exporting photos

The backup techniques that we've discussed so far all produce backup files that can be read only by Lightroom or another application that is capable of reading and interpreting the exported XMP metadata. If you wish to send your work to somebody who doesn't have Lightroom installed on their computer, you'll first need to convert the images to an appropriate file format. This is comparable to saving a Word document as plain text or as a PDF document for distribution; some of the functionality is lost but at least the recipient can see what you're working on. Your choice of file format will depend on the purpose for which the images are intended.

• To export a photo for use as an e-mail attachment intended to be viewed on screen, use the JPEG file format and minimize the file size by reducing the resolution and dimensions of the image.

• To export an image to be edited in another application, convert the photo to either the PSD or TIFF file format at full size.

• For archival purposes, export the images in their original file format or convert them to DNG.

Exporting JPEG files for on-screen viewing

For this exercise, you'll use a saved preset to edit the lesson images before you export them so that you'll be able to see at a glance that your develop settings have been applied to the exported copies.

1   In the Folders panel, select the Lesson 11 folder; then, choose Edit > Select All. From the Saved Preset menu at the top of the Quick Develop panel, choose Lightroom B&W Toned Presets > Split Tone 4.

2   With all six images still selected in the Grid view, choose File > Export.

3   Under Export Location in the Export dialog box, choose Specific Folder from the Export To menu, and then click the Choose button below it to specify a destination folder *(see illustration after step 4)*. Navigate to your Lessons folder, select the Lesson 11 folder, and click OK / Choose.

4   Activate the Put In Subfolder option and type **Export** as the name for the new subfolder. Disable the option Add To This Catalog.

5   Under File Naming in the Export dialog box, click the checkbox to activate the Rename To option; then, choose Date - Filename from the menu.

6   Under File Settings, choose JPEG from the Image Format menu and set a Quality value of between 70% and 80%—a range that generally makes an acceptable compromise between image quality and file size. From the Color Space menu choose sRGB. The sRGB color space is a good choice for images intended to be viewed on the web—or in other circumstances where you are unsure what form of color management is used, if any at all.

7   Scroll down in the Export dialog box, if necessary, so that you can see the Image Sizing controls. Activate the Resize To Fit option and choose Width & Height from the menu. Enter **750** for both width (W) and height (H) and choose Pixels from the units menu. This will proportionally scale each image so that its longest side is 750 pixels. Activate Don't Enlarge to avoid smaller images being upsampled. Set the Resolution to **72** Pixels Per Inch—although resolution settings are in general ignored for on-screen display. The reduction in file size is the result of reducing the total number of pixels that make up the image.

8 In the Output Sharpening settings, activate the Sharpen For Screen option and set the Amount to Standard. Under Metadata, choose the Copyright Only option. Note the other options available under Metadata; even with the All metadata option selected, you can still protect your privacy by removing GPS location information. Disable Watermarking. Choose Show In Explorer / Show In Finder from the After Export menu under Post-Processing.

9 Click Export; then, watch the progress bar on the left side of the top panel in the Lightroom workspace. When the export process is complete, your Export folder inside the Lesson 11 folder will open in Windows Explorer / the Finder.

● **Note:** To have Lightroom notify you by playing a sound when the export process is complete, choose a sound from the menu under Completion Sounds on the General tab in the Preferences dialog box.

Using export plug-ins

You can use third-party Lightroom plug-ins to extend almost any aspect of Lightroom's functionality, including the export options.

There are export plug-ins available that enable you to upload photos directly from within Lightroom to your SmugMug, Zenfolio, or Picasa Web accounts, amongst others. Worth mentioning also are the plug-ins SlideShowPro, and iStockPhoto.

Other plug-ins add search criteria to the Filter bar, enable you to automate and compress backups, help you to create photo-collages or design and upload web galleries, give you access to professional effects and filters, or let you work with Photoshop-style layers in the Develop module.

Click the Plug-in Manager button in the lower left corner of the Export dialog box, and then click Plug-in Exchange to browse Lightroom Exchange online, where you'll find plug-ins from third-party developers offering additional functionality or helping you to automate tasks, customize workflows, and create stylish effects.

You can search the available Lightroom plug-ins by category, browsing for camera raw profiles, develop presets, export plug-ins, and even web gallery templates.

10 In Windows Explorer, show the Preview Pane or click Slideshow view to see a preview of the images in the folder. In the Mac OS Finder, select an image in Column view or in Cover Flow to see its preview. You can see that the duo-tone preset has been applied to these copies of the lesson photos during the export process. The copies are 750 pixels wide and have much reduced file sizes.

11 Delete the images from the Export folder, and then return to Lightroom. With the six images still selected, choose Photo > Develop Settings > Reset to revert all six images to their original colors.

Exporting as PSD or TIFF for further editing

1 In the Grid view, choose Edit > Select None, and then click to select the image Texture-3.jpg. In the right panel group, expand the Quick Develop panel and choose Lightroom Color Presets > Cross Process 3 from the Saved Preset menu.

2 Choose File > Export. In the Export dialog box, you'll notice that all your settings from the previous exercise are still in place.

3 In File Settings, choose TIFF from the Image Format menu. When saving in TIFF format, you have the option to apply ZIP data compression—a lossless form of compression—to reduce the resulting file size. From the Color Space menu, choose AdobeRGB (1998).

Tip: To export more images using the same settings that you used for the previous export (and without calling up the Export dialog box) choose File > Export With Previous.

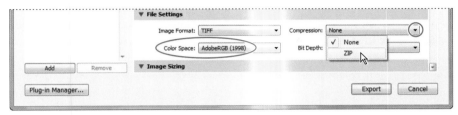

When you intend to edit an image in an external application after exporting it, you should use the AdobeRGB (1998) color profile rather than the sRGB color profile. The AdobeRGB (1998) color profile has a larger color gamut, which results in fewer colors being clipped and the original appearance of your images being better preserved. The ProPhoto RGB color gamut is even larger, capable of representing any color from the original raw image. However, to correctly display images using the AdobeRGB (1998) or ProPhoto RGB color profiles on screen you need an image editing application capable of reading these color profiles.

You'll also need to turn color management on and calibrate your computer display. Without taking these measures, your images will look bad on screen with the AdobeRGB (1998) color profile—and even worse with ProPhoto RGB.

4 Change the image format to PSD. Choose 8 Bits/Component from the Bit Depth menu. Unless you have a particular need to output 16 bit files as part of your workflow, 8-bit files are smaller and compatible with more programs and plug-ins, but do not preserve fine tonal detail as well as 16-bit files. Lightroom actually operates in a 16 bit color space but by the time you're ready to export images you've usually already made any important corrections or adjustments that were necessary, so you won't lose much in terms of editing capability by converting the files to 8 bits for export.

Tip: Choose your preferred external editor, file format, color space, bit depth, compression settings, and file naming options on the External Editing tab of the Preferences dialog box. In the Lightroom workspace, choose Photo > Edit In, and then choose your preferred external image editing application from the menu. Lightroom will automatically export an image in the appropriate file format, open it in the external editor, and add the converted file to the Lightroom library.

5 In Image Sizing, disable Resize To Fit; to preserve all the image information for further editing, we wish to export every pixel of the original image.

6. Leave the Output Sharpening and Metadata settings unchanged. If you have Adobe Photoshop CS2 or later installed on your computer, choose that application from the After Export menu in the Post-Processing options. Alternatively, choose Open In Other Application, and then click Choose to select your preferred image editor. Click Export.

7. Wait until the export is complete and the photo has opened in the external editor. The image has been exported with the Color Presets - Cross Process 3 preset that you applied in the Quick Develop panel. Its dimensions are the same as those of the original image—2500 by 1660 pixels.

8. Quit the external editor, delete the file from the Export folder in Windows Explorer / the Finder, and then return to Lightroom.

Exporting as Original or DNG for archiving

Note: When you choose to export images in DNG file format you have additional options that affect the way the DNG files are created, but the original image data remains essentially unchanged.

1. In the Folders panel, click the Lesson 6 folder. In the Grid view, select the Raw image DSC_0151.NEF, a photograph of two sculpted marble horses.

2. Choose File > Export. In the Export dialog box, leave the Export Location unchanged, but disable the renaming option under File Naming.

3. In File Settings, choose Original from the Image Format menu. Note that there are now no other File Settings, Image Settings, or Output Sharpening options available; Lightroom will export the original image data unaltered.

4. In the Post-Processing options, choose Show In Explorer / Show In Finder from the After Export menu; then, click Export.

5 Wait until the export process completes and the Export folder inside the Lesson 11 folder opens in Windows Explorer / the Finder. In the Windows Explorer / Finder window, note that an XMP sidecar file has been saved together with the copy of the original RAW image. This XMP file records changes to the image's metadata as well as its detailed editing history.

6 In Windows Explorer / the Finder, delete both files from the Export folder, and then return to Lightroom.

Using export presets

Lightroom provides presets for commonly performed export tasks. You can use a preset as is or as a starting point for setting up your own.

If you find yourself performing the same operations over and over again you should create your own presets to automate your workflow.

1 Click the Lesson 11 folder in the Folders panel. In the Grid view, select any of the images in the Lesson 11 folder and then choose File > Export.

2 In the list of presets on the left side of the Export dialog box, choose For Email from the Lightroom Presets.

3 Examine the settings associated with this preset. With the current File Settings, an exported file will be an sRGB JPEG file with a Quality setting of 60 (%). Under Image Sizing, the exported image is set to be scaled down so that its longest side will be 500 pixels. Output Sharpening and Watermarking are disabled and the Metadata options are set to export copyright details only. Note that there are no export location or post-processing settings.

▶ **Tip:** For more detail on exporting photos as e-mail attachments, see "Sharing your work by e-mail" in Lesson 1.

Lightroom will export the image directly to an e-mail, so there are no export location settings associated with this preset. Post-processing options are also unnecessary; Lightroom automatically generates an e-mail and attaches the photo; your e-mail will be sent from within Lightroom, with no need to launch an e-mail client.

4 In the list of presets on the left side of the Export dialog box, click to select the Burn Full-Sized JPEGs export preset.

5 Note the changes in the export settings. CD / DVD is now selected in the Export To menu at the top of the Export dialog box, instead of Email (so, once again, export location settings are redundant). Under File Settings, the JPEG Quality setting has been set to 100 (%).

6 Scroll down in the Export dialog box to examine the rest of the preset options. Under Image Sizing, the Resize To Fit option is disabled, and the file will be exported with all of its metadata intact, including GPS location information.

You can adjust any of the preset settings if you wish, and then save your custom configuration as a new preset by clicking the Add button below the Presets list.

Once again, there are no post-processing options; if you go ahead and click the Export button, Lightroom will automatically open the Choose Burner / Burn Disc dialog box, where you can nominate your disk burner and specify the burn speed before clicking Burn.

Setting up post-processing actions

You can streamline your export workflow by setting up automated post-processing actions. For example, if you prefer to set up an e-mail in your default e-mail client, you could have Lightroom automatically launch your mail application and prepare a new message with the exported image attached.

1   Choose For Email (Hard Drive) from the Lightroom Presets. For this preset, Lightroom exports the file to disk at an appropriate file size for e-mailing.

2   Under Export Location in the Export dialog box, choose Specific Folder from the Export To menu, and then click the Choose button below it to select your Lesson 11 folder as the export destination. Activate the Put In Subfolder option and type **For Email** as the name for the new subfolder. Disable the option Add To This Catalog.

3   In the Post-Processing options, choose Go To Export Actions Folder Now from the After Export menu.

Lightroom opens a Windows Explorer / Finder window with the Export Actions folder already selected. The next step in setting up your automated export is to place a shortcut or alias for your e-mail application into this folder.

4   Open a second Windows Explorer / Finder window and navigate to the folder containing your e-mail application. Right-click / Control-click the e-mail application, choose Create Shortcut / Make Alias from the context menu, and then drag the new shortcut or alias into the Export Actions folder. When you're done, return to the Export dialog box in Lightroom.

5   In the Post-Processing settings, choose the new shortcut or alias to your e-mail application from the After Export menu.

With the current settings you could export an image as a small JPEG file and Lightroom would automatically launch your e-mail application and open a new message with the image already attached. But first, there's one more step that can help automate the process even further.

Creating user presets

You can save your customized export settings as a new user preset. Export presets are always available from the File menu (File > Export With Preset) where you can start your export without having to open the Export dialog first.

1   Click the Add button in the lower left corner of the Export dialog box. In the New Preset dialog box, type To **My Email and Attach** as the name for your new preset, choose User Presets from the Folder menu, and then click Create.

In the Export dialog box, your new preset is now listed under User Presets.

2   Click Cancel to close the Export dialog box without exporting any images.

3   Select one or more images in the Grid view and choose File > Export With Preset > To My Email And Attach.

The export process will begin immediately. When exporting is complete, your e-mail application will be launched automatically and will open a new message with your exported photo or photos already attached; all you need to do is to enter the recipient's e-mail address and you're ready to send.

Review questions

1 What are the two basic components of your photo library that need to be backed up?

2 How can you move a selection of images or your entire image library with all the associated catalog information from one computer to another?

3 How can you do an incremental backup of your photo library?

4 How would you choose between file formats for exporting your photos?

5 What is a post-processing action?

Review answers

1 The two basic components of the image library are the original image files (or master files) and the library catalog file, which records all the metadata and the complete editing history for every image in the library as well as information about collections, user templates and presets, and output settings.

2 On one computer, use the Export As Catalog command to create a catalog file together with copies of the original images and the available previews. On the other computer, use the Import From Another Catalog command.

3 Once you have created a full backup of the library using Export As Catalog, you can switch to the backup catalog regularly and use the Import From Another Catalog command to update it. You can configure the import settings so only those images that have been modified since the last backup are imported from the main catalog. In this way, you can keep your existing backup catalog updated incrementally— avoiding the more time consuming process of making a full new backup.

4 The appropriate choice of a file format depends on the intended use of the exported images. To export images for on-screen viewing as e-mail attachments, you'd use the JPEG file format and minimize the file size. To export an image to an external image editing application you'd use PSD or TIFF and export the image at full size. For archival purposes, export the images in their original format or convert them to DNG.

5 A post-processing action is a preset that can help to automate your workflow. You can choose a preset that will automatically burn your images to a CD or DVD after export, or one that will launch your e-mail application and attach your exported images to a new message. You can save your own action presets, which will be listed beside the Lightroom presets in the Export dialog box.

INDEX

Production notes

The *Adobe Photoshop Lightroom 5 Classroom in a Book* was created electronically using Adobe InDesign CS5. Art was produced using Adobe InDesign, Adobe Illustrator, and Adobe Photoshop.

References to company names in the lessons are for demonstration purposes only and are not intended to refer to any actual organization or person.

Team credits

The following individuals contributed to the development of this edition of the *Adobe Photoshop Lightroom 5 Classroom in a Book*:

Project coordinators, technical writers: John Evans & Katrin Straub

Production: Manneken Pis Productions (www.manneken.be)

Copyediting & Proofreading: John Evans, Katrin Straub and Torsten Buck

Keystroker: Megan Ahearn

Designer: Katrin Straub

Special thanks to Victor Gavenda, Eric Geoffroy, Connie Jeung-Mills, Tracey Croom, and Christine Yarrow.

Typefaces used

Adobe Clean, Adobe Myriad Pro, and Adobe Warnock Pro are used throughout the lessons. For more information about OpenType and Adobe fonts, visit www.adobe.com/type/opentype/.

Photo Credits

Photographic images and illustrations supplied by John Batdorff, Colby Brown, Torsten Buck, Michael Clark, John Evans, Chris Orwig, Seth Resnick, Carsten Schael, Katrin Straub, Nicole Young, and Adobe Systems Incorporated. Photos are for use only with the lessons in the book.

Contributors

John Evans has worked in computer graphics and design for more than 25 years, initially as a graphic designer, and then since 1993 as a multimedia author, software interface designer, and technical writer. His multimedia and digital illustration work associated with Japanese type attracted an award from Apple Computer Australia. His other projects range from music education software for children to interface design for innovative Japanese font design software. As a technical writer his work includes software design specifications, user manuals, and more recently several editions of *Adobe Photoshop Elements Classroom in a Book* and *Adobe Photoshop Lightroom Classroom in a Book*.

Katrin Straub is an artist, a graphic designer, and author. Her award-winning print, painting, and multimedia work has been exhibited worldwide. With more than 15 years experience in design, Katrin has worked as Design Director for companies such as Landor Associates and Fontworks in the United States, Hong Kong, and Japan. Her work includes packaging, promotional campaigns, multimedia, website design, and internationally recognized corporate and retail identities. She holds degrees from the FH Augsburg, ISIA Urbino, and The New School University in New York. Katrin has authored many books, from the *Adobe Creative Suite Idea Kit* to Classroom in a Book titles for Adobe Photoshop Lightroom 4, Adobe Creative Suite 4, Adobe Soundbooth, and several versions of *Adobe Photoshop Elements Classroom in a Book* and *Adobe Premiere Elements Classroom in a Book*.

Torsten Buck has been involved in the development of software for the design and desktop publishing industries in Japan, China and the United States for almost 20 years. A Masters in Computer Science combined with a passion for typography have shaped a career that took Torsten from the development of ground-breaking Asian font technology in Hong Kong to a position as Head of Type Development at Adobe Systems in the USA. As director of Manneken Pis Productions he has authored a wide range of design software training books.

The fastest, easiest, most comprehensive way to learn
Adobe® Creative Cloud™

Classroom in a Book®, the best-selling series of hands-on software training books, helps you learn the features of Adobe software quickly and easily.

The **Classroom in a Book** series offers what no other book or training program does—an official training series from Adobe Systems, developed with the support of Adobe product experts.

To see a complete list of our Adobe Creative Cloud titles go to:
www.adobepress.com/adobecc

Adobe Photoshop CC Classroom in a Book
ISBN: 9780321928078

Adobe Illustrator CC Classroom in a Book
ISBN: 9780321929495

Adobe InDesign CC Classroom in a Book
ISBN: 9780321926975

Adobe Dreamweaver CC Classroom in a Book
ISBN: 9780321919410

Adobe Flash Professional CC Classroom in a Book
ISBN: 9780321927859

Adobe Premiere Pro CC Classroom in a Book
ISBN: 9780321919380

Adobe After Effects CC Classroom in a Book
ISBN: 9780321929600

Adobe Audition CC Classroom in a Book
ISBN: 9780321929532

Adobe SpeedGrade CC Classroom in a Book
ISBN: 9780321927002

Digital Video with Adobe Creative Cloud Classroom in a Book
ISBN: 9780321934024

Design with the Adobe Creative Cloud Classroom in a Book
ISBN: 9780321940513

AdobePress

CLASSROOM IN A BOOK®
Digital Features Access Code Inside!

Inside this envelope is a unique code that will allow you to unlock the digital features of this book, including all of the lesson files and access to online resources to help you learn more about Adobe software. You can also get updates on changes to the software.

F966BC3A531C

Please see other side of this card for registration instructions.

Adobe

CLASSROOM IN A BOOK®
Digital Features Access Code Inside!

To access the Classroom in a Book files:

1. Go to www.peachpit.com/redeem and enter the code inside this card.

2. If you do not have a Peachpit.com account, you will be prompted to create one.

3. The downloadable files will be listed under Lesson & Update Files tab on your Account page.

4. Click the lesson file links to download them to your computer.